Cambridge School
Shakespeare

Othello

Edited by Jane Coles

Series Editor: Rex Gibson
Director, Shakespeare and Schools Project

CAMBRIDGE
UNIVERSITY PRESS

CAMBRIDGE UNIVERSITY PRESS
Cambridge, New York, Melbourne, Madrid, Cape Town, Singapore, São Paulo

Cambridge University Press
The Edinburgh Building, Cambridge CB2 2RU, UK

www.cambridge.org
Information on this title: www.cambridge.org/9780521618762

First published 1992
Second edition 2005
Reprinted 2006

Printed in the United Kingdom at the University Press, Cambridge

A catalogue record for this publication is available from the British Library

ISBN-13   978-0-521-61876-2 paperback
ISBN-10   0-521-61876-2 paperback

ACKNOWLEDGEMENTS
Thanks are due to the following for permission to reproduce illustrations:
Cover, v, vi, vii, viii, ix, x, xi, xii, 70, 116, 122, 134, 143*tl*, 152, 174, 180, 182, 200,
224*tl*, Donald Cooper/Photostage; 20, from Giacomo Franco, *Habiti d'huomeni et donne
Venetia*, by permission of the Folger Shakespeare Library; 42, 108, 224*cr*, 224*b*, Richard
Mildenhall; 64, 241, British Home Entertainment plc/photo BFI; 91, 196, Philip Sayer;
92, Pepys Library, Magdalene College, Cambridge; 112, 143*tr*, Martha Swope Pho-
tography Inc; 132, photographer Reg Wilson © Royal Shakespeare Company; 143*bl*,
242*tr*, Billy Rose Theatre Collection, New York Public Library at Lincoln Center, Astor,
Lenox and Tilden Foundations; 143*br*, Raymond Mander & Joe Mitchenson Theatre
Collection; 221, by permission of the Shakespeare Birthplace Trust; 232, University of
Birmingham Collections; 242*br*, The Harvard Theatre Collection, Houghton Library;
242*cl*, Shakespeare Theatre Company, Washington DC; 243, Miramax/Dimension
Films/The Kobal Collection/Basha, Bob.

Thanks are due to the following for permission to reproduce from copyright material:
234, 'White Lies' ('To whom it may concern') by Stanley Mogoba, 1973, reproduced by
permission of Ad Donker (Pty) Limited, Johannesburg, SA; 236, extract from 'Diabolic
intellect and the noble hero' from *The Common Pursuit* by F. R. Leavis, 1952, published
by Chatto & Windus, reprinted by permission of the Random House Group Ltd; 237,
extract from *The Noble Moor* by Helen Gardner, *Proceedings of the British Academy*, volume
LXI, 1955, reproduced by permission of the British Academy; 237, extract from *Shakespeare* by Germaine Greer, 1986, reproduced by permission of Oxford University Press;
237, extract from *Shakespeare* by Kiernan Ryan, 1989, published by Pearson Education
Ltd; 237, extract from 'Cultural materialism, *Othello* and the politics of plausibility' by
Alan Sinfield and from 'Othello's identity, postcolonial theory and contemporary African
rewritings of *Othello*' by Jyotsna Singh in Lena Cowen Orlin (ed.), *Othello*, New Casebook
series, 2004, published by Palgrave Macmillan.

Cover design by Smith

£4.99

SFCO3207✓

Contents

Cambridge School
Shakespeare

This edition of *Othello* is part of the **Cambridge School Shakespeare** series. Like every other play in the series, it has been specially prepared to help all students in schools and colleges.

This *Othello* aims to be different from other editions of the play. It invites you to bring the play to life in your classroom, hall or drama studio through enjoyable activities that will increase your understanding. Actors have created their different interpretations of the play over the centuries. Similarly, you are encouraged to make up your own mind about *Othello*, rather than having someone else's interpretation handed down to you.

Cambridge School Shakespeare does not offer you a cut-down or simplified version of the play. This is Shakespeare's language, filled with imaginative possibilities. You will find on every left-hand page: a summary of the action, an explanation of unfamiliar words, and a choice of activities on Shakespeare's language, characters and stories.

Between the acts and in the pages at the end of the play, you will find notes, illustrations and activities. These will help to increase your understanding of the whole play.

There are a large number of activities to give you the widest choice to suit your own particular needs. Please don't think you have to do every one. Choose the activities that will help you most.

This edition will be of value to you whether you are studying for an examination, reading for pleasure, or thinking of putting on the play to entertain others. You can work on the activities on your own or in groups. Many of the activities suggest a particular group size, but don't be afraid to make up larger or smaller groups to suit your own purposes.

Although you are invited to treat *Othello* as a play, you don't need special dramatic or theatrical skills to do the activities. By choosing your activities, and by exploring and experimenting, you can make your own interpretations of Shakespeare's language, characters and stories. Whatever you do, remember that Shakespeare wrote his plays to be acted, watched and enjoyed.

Rex Gibson

This edition of *Othello* uses the text of the play established by Norman Sanders in **The New Cambridge Shakespeare**.

Othello is the dramatised story of a black army general who has secretly married the white daughter of a leading politician. Will their marriage survive in the face of racism, jealousy and a struggle for power?

'I am not what I am': Othello has no idea that his trusted ensign (standard-bearer), Iago, is plotting against him.

Iago enlists the help of Roderigo to stir up trouble for Othello and Desdemona. They tell Desdemona's father about the secret marriage and spread racist lies.

Meanwhile, a Turkish fleet threatens the island of Cyprus, and Othello is sent to command the forces.

'. . . our noble and valiant general!' A terrible storm scatters and destroys the Turkish invasion fleet, and Othello lands safely in Cyprus.

Othello is reunited with Desdemona, and he takes up official duties as commander of the occupying forces in Cyprus . . .

. . . unaware that Iago (centre back in picture below) is watching their every move. He plans to destroy Othello by suggesting that Desdemona is having an affair with Cassio, a handsome lieutenant.

Iago tricks Cassio into getting drunk at a barracks party. After Cassio is involved in a drunken brawl, Othello dismisses him from office and promotes Iago in his place.

Meanwhile, Iago tells his wife (Emilia) to steal Desdemona's special handkerchief – an antique love-token given to her as a wedding gift by Othello. Iago later places it in Cassio's lodgings, as if proof of Desdemona's adultery.

Iago continues to
rouse Othello's
jealousy . . .

. . . whilst pretending to
be Desdemona's friend
and confidant.

'jealousy: / It is the green-eyed monster which doth mock / The meat it feeds on'. Eventually, Iago's lies and tricks move Othello to a jealous rage . . .

. . . and he attacks Desdemona, refusing to listen to reason.

Only after he has killed Desdemona does Othello discover the truth about her innocence.

'. . . to die upon a kiss'. Grief-stricken and full of remorse, Othello kills himself. Iago is arrested and charged.

List of characters

OTHELLO	A black army general in the service of the Duke of Venice
DESDEMONA	Othello's wife, daughter of Brabantio
IAGO	Othello's ensign (standard-bearer)
EMILIA	Iago's wife, companion to Desdemona
CASSIO	Othello's lieutenant
BIANCA	in love with Cassio
DUKE OF VENICE	
BRABANTIO	A Venetian senator, father of Desdemona
RODERIGO	A Venetian gentleman, in love with Desdemona
GRATIANO	Brabantio's brother
LODOVICO	Brabantio's relative
MONTANO	Governor of Cyprus

Senators of Venice
Gentlemen of Cyprus

CLOWN	Servant to Othello

Herald
Messenger
Musicians, soldiers, attendants, servants
Sailor

The action of the play takes place in Venice and Cyprus.

Two men are in the middle of an argument. Roderigo accuses Iago of cheating him. Iago is angry about failing to gain the promotion that has gone instead to Michael Cassio.

1 A dramatic opening (in pairs)

In the theatres of Shakespeare's time there was no electric lighting and no stage curtain. The playwright had to signal the start of the play by means of a dramatic opening scene. Here, the noisy audience would be silenced by two men in the middle of a heated argument, with much swearing.

a Read this opening conversation (lines 1–34) aloud. Try reading it in several different ways to find which way sounds best. Discuss which words in the script gave you clues as to how it should be spoken.

b Film and theatre directors have chosen various ways in which to begin the play (see pp. 240–1 for a detailed activity exploring some of these). Think about ways in which you might want to set the scene, how you might have actors enter the stage, and what sound and lighting effects might suggest a street at night.

c The play opens half-way through an argument. Make up what you think Iago and Roderigo have been saying *before* the play begins. End your dialogue on the first line of the play.

2 Michael Cassio – why does Iago dislike him?

Iago explains why he believes he has not been promoted to the rank of lieutenant (lines 8–27). Look carefully at the way Iago describes Cassio (lines 19–26) and pick out four key phrases which suggest why Iago is jealous of him.

'Sblood by God's blood (a swear-word)
suit attendance
bombast circumstance fancy excuse
Certes certainly
arithmetician theorist

Florentine from Florence
devision strategical placing of soldiers
togèd consuls senators wearing the robes of peace
had the election was chosen

Othello, the Moor of Venice

Act 1 Scene 1
Venice   A street at night

Enter RODERIGO and IAGO.

RODERIGO Tush, never tell me, I take it much unkindly
    That thou, Iago, who hast had my purse
    As if the strings were thine shouldst know of this.
IAGO 'Sblood, but you will not hear me.
    If ever I did dream of such a matter,   5
    Abhor me.
RODERIGO Thou told'st me thou didst hold him in thy hate.
IAGO Despise me if I do not: three great ones of the city,
    In personal suit to make me his lieutenant,
    Off-capped to him; and by the faith of man,   10
    I know my price, I am worth no worse a place.
    But he, as loving his own pride and purposes,
    Evades them with a bombast circumstance,
    Horribly stuffed with epithets of war,
    And in conclusion,   15
    Non-suits my mediators. For 'Certes', says he,
    'I have already chosen my officer.'
    And what was he?
    Forsooth, a great arithmetician,
    One Michael Cassio, a Florentine,   20
    A fellow almost damned in a fair wife,
    That never set a squadron in the field,
    Nor the devision of a battle knows
    More than a spinster, unless the bookish theoric,
    Wherein the togèd consuls can propose   25
    As masterly as he. Mere prattle without practice
    Is all his soldiership. But he, sir, had the election,

Iago continues to complain about 'the Moor' and the system of promotion. He says he pretends to be a faithful officer, but follows Othello only to serve his own purposes.

1 First impressions of Iago (in small groups)

Read the page of script aloud several times, sharing out the lines.

On a large plain piece of paper, write IAGO in the centre (see the diagram below) and collect together any key things Iago seems to say about himself. Include anything that reveals something about his character or motivation. On the outer layer of the diagram explain in your own words what you believe each quotation might indicate about him.

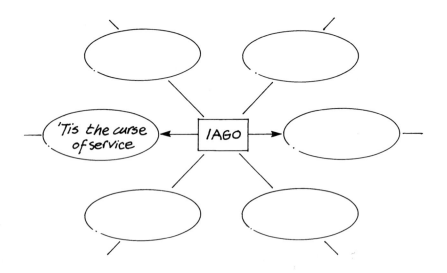

When you have finished, join together with other groups and compare your sheet with theirs. Explain how and why you chose your particular words/phrases/lines.

Pool your ideas to produce one final diagram for display on your classroom wall.

---

lee'd pacified (sailing terminology)
counter-caster accountant
ancient ensign, standard-bearer
Preferment promotion
letter academic qualifications

affection favouritism
affined bound
provender food and drink
cashiered dismissed from service
forms outward shows
complement extern outward show

And I, of whom his eyes had seen the proof
At Rhodes, at Cyprus, and on other grounds
Christian and heathen, must be lee'd and calmed   30
By debitor and creditor; this counter-caster,
He, in good time, must his lieutenant be,
And I, God bless the mark, his Moorship's ancient.

RODERIGO By heaven, I rather would have been his hangman.

IAGO Why, there's no remedy. 'Tis the curse of service;   35
Preferment goes by letter and affection,
Not by the old gradation, where each second
Stood heir to the first. Now sir, be judge yourself
Whether I in any just term am affined
To love the Moor.

RODERIGO   I would not follow him then.   40

IAGO O sir, content you.
I follow him to serve my turn upon him.
We cannot all be masters, nor all masters
Cannot be truly followed. You shall mark
Many a duteous and knee-crooking knave,   45
That doting on his own obsequious bondage,
Wears out his time much like his master's ass
For nought but provender, and when he's old, cashiered.
Whip me such honest knaves. Others there are
Who, trimmed in forms and visages of duty,   50
Keep yet their hearts attending on themselves,
And throwing but shows of service on their lords,
Do well thrive by them; and when they have lined their coats,
Do themselves homage. These fellows have some soul,
And such a one do I profess myself.   55
For, sir,
It is as sure as you are Roderigo,
Were I the Moor, I would not be Iago;
In following him, I follow but myself.
Heaven is my judge, not I for love and duty,   60
But seeming so for my peculiar end.
For when my outward action doth demonstrate
The native act and figure of my heart
In complement extern, 'tis not long after
But I will wear my heart upon my sleeve   65
For daws to peck at. I am not what I am.

Iago suggests a way of taking revenge against Othello. They shout in the street outside Brabantio's house, and tell him the news that he has been 'robbed'.

1 'BRABANTIO [*appears*] *above at a window*' (in pairs)

Turn to page 186, where you will find an illustration of an Elizabethan theatre. It has a deep 'thrust' stage, with two exits at the back and a balcony above. Some of the audience stood crammed in 'the pit' (the 'groundlings'), others sat in tiers of seating around the walls, and a few even sat on the stage.

Talk together about how you would stage lines 68–93:

- on the Elizabethan stage
- on a modern acting space.

Think about use of lighting, and any props which seem appropriate.

2 Iago's role (in groups of three)

Take parts and read lines 68–143 (to 'Light, I say, light!'). Notice the differences in the way the three characters speak. Do Iago and Roderigo take an equal share in giving information to Brabantio? Now look more closely at the way Iago speaks:

a Identify each occasion on which Iago uses the imperative form of a verb (lines 68–74).

b Find any times Iago uses animal imagery between lines 68 and 92. What kind of animals are they and what are they doing? (This activity is continued on p. 8.)

c On the previous page Iago has talked a good deal about himself – count how many times he uses the first-person pronoun in approximately ten lines of script (see lines 57–66).

Discuss what Shakespeare's use of language suggests about Iago and his relationship with the other men at this point in the play.

---

owe own
timorous frightening or fearful
tupping mating or copulating with

snorting snoring
devil in old church paintings devils were commonly portrayed as black

RODERIGO What a full fortune does the thick-lips owe,
      If he can carry it thus!
IAGO   Call up her father:
      Rouse him, make after him, poison his delight,
      Proclaim him in the street, incense her kinsmen,   70
      And though he in a fertile climate dwell,
      Plague him with flies: though that his joy be joy,
      Yet throw such chances of vexation on't
      As it may lose some colour.
RODERIGO Here is her father's house; I'll call aloud.   75
IAGO Do, with like timorous accent and dire yell,
      As when, by night and negligence, the fire
      Is spied in populous cities.
RODERIGO What ho, Brabantio! Signior Brabantio, ho!
IAGO Awake! What ho, Brabantio! Thieves, thieves!   80
      Look to your house, your daughter, and your bags!
      Thieves, thieves!

      BRABANTIO [*appears*] *above at a window.*

BRABANTIO What is the reason of this terrible summons?
      What is the matter there?
RODERIGO Signior, is all your family within?   85
IAGO Are your doors locked?
BRABANTIO   Why, wherefore ask you this?
IAGO Zounds, sir, you're robbed; for shame, put on your gown;
      Your heart is burst; you have lost half your soul;
      Even now, now, very now, an old black ram
      Is tupping your white ewe. Arise, arise;   90
      Awake the snorting citizens with the bell,
      Or else the devil will make a grandsire of you.
      Arise, I say!

Brabantio suspects the two men are drunk. He learns Roderigo's name, but not Iago's. Iago obscenely tells him that Desdemona and Othello are having sexual intercourse and that his descendants will be mere animals.

1 Animals

Read through the script on pages 7 and 9. Identify any references to animals or insects in the dialogue. It may help you to know that a 'Barbary horse' is a North African breed, 'coursers' are racehorses, and 'jennets' are a breed of small Spanish horse.

Write down which characters make the comments, and what significance the choice of each animal image carries for you. Discuss what effect this choice of language might be intended to have. You will find further examples of this type of imagery on page 229.

2 Verse and prose

Brabantio and Roderigo speak in verse. When Iago interjects (at line 109), the script switches to prose. Read 'Verse and prose' on page 228, then suggest why Shakespeare gives Iago prose here.

3 A different perspective (in pairs)

Imagine you are two servants in Brabantio's house, intrigued by the commotion outside. What can you make of the rag-bag of information shouted by the two men in the street? Improvise a 'below-stairs' scene between the two servants.

---

distempering draughts alcohol
start disturb
place position
grange house in the country

germans relatives
profane foul-mouthed
making the beast with two backs
  having sexual intercourse

BRABANTIO   What, have you lost your wits?

RODERIGO Most reverend signior, do you know my voice?

BRABANTIO Not I; what are you?   95

RODERIGO My name is Roderigo.

BRABANTIO   The worser welcome;
    I have charged thee not to haunt about my doors;
    In honest plainness thou hast heard me say
    My daughter is not for thee. And now in madness,
    Being full of supper and distempering draughts,   100
    Upon malicious bravery dost thou come
    To start my quiet.

RODERIGO Sir, sir, sir –

BRABANTIO   But thou must needs be sure
    My spirit and my place have in them power
    To make this bitter to thee.

RODERIGO   Patience, good sir.   105

BRABANTIO What tell'st thou me of robbing? This is Venice;
    My house is not a grange.

RODERIGO   Most grave Brabantio,
    In simple and pure soul I come to you.

IAGO Zounds, sir; you are one of those that will not serve God if the
    devil bid you. Because we come to do you service and you think   110
    we are ruffians, you'll have your daughter covered with a Barbary
    horse, you'll have your nephews neigh to you, you'll have
    coursers for cousins, and jennets for germans.

BRABANTIO What profane wretch art thou?

IAGO I am one, sir, that comes to tell you your daughter and the Moor   115
    are now making the beast with two backs.

BRABANTIO Thou art a villain.

IAGO   You are a senator.

Roderigo tells Brabantio that Desdemona has run away to live with Othello. Brabantio leaves to check if the story is true, saying he has already dreamt of such a happening.

---

1 Desdemona's flight (in groups of three)

Read Roderigo's report of Desdemona's secret departure from home (lines 119–36).

Mime her flight, using captions taken from Roderigo's story. Share your version with the rest of the class.

2 '. . . a gross revolt' (in small groups)

Desdemona has run away from home to marry a man of whom her father disapproves. There are several of Shakespeare's plays in which young people rebel against their parents' wishes (most famously *Romeo and Juliet*). Generally speaking, in Shakespeare's comedies the young people are eventually forgiven; in tragedies the situation ends with disaster for them.

Talk together about other stories you have read or films you have seen which include a similar plot element. How is the family split resolved in those stories?

3 Word association (in pairs)

In lines 119–39 Roderigo refers to Desdemona in positive terms (e.g. 'fair'), whereas he uses derogatory language to refer to Othello (e.g. 'gross clasps'). Identify all words/phrases he uses to talk about Othello and Desdemona. Discuss with your partner why you think he makes this distinction.

---

odd-even   just after midnight
lascivious   lustful
Strike on the tinder   make a light
taper   candle

gall   hurt
cast   dismiss
loud reason   strong support from the Senate

BRABANTIO This thou shalt answer; I know thee, Roderigo.

RODERIGO Sir, I will answer anything. But I beseech you
     If't be your pleasure and most wise consent   120
     (As partly I find it is) that your fair daughter,
     At this odd-even and dull watch o'the night,
     Transported with no worse nor better guard,
     But with a knave of common hire, a gondolier,
     To the gross clasps of a lascivious Moor: 125
     If this be known to you, and your allowance,
     We then have done you bold and saucy wrongs.
     But if you know not this, my manners tell me,
     We have your wrong rebuke. Do not believe
     That from the sense of all civility   130
     I thus would play and trifle with your reverence.
     Your daughter, if you have not given her leave,
     I say again, hath made a gross revolt,
     Tying her duty, beauty, wit, and fortunes
     In an extravagant and wheeling stranger   135
     Of here and everywhere. Straight satisfy yourself.
     If she be in her chamber or your house,
     Let loose on me the justice of the state
     For thus deluding you.

BRABANTIO   Strike on the tinder, ho!
     Give me a taper; call up all my people.   140
     This accident is not unlike my dream;
     Belief of it oppresses me already.
     Light, I say, light!   *Exit*

IAGO   Farewell, for I must leave you.
     It seems not meet nor wholesome to my place
     To be produced, as if I stay I shall,   145
     Against the Moor. For I do know the state,
     However this may gall him with some check,
     Cannot with safety cast him; for he's embarked
     With such loud reason to the Cyprus wars,

Iago slips away, not wishing to be identified as a trouble-maker. Brabantio discovers his daughter is indeed missing. He goes off with Roderigo to seek assistance from neighbours and the police.

1 'The Moor' (in small groups)

Throughout the whole of this first scene, no one has used Othello's *name* – although all three men have referred to him several times. Collect all the terms used to describe Othello in Scene 1. Try to decide what aspect of Othello is being highlighted in each instance; is it a complimentary term or a derogatory one? Also, decide what these descriptive terms tell you about the *speaker* in each case.

Copy the following table and use it to record your findings:

Term used (line)	Aspect of Othello	Spoken by?	What does it say about the speaker?
the Moor (40)	his ethnicity or 'race'	Iago	He's trying to take away Othello's individuality.
the thick-lips (67)	his physical features (stereotype)		Racist! Purposely insulting.
the devil . . .			

When you have completed your table, compare your ideas with those of other groups.

---

fathom capability
life livelihood, occupation
flag outward appearance
Sagittary (the name of an inn)

despisèd time time of great dishonour
charms spells, love potions
deserve your pains reward you for your trouble

Which even now stands in act, that, for their souls,   150
Another of his fathom they have none
To lead their business; in which regard,
Though I do hate him as I do hell's pains,
Yet, for necessity of present life,
I must show out a flag and sign of love,   155
Which is indeed but sign. That you shall surely find him,
Lead to the Sagittary the raisèd search,
And there will I be with him. So farewell.   *Exit*

Enter Brabantio in his nightgown, and SERVANTS *with torches.*

BRABANTIO It is too true an evil. Gone she is,
    And what's to come of my despisèd time   160
    Is nought but bitterness. Now Roderigo,
    Where didst thou see her? O unhappy girl!
    With the Moor, say'st thou? Who would be a father?
    How didst thou know 'twas she? O she deceives me
    Past thought! What said she to you? Get more tapers,   165
    Raise all my kindred. Are they married, think you?
RODERIGO Truly I think they are.
BRABANTIO O heaven! How got she out? O treason of the blood!
    Fathers, from hence trust not your daughters' minds
    By what you see them act. Is there not charms   170
    By which the property of youth and maidhood
    May be abused? Have you not read, Roderigo,
    Of some such thing?
RODERIGO   Yes, sir, I have indeed.
BRABANTIO Call up my brother. O that you had had her!
    Some one way, some another. Do you know   175
    Where we may apprehend her and the Moor?
RODERIGO I think I can discover him, if you please
    To get good guard and go along with me.
BRABANTIO Pray you lead on. At every house I'll call;
    I may command at most. Get weapons, ho!   180
    And raise some special officers of night:
    On, good Roderigo; I'll deserve your pains.
                                Exeunt

Iago, pretending to be Othello's faithful supporter, warns Othello that Brabantio will attempt to break up the marriage. Othello is confident that his service to Venice and his noble descent will make all well.

1 Iago's version (in pairs)

In lines 6–10, Iago tells of the conversation he had with Roderigo. Talk together about how this version compares with what was actually said in the previous scene.

2 Enter Othello

Shakespeare has chosen to delay Othello's entrance until the second scene of the play. We have heard a lot about Othello from others. Now we meet him for the first time.

a Look closely at what Othello says in lines 17–28. Write a paragraph comparing your first impressions with the descriptions given of him in Scene 1.

b If you were directing a production of the play, what effect would you want to create with Othello's entrance? For example, in Trevor Nunn's 1990 Royal Shakespeare Company production, the imposing figure of Othello (played by Willard White) is framed in a doorway illuminated by brilliant light. He is dressed in smart military uniform. In Janet Suzman's 1987 Market Theatre of Johannesburg production, the more physically slight figure of John Kani (Othello) is leaning against a wall, dressed in a flowing white shirt and brushing a rose against his lips. What impression do you think each of these directors is trying to make?

c In groups of four or five create a freeze-frame (or tableau) of the stage direction 'Enter OTHELLO, IAGO and ATTENDANTS with torches'. Compare your ideas with other groups and talk about the effects of each.

---

stuff essence
I lack ... service sometimes I'm too nice for my own good
yerked stabbed
magnifico nobleman (Brabantio)
give him cable allow him

signiory the Venetian government
provulgate make public
siege rank
demerits deserts, worth
circumscription restriction

Act 1 Scene 2
Venice   Outside the Sagittary

Enter OTHELLO, IAGO *and* ATTENDANTS *with torches.*

IAGO Though in the trade of war I have slain men,
      Yet do I hold it very stuff o'the conscience
      To do no contrived murder. I lack iniquity
      Sometimes to do me service. Nine or ten times
      I had thought to have yerked him here, under the ribs.   5
OTHELLO 'Tis better as it is.
IAGO   Nay, but he prated,
      And spoke such scurvy and provoking terms
      Against your honour,
      That, with the little godliness I have,
      I did full hard forbear him. But I pray, sir,   10
      Are you fast married? For be sure of this,
      That the magnifico is much beloved,
      And hath in his effect a voice potential
      As double as the duke's. He will divorce you,
      Or put upon you what restraint and grievance   15
      The law, with all his might to enforce it on,
      Will give him cable.
OTHELLO   Let him do his spite;
      My services which I have done the signiory
      Shall out-tongue his complaints. 'Tis yet to know –
      Which, when I know that boasting is an honour,   20
      I shall provulgate – I fetch my life and being
      From men of royal siege, and my demerits
      May speak unbonneted to as proud a fortune
      As this that I have reached. For know, Iago,
      But that I love the gentle Desdemona,   25
      I would not my unhousèd free condition
      Put into circumscription and confine
      For the sea's worth. But look what lights come yond!

Cassio arrives on an urgent mission from the Duke to find Othello. He reports that war is imminent and the Senate urgently needs Othello. Iago tells Cassio of Othello's marriage.

1 Two-faced Janus (in pairs)

Why is it significant that Iago swears 'By Janus'? Stand back to back. One partner reads Iago's words in lines 1–53 aloud, pausing at the end of each sentence. The other partner speaks in each pause, saying what Iago's real thoughts might be.

2 Greetings (in groups of seven or more)

Two separate search parties come looking for Othello in lines 34–61, one on official war business, the other pursuing a personal grievance. Work out how each search party might enter and how they would greet Othello and Iago. Freeze each scene at the moment of greeting, making it clear from the way characters are looking or standing who they are, and what their intentions are. Show your two freeze-frames to the rest of the class. Can they guess whom you are representing in each tableau?

3 '. . . boarded a land carrack'

When Cassio wonders why Othello is staying at the Sagittary, Iago tells him it is because Othello has 'boarded a land carrack' (taken a treasure ship by an act of 'land' piracy). Write down what you think Iago means by this cryptic comment, and how appropriate the choice of words seems to be.

---

raisèd awakened and indignant
Janus (a two-faced Roman god; January is named after him, as it faces back to winter and forward to summer)

divine guess
sequent one after the other
lawful prize legal capture

IAGO Those are the raisèd father and his friends;
        You were best go in.
OTHELLO   Not I; I must be found.   30
        My parts, my title, and my perfect soul
        Shall manifest me rightly. Is it they?
IAGO By Janus, I think no.

            Enter CASSIO, *with* OFFICERS *and torches.*

OTHELLO The servants of the duke and my lieutenant!
        The goodness of the night upon you, friends.   35
        What is the news?
CASSIO   The duke does greet you, general,
        And he requires your haste-post-haste appearance
        Even on the instant.
OTHELLO   What is the matter, think you?
CASSIO Something from Cyprus, as I may divine.
        It is a business of some heat. The galleys   40
        Have sent a dozen sequent messengers
        This very night at one another's heels;
        And many of the consuls, raised and met,
        Are at the duke's already. You have been hotly called for,
        When, being not at your lodging to be found,   45
        The senate hath sent about three several quests
        To search you out.
OTHELLO   'Tis well I am found by you.
        I will but spend a word here in the house,
        And go with you.   [*Exit*]
CASSIO   Ancient, what makes he here?
IAGO Faith, he tonight hath boarded a land carrack;   50
        If it prove lawful prize, he's made for ever.
CASSIO I do not understand.
IAGO   He's married.
CASSIO   To who?

                [Enter Othello.]

IAGO Marry, to – Come, captain, will you go?
OTHELLO   Have with you.
CASSIO Here comes another troop to seek for you.

Brabantio abuses Othello and physically threatens him. He accuses Othello of enchanting Desdemona with bad magic and drugs, and orders his arrest. Othello reacts calmly.

1 Direct Othello and Brabantio (in pairs)

If you were directing a production of *Othello*, what advice would you give to the two actors playing Othello and Brabantio at line 57, 'Down with him, thief!', and lines 59–61, 'Keep up your bright swords . . .'? Experiment with ways of saying the lines and then explain to the rest of the class how you came to make your decision.

2 Brabantio's accusations (in groups of four)

Read lines 62–81. First, pick out the precise accusations Brabantio makes against Othello. Then identify all the insulting terms Brabantio uses to refer directly or indirectly to Othello. Next, take everything Othello says opposite and divide it up into separate meaningful sections (words, phrases, lines). Three of you share Brabantio's accusations and insults between you, the fourth member of the group takes Othello's language.

Explore ways of presenting your words or lines so that the characters' relationships, moods and situation are clearly communicated.

3 Role reversal

Brabantio is a politician; Othello is a soldier, a man of action. Write a paragraph telling how their roles are reversed in this scene.

Keep up put away
refer me . . . sense appeal to common sense
guardage guardianship, safety of her home

gross in sense quite obvious
out of warrant against the law
of my inclining my supporters

Enter BRABANTIO, RODERIGO *and* OFFICERS *with lights and weapons.*

IAGO It is Brabantio; general, be advised,   55
      He comes to bad intent.
OTHELLO   Holla, stand there!
RODERIGO Signior, it is the Moor.
BRABANTIO   Down with him, thief!
IAGO You, Roderigo? Come, sir, I am for you.
OTHELLO Keep up your bright swords, for the dew will rust them.
      Good signior, you shall more command with years   60
      Than with your weapons.
BRABANTIO O thou foul thief! Where hast thou stowed my
        daughter?
      Damned as thou art, thou hast enchanted her,
      For I'll refer me to all things of sense,
      If she in chains of magic were not bound,   65
      Whether a maid so tender, fair, and happy,
      So opposite to marriage that she shunned
      The wealthy curlèd darlings of our nation,
      Would ever have, t'incur a general mock,
      Run from her guardage to the sooty bosom   70
      Of such a thing as thou – to fear, not to delight.
      Judge me the world, if 'tis not gross in sense
      That thou hast practised on her with foul charms,
      Abused her delicate youth with drugs or minerals
      That weakens motion. I'll have't disputed on;   75
      'Tis probable and palpable to thinking.
      I therefore apprehend and do attach thee
      For an abuser of the world, a practiser
      Of arts inhibited and out of warrant.
      Lay hold upon him. If he do resist,   80
      Subdue him at his peril.
OTHELLO   Hold your hands,
      Both you of my inclining and the rest.
      Were it my cue to fight, I should have known it
      Without a prompter. Where will you that I go
      To answer this your charge?
BRABANTIO   To prison, till fit time   85
      Of law and course of direct session
      Call thee to answer.

Brabantio is certain that the Duke will decide in his favour. In the next scene the Duke and Venetian senators are considering news of the Turkish threats of war on Cyprus, a Venetian colony.

1 Setting Scene 3 – the Council Chamber

Scene 3 marks a change from private matters (even secrecy) to public affairs of state. If you were directing this scene on stage, what kind of room would you imagine it taking place in? Consider how you would show the change of location from the previous street scene on stage, using a bare minimum of props or music. Remember that in most modern productions, scene-changing is very swift indeed and one scene flows quickly into the next.

A contemporary drawing of the Duke (Doge) of Venice (1609).

---

brothers of the state fellow senators
composition agreement
disproportioned inconsistent

jump not on a just accompt do not agree precisely
bearing up sailing towards

OTHELLO　　　　　　　What if I do obey?
　　　How may the duke be therewith satisfied,
　　　Whose messengers are here about my side
　　　Upon some present business of the state　　　　　　90
　　　To bring me to him?
OFFICER　　　　　　　　'Tis true, most worthy signior;
　　　The duke's in council, and your noble self
　　　I am sure is sent for.
BRABANTIO　　　　　　How? The duke in council?
　　　In this time of the night? Bring him away;
　　　Mine's not an idle cause. The duke himself,　　　　95
　　　Or any of my brothers of the state,
　　　Cannot but feel this wrong as 'twere their own;
　　　For if such actions may have passage free,
　　　Bondslaves and pagans shall our statesmen be.

　　　　　　　　　　　　　　　　　　　Exeunt

Act 1 Scene 3
Venice   The Council Chamber

Enter DUKE and SENATORS, set at a table with lights, and
　　　　　　　　　ATTENDANTS.

DUKE There is no composition in these news
　　　That gives them credit.
1 SENATOR　　　　　　　　Indeed they are disproportioned.
　　　My letters say a hundred and seven galleys.
DUKE And mine, a hundred and forty.
2 SENATOR　　　　　　　　　And mine, two hundred;
　　　But though they jump not on a just accompt –　　　　5
　　　As in these cases where the aim reports
　　　'Tis oft with difference – yet do they all confirm
　　　A Turkish fleet, and bearing up to Cyprus.

Amid uncertainty about the size of the Turkish fleet, a sailor brings news that it is now sailing towards Rhodes. However, a senator and the Duke agree that the Turks intend to attack Cyprus.

1 The Mediterranean – the commercial empire of Venice

In the sixteenth century, Venice was the dominant colonial force in the Mediterranean. It was a thriving commercial centre. The powerful merchants protected their commercial empire with military strength, including mercenary forces. Cyprus was particularly valued as a colony for being a profitable source of sugar and cotton.

Use the map below, which shows the extent of the Ottoman (Turkish) Empire, to help your understanding of the reports of Turkish invasion plans in lines 14–46.

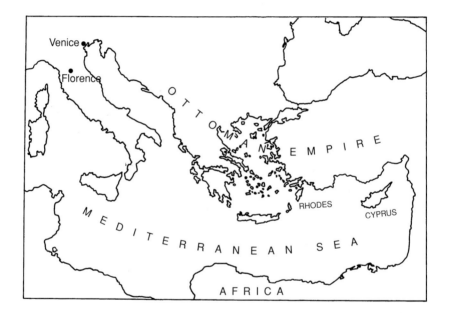

secure me feel confident	**pageant** show, diversion
approve accept	**brace** readiness
In fearful sense as a cause for alarm	**wake** bustle about
assay test	**wage** risk

DUKE Nay, it is possible enough to judgement:
        I do not so secure me in the error,   10
        But the main article I do approve
        In fearful sense.
SAILOR *(Within)*   What ho! What ho! What ho!
OFFICER A messenger from the galleys.

Enter a SAILOR.

DUKE   Now, what's the business?
SAILOR The Turkish preparation makes for Rhodes;
        So was I bid report here to the state   15
        By Signior Angelo.
DUKE How say you by this change?
I SENATOR   This cannot be,
        By no assay of reason. 'Tis a pageant
        To keep us in false gaze. When we consider
        The importancy of Cyprus to the Turk,   20
        And let ourselves again but understand
        That as it more concerns the Turk than Rhodes,
        So may he with more facile question bear it,
        For that it stands not in such warlike brace,
        But altogether lacks the abilities   25
        That Rhodes is dressed in. If we make thought of this,
        We must not think the Turk is so unskilful
        To leave that latest which concerns him first,
        Neglecting an attempt of ease and gain
        To wake and wage a danger profitless.   30
DUKE Nay, in all confidence he's not for Rhodes.
OFFICER Here is more news.

A messenger from Montano, the governor of Cyprus, brings more news: the Turkish fleet, reinforced, sails towards Cyprus. Discussion of war tactics is interrupted by Brabantio's and Othello's arrival.

1 Valiant Othello – the statue! (in pairs)

It has been common practice to erect statues to commemorate military leaders who have been considered to have performed 'great' deeds. One person becomes the sculptor, the other the 'raw material'. Create your own statue to commemorate 'Valiant Othello' (line 48).

2 Brabantio's grief (in small groups)

In lines 52–8, Brabantio is trying to convey the extent of his grief, and ends up using an image of a flood-gate to do it. Do you think it is an appropriate image? Talk together about your response to the image, then:

Either create a graphic design based on lines 55–8.

Or represent these lines, matching words with movement.

3 Public affairs and private anxiety (in small groups)

Brabantio says his 'particular grief' overcomes 'the general care' (matters of state). Some people claim he is being particularly selfish here. But what do you think? Write a paragraph explaining whether you believe Brabantio is being selfish to impose his personal complaint on the Senate at a time of war, and whether 'particular grief' does always overwhelm 'the general care'.

Ottomites   Turks (from the Ottoman Empire)
injointed   linked up

free duty   respect
straight   straight away
engluts   engulfs, overwhelms

Enter a MESSENGER.

MESSENGER The Ottomites, reverend and gracious,
    Steering with due course toward the isle of Rhodes
    Have there injointed with an after fleet.   35
I SENATOR Ay, so I thought. How many, as you guess?
MESSENGER Of thirty sail, and now they do restem
    Their backward course, bearing with frank appearance
    Their purposes toward Cyprus. Signior Montano,
    Your trusty and most valiant servitor,   40
    With his free duty recommends you thus,
    And prays you to believe him.
DUKE 'Tis certain then for Cyprus.
    Marcus Luccicos, is not he in town?
I SENATOR He's now in Florence.
DUKE   Write from us to him   45
    Post-post-haste dispatch.
I SENATOR Here comes Brabantio and the valiant Moor.

Enter BRABANTIO, OTHELLO, CASSIO, IAGO, RODERIGO *and*
OFFICERS.

DUKE Valiant Othello we must straight employ you
    Against the general enemy Ottoman.
    [*To Brabantio*] I did not see you: welcome, gentle
      signior;   50
    We lacked your counsel and your help tonight.
BRABANTIO So did I yours. Good your grace, pardon me:
    Neither my place nor aught I heard of business
    Hath raised me from my bed, nor doth the general care
    Take hold on me; for my particular grief   55
    Is of so flood-gate and o'erbearing nature
    That it engluts and swallows other sorrows
    And yet is still itself.

Brabantio publicly accuses Othello of abducting and seducing his daughter. Othello offers to explain what has really happened.

---

1 Brabantio's story (in groups of four)

Myths and stories play an important part in *Othello* (see, e.g., p. 132). Here, in lines 59–64, Brabantio composes his preferred version of his daughter's flight. Present three moments from that story:

- how Desdemona was charmed
- how she was stolen
- how she was abused.

2 'Rude am I in my speech' (in groups of four to six)

As a group, read through Othello's speech (lines 76–94), each person handing over to the next person at every punctuation mark. Once you've read it through once, try reading it round the circle in different styles or moods. Experiment with the sound of it until you can decide on the way that best fits the words. Then talk together about whether you think that Othello is 'rude' in his speech.

3 Freeze-frame: 'Here is the man' (in groups of seven or more)

At one precise moment (line 71), there are at least seven characters on stage. Work out who they all are and discuss how each might be reacting.

Present this stage moment as a freeze-frame to the rest of the class. They guess who is who. After identification, the class can ask certain characters to step forward out of the tableau, and to reveal what their thoughts are at that moment.

---

of mountebanks from dubious dealers
Sans without
bloody book of law laws including the death penalty
After your own sense however you want

our proper son my own son
pith strength
field battlefield
conjuration spells

DUKE   Why, what's the matter?

BRABANTIO My daughter! O, my daughter!

SENATORS   Dead?

BRABANTIO   Ay, to me.
    She is abused, stol'n from me, and corrupted   60
    By spells and medicines bought of mountebanks;
    For nature so preposterously to err,
    Being not deficient, blind, or lame of sense,
    Sans witchcraft could not.

DUKE Whoe'er he be that in this foul proceeding   65
    Hath thus beguiled your daughter of herself,
    And you of her, the bloody book of law
    You shall yourself read in the bitter letter
    After your own sense, yea, though our proper son
    Stood in your action.

BRABANTIO   Humbly I thank your grace.   70
    Here is the man: this Moor, whom now it seems
    Your special mandate for the state affairs
    Hath hither brought.

ALL   We are very sorry for't.

DUKE [*To Othello*] What in your own part can you say to this? ·

BRABANTIO Nothing, but this is so.   75

OTHELLO Most potent, grave, and reverend signiors,
    My very noble and approved good masters,
    That I have tane away this old man's daughter,
    It is most true; true I have married her;
    The very head and front of my offending   80
    Hath this extent, no more. Rude am I in my speech
    And little blessed with the soft phrase of peace,
    For since these arms of mine had seven years' pith
    Till now some nine moons wasted, they have used
    Their dearest action in the tented field;   85
    And little of this great world can I speak
    More than pertains to feats of broil and battle;
    And therefore little shall I grace my cause
    In speaking for myself. Yet, by your gracious patience,
    I will a round unvarnished tale deliver   90
    Of my whole course of love: what drugs, what charms,
    What conjuration and what mighty magic –
    For such proceedings I am charged withal –
    I won his daughter.

Brabantio again accuses Othello of drugging his daughter. The Duke asks for proof. Othello suggests Desdemona is sent for to give her side of the story. Iago goes to fetch her.

1 '. . . perfection' in a woman?

According to Brabantio, his daughter is a perfect mixture of womanly virtues. Gather from lines 94–8 the aspects he seems to admire in a woman. Write a paragraph explaining your opinion of his views.

2 'Against all rules of nature' (in small groups)

Discuss whether you think that today's society is any more tolerant of so-called 'mixed-race' marriages. What do you think *your* family's reaction to you would be in a similar situation? Then think of any particular places or countries where other circumstances (political, religious) might create illicit relationships.

Improvise a short drama called *Forbidden Friendships*.

3 The case against Othello (in groups of five or more)

With all the talk of criminal acts and sentencing (e.g. in 'the bloody book of law'), it is almost as though Othello were on trial. What exactly is the 'case' against him?

Work out which of the characters on stage you would cast as judge, prosecutor, defendant and witnesses. Choose a significant moment from the script and show where characters would be positioned on stage, in such a way as to illustrate the formality at a court trial of a serious offence. Each major character then summarises what they feel the main 'case' against Othello to be.

motion emotion, desires	**thin habits** outward appearances
credit reputation	**poor likelihoods** weak possibilities
dram potion	**modern seeming** common beliefs
vouch assert	

BRABANTIO   A maiden never bold;
    Of spirit so still and quiet that her motion   95
    Blushed at herself; and she, in spite of nature,
    Of years, of country, credit, everything,
    To fall in love with what she feared to look on?
    It is a judgement maimed and most imperfect
    That will confess perfection so could err   100
    Against all rules of nature, and must be driven
    To find out practices of cunning hell
    Why this should be. I therefore vouch again
    That with some mixtures powerful o'er the blood
    Or with some dram conjured to this effect   105
    He wrought upon her.
DUKE   To vouch this is no proof
    Without more wider and more overt test
    Than these thin habits and poor likelihoods
    Of modern seeming do prefer against him.
I SENATOR But, Othello, speak: 110
    Did you by indirect and forcèd courses
    Subdue and poison this young maid's affections?
    Or came it by request and such fair question
    As soul to soul affordeth?
OTHELLO   I do beseech you
    Send for the lady to the Sagittary   115
    And let her speak of me before her father.
    If you do find me foul in her report,
    The trust, the office I do hold of you,
    Not only take away, but let your sentence
    Even fall upon my life.
DUKE   Fetch Desdemona hither.   120
OTHELLO Ancient, conduct them: you best know the place.
               [*Exit Iago with two or three Attendants*]
    And till she come, as truly as to heaven
    I do confess the vices of my blood,
    So justly to your grave ears I'll present
    How I did thrive in this fair lady's love,   125
    And she in mine.
DUKE   Say it, Othello.

Othello tells how he was introduced to Brabantio's household. He recounts how his relationship with Desdemona began when he entertained her with the story of his life.

---

1 Othello's life story (in groups of four or five)

As a whole class, divide up Othello's summary of his life (lines 128–44) into sections. Each group chooses one of the incidents from Othello's life and creates a short improvisation or a series of tableaux based on their lines. Then put all the sections together.

Come back together as a class and show your collective version of Othello's life history.

2 Two contrasting stories (in pairs)

Othello's account of his courtship of Desdemona gives a very different picture of their relationship from that told by Brabantio. Improvise (or storyboard) two scenes between Othello and Desdemona, one taken from Brabantio's version of events (see lines 59–64 and 94–106) and the other illustrating how Othello claims the courtship happened (lines 144–69).

Discuss which version you think is true, based on your impressions of Brabantio and Othello.

3 Othello's 'soft phrase of peace'

Othello claimed to be 'little blessed with the soft phrase of peace' (line 82). What do you think? Write a paragraph describing the way Othello speaks. As you read on, you will find other activities on Othello's language; add to your description as you discover more.

---

chances events
by flood and field on sea and
  on land
antres caves

Anthropophagi man-eaters,
  cannibals
pliant favourable
intentively altogether

OTHELLO Her father loved me, oft invited me,
       Still questioned me the story of my life
       From year to year – the battles, sieges, fortunes
       That I have passed. 130
       I ran it through, even from my boyish days
       To the very moment that he bade me tell it;
       Wherein I spake of most disastrous chances,
       Of moving accidents by flood and field,
       Of hair-breadth scapes i'th'imminent deadly breach, 135
       Of being taken by the insolent foe
       And sold to slavery; of my redemption thence,
       And with it all my travels' history:
       Wherein of antres vast and deserts idle,
       Rough quarries, rocks, and hills whose heads touch
          heaven, 140
       It was my hint to speak – such was the process:
       And of the cannibals that each other eat,
       The Anthropophagi, and men whose heads
       Do grow beneath their shoulders. This to hear
       Would Desdemona seriously incline; 145
       But still the house affairs would draw her thence,
       Which ever as she could with haste dispatch
       She'd come again, and with a greedy ear
       Devour up my discourse; which I observing
       Took once a pliant hour and found good means 150
       To draw from her a prayer of earnest heart
       That I would all my pilgrimage dilate
       Whereof by parcels she had something heard,
       But not intentively. I did consent,
       And often did beguile her of her tears 155
       When I did speak of some distressful stroke
       That my youth suffered. My story being done,
       She gave me for my pains a world of sighs:

Othello completes the story of his courtship just as Desdemona arrives. Brabantio demands to know where her duty lies, and she answers him diplomatically, but makes it clear that she now obeys Othello before her father.

1 'She loved me for the dangers I had passed' (in groups of three or four)

Improvise a short scene, or write a story, using line 166 as the title. Experiment with different styles of presentation, both serious and comic.

Afterwards, as a whole class, discuss whether you think this is a sound foundation for a marriage. What is it, do you think, that Desdemona is looking for in a man?

2 Desdemona's 'divided duty' (in pairs)

Brabantio directly challenges his daughter to say 'Where most you owe obedience?' Discuss whether you believe this to be a fair question and to whom *you* feel you 'owe obedience' – if anyone.

On a large sheet of paper, create a design based on an image of scales. Enter on each side of the scales what balanced argument Desdemona gives in answer to her father's challenge. Add what other items you think belong in each scale.

From the play so far, deduce what you can about the position of women in Othello's society. Make notes that you can add to as you work through the play.

3 The effect of Othello's words

The Duke seems very impressed by Othello's story. He tells Brabantio: 'Men do their broken weapons rather use / Than their bare hands.' What do you think is meant by this? Consider whether it seems to you to be sound advice. Write a paragraph on a modern situation that would illustrate the Duke's words.

passing exceedingly	**learn me** teach me	
witness give evidence about	**challenge** claim	
Light fall		

She swore, in faith, 'twas strange, 'twas passing strange,
'Twas pitiful, 'twas wondrous pitiful;   160
She wished she had not heard it, yet she wished
That heaven had made her such a man. She thanked me,
And bade me, if I had a friend that loved her,
I should but teach him how to tell my story,
And that would woo her. Upon this hint I spake: 165
She loved me for the dangers I had passed,
And I loved her that she did pity them.
This only is the witchcraft I have used.
Here comes the lady: let her witness it.

Enter DESDEMONA, *Iago and Attendants.*

DUKE I think this tale would win my daughter too.   170
Good Brabantio, take up this mangled matter at the best:
Men do their broken weapons rather use
Than their bare hands.
BRABANTIO   I pray you hear her speak.
If she confess that she was half the wooer,
Destruction on my head if my bad blame   175
Light on the man! Come hither, gentle mistress;
Do you perceive in all this noble company
Where most you owe obedience?
DESDEMONA   My noble father,
I do perceive here a divided duty:
To you I am bound for life and education;   180
My life and education both do learn me
How to respect you. You are lord of all my duty;
I am hitherto your daughter. But here's my husband;
And so much duty as my mother showed
To you, preferring you before her father,   185
So much I challenge that I may profess
Due to the Moor my lord.

Brabantio grudgingly gives up his accusations against Othello. The Duke attempts to cheer him up, but Brabantio refuses comfort. The Duke appoints Othello to supreme charge of the defence of Cyprus.

1 Brabantio as a father (in pairs)

Reread Brabantio's lines 187–96 and 208–18. How do you respond? Identify which of his words might have the greatest effect on you (moving you to anger, pity or regret, etc.). Talk together with your partner about your reactions.

2 Rhyming proverbs and clichés (in groups of three)

The Duke sounds a little like an Elizabethan agony aunt! He speaks a series of clichés and proverbs (along the lines of 'every cloud has a silver lining'). Read aloud lines 200–7 to hear what it sounds like. Why do you think Shakespeare writes in rhyming couplets here?

Pick out the three distinct pieces of advice the Duke gives to Brabantio, and express them in your own words.

3 Back to business – in prose

The Duke stops speaking in verse when he begins to discuss affairs of state. Some critics argue that the reason for the switch from verse to prose is that he urgently wishes to get on to affairs of state, rather than Brabantio's private matters. If you were directing this scene, how would you mark this change on stage (e.g. in tone of voice, movement, position of characters)?

God bu'y!   God be with you!
 (Goodbye!)
clogs   blocks of wood tied to horses'
 legs to stop them escaping
grise   step on a staircase

The robbed   a person who has
 been robbed
bootless   useless
gall   bitterness
slubber   spoil

BRABANTIO   God bu'y! I have done.
        Please it your grace, on to the state affairs.
        I had rather to adopt a child than get it.
        Come hither, Moor: 190
        I here do give thee that with all my heart
        Which, but thou hast already, with all my heart
        I would keep from thee. For your sake, jewel,
        I am glad at soul I have no other child,
        For thy escape would teach me tyranny   195
        To hang clogs on them. I have done, my lord.
DUKE Let me speak like yourself and lay a sentence
        Which as a grise or step may help these lovers
        Into your favour.
        When remedies are past the griefs are ended   200
        By seeing the worst which late on hopes depended.
        To mourn a mischief that is past and gone
        Is the next way to draw new mischief on.
        What cannot be preserved when fortune takes,
        Patience her injury a mockery makes.   205
        The robbed that smiles steals something from the thief;
        He robs himself that spends a bootless grief.
BRABANTIO So let the Turk of Cyprus us beguile,
        We lose it not so long as we can smile;
        He bears the sentence well that nothing bears   210
        But the free comfort which from thence he hears;
        But he bears both the sentence and the sorrow
        That to pay grief must of poor patience borrow.
        These sentences, to sugar or to gall,
        Being strong on both sides, are equivocal.   215
        But words are words; I never yet did hear
        That the bruised heart was piercèd through the ear.
        Beseech you now, to the affairs of the state.
DUKE The Turk with a most mighty preparation makes for Cyprus.
        Othello, the fortitude of the place is best known to you; and   220
        though we have there a substitute of most allowed sufficiency,
        yet opinion, a more sovereign mistress of effects, throws a
        more safer voice on you. You must therefore be content to
        slubber the gloss of your new fortunes with this more stubborn
        and boisterous expedition.   225

Othello promises to depart immediately for Cyprus, asking only that Desdemona be provided for. Neither Brabantio nor Desdemona wishes her to return to her father's house. Desdemona asks if she might accompany Othello.

1 'A maiden never bold'?

Remember, Desdemona's father said of her:

> A maiden never bold;
> Of spirit so still and quiet that her motion
> Blushed at herself . . .
> *Act 1 Scene 3, lines 94–6*

How well does her father really know her?

Reread all that Desdemona says on the opposite page. Identify all the things she says that appear to challenge her father's description, and that also challenge the convention that a wife does not accompany her husband to war. Then think about all of Desdemona's actions in the play so far. Try to decide what kind of a woman she appears to be. Don't forget to provide evidence for your ideas.

2 '. . . storm of fortunes' (in pairs)

This comment at line 245 by Desdemona may mean either 'taking my future by storm' or 'creating a stormy future'. One edition of the play uses the word 'scorn' instead of 'storm', so that she is saying that she loves Othello so much she has sacrificed her secure family life for him. Talk together about whether you think 'storm' or 'scorn' is most appropriate and why.

3 'I saw Othello's visage in his mind' (in pairs)

Spend five minutes discussing what you think Desdemona means by line 248. Can you decide why she feels it important to make the point at this moment?

---

thrice-driven bed of down a feather bed of the very finest quality
agnise acknowledge
Ottomites Turks

disposition arrangements
exhibition financial support
besort servants
downright violence open rebellion

OTHELLO   The tyrant custom, most grave senators,
          Hath made the flinty and steel couch of war
          My thrice-driven bed of down. I do agnise
          A natural and prompt alacrity
          I find in hardness, and do undertake   230
          These present wars against the Ottomites.
          Most humbly, therefore, bending to your state,
          I crave fit disposition for my wife,
          Due reference of place and exhibition
          With such accommodation and besort   235
          As levels with her breeding.
DUKE   If you please,
          Be't at her father's.
BRABANTIO   I'll not have it so.
OTHELLO   Nor I.
DESDEMONA   Nor I; I would not there reside
          To put my father in impatient thoughts
          By being in his eye. Most gracious duke,   240
          To my unfolding lend your prosperous ear
          And let me find a charter in your voice
          T'assist my simpleness.
DUKE   What would you, Desdemona?
DESDEMONA That I did love the Moor to live with him,
          My downright violence and storm of fortunes   245
          May trumpet to the world. My heart's subdued
          Even to the very quality of my lord.
          I saw Othello's visage in his mind
          And to his honours and his valiant parts
          Did I my soul and fortunes consecrate.   250
          So that, dear lords, if I be left behind
          A moth of peace, and he go to the war,
          The rites for which I love him are bereft me,
          And I a heavy interim shall support
          By his dear absence. Let me go with him.   255

Othello wishes Desdemona to accompany him, and asserts that she will not distract him from his military duties. The Duke orders that they must depart that very night for Cyprus. Brabantio warns Othello of Desdemona's deceit.

---

1 'Let housewives make a skillet of my helm' (in pairs)

Othello assures the senators that he will not be distracted by Desdemona's presence. In lines 262–70 he uses two images to under-line his assertion: first, that of Cupid blindfolding him; and, second, his helmet converted to a cooking pot (skillet). Locate the exact words in the script, then design a visual representation of both images.

2 Dramatic irony (in small groups)

Othello says of Iago, 'A man he is of honesty and trust' (line 280). This is an example of **dramatic irony**, where the audience knows more than a character on stage. There are numerous examples of it in *Othello*. Talk together about the dramatic effect of such lines.

3 A 'fair' comment?

The Duke comments: 'If virtue no delighted beauty lack, / Your son-in-law is far more fair than black.' This is meant to be a compliment about Othello! Jot down what you think this comment suggests about the Duke's attitude to Othello as a black man.

4 Foreboding

Brabantio's parting words are to warn Othello that Desdemona is untrustworthy (line 289). Othello swears that he entrusts his life upon Desdemona's loyalty (line 290). How does this exchange shape your expectations, particularly given that Othello wholeheartedly trusts Iago?

---

scant neglect
seel close up
disports sexual pleasures
indign unworthy

Make head against attack
estimation reputation
import concern

OTHELLO Let her have your voice.
        Vouch with me, heaven, I therefore beg it not
        To please the palate of my appetite,
        Nor to comply with heat the young affects
        In my distinct and proper satisfaction,   260
        But to be free and bounteous to her mind.
        And heaven defend your good souls that you think
        I will your serious and great business scant
        For she is with me. No, when light-winged toys
        Of feathered Cupid seel with wanton dullness   265
        My speculative and officed instruments,
        That my disports corrupt and taint my business,
        Let housewives make a skillet of my helm,
        And all indign and base adversities
        Make head against my estimation!   270
DUKE Be it as you shall privately determine,
        Either for her stay or going. Th'affair cries haste,
        And speed must answer it. You must hence tonight.
DESDEMONA Tonight, my lord?
DUKE   This night.
OTHELLO   With all my heart.
DUKE At nine i'the morning, here we'll meet again.   275
        Othello, leave some officer behind
        And he shall our commission bring to you
        With such things else of quality and respect
        As doth import you.
OTHELLO   So please your grace, my ancient:
        A man he is of honesty and trust.   280
        To his conveyance I assign my wife,
        With what else needful your good grace shall think
        To be sent after me.
DUKE   Let it be so.
        Good night to everyone. [*To Brabantio*] And noble
                signior,
        If virtue no delighted beauty lack,   285
        Your son-in-law is far more fair than black.
I SENATOR Adieu, brave Moor; use Desdemona well.
BRABANTIO Look to her, Moor, if thou hast eyes to see:
        She has deceived her father and may thee.
OTHELLO My life upon her faith!
        Exeunt [Duke, Brabantio, Cassio, Senators and Attendants]

Othello charges Iago to look after Desdemona. Roderigo is despondent, but Iago scorns his love-sickness and argues that will and reason govern men's appetites.

---

1 Contrasting characters (in groups of three)

Read the exchange between Iago and Roderigo, then try different ways of acting it out. The third member of the group is the director. Try to distinguish between the two characters in the way you present it. (Remember, Roderigo is a 'gentleman', whilst Iago is a professional soldier.) Try reading it in a variety of styles (e.g. serious, funny, threatening). Which one sounds best?

2 Iago's garden imagery (in pairs)

Writers use **imagery** to help create an image or association in the reader's or listener's mind. Garden imagery is used by Shakespeare in other plays too (e.g. in *King Richard II* the whole kingdom is likened to an unkempt garden). How successful is Iago at creating a picture for you, and does it help to make clearer what he is saying to Roderigo?

Talk with your partner about whether you agree with Iago's view that 'our wills are gardeners' where our emotions are concerned, and that love is 'a sect or scion' (grafted on). Can love be controlled by reason?

3 Sexist language

Some readers find the terms Iago uses to describe women highly offensive. Examples are his derogatory terms like 'guinea-hen' (a 'tart'), and his exclamation of 'A fig!' – a contemptuous remark usually accompanied by making a rude gesture (thrusting the thumb between the first and second fingers). Why do you think Iago uses sexist language?

---

incontinently immediately
hyssop, thyme aromatic herbs
gender type
corrigible authority ability to control

poise counterbalance
carnal stings sexual urges
unbitted unbridled

Honest Iago 290
My Desdemona must I leave to thee;
I prithee, let thy wife attend on her,
And bring her after in the best advantage.
Come, Desdemona, I have but an hour
Of love, of worldly matters and direction 295
To spend with thee. We must obey the time.

Exeunt Othello and Desdemona

RODERIGO Iago.

IAGO What say'st thou, noble heart?

RODERIGO What will I do, think'st thou?

IAGO Why, go to bed and sleep. 300

RODERIGO I will incontinently drown myself.

IAGO If thou dost, I shall never love thee after. Why, thou silly
gentleman?

RODERIGO It is silliness to live, when to live is torment: and then we
have a prescription to die, when death is our physician. 305

IAGO O villainous! I have looked upon the world for four times seven
years, and since I could distinguish betwixt a benefit and an
injury, I never found a man that knew how to love himself. Ere
I would say I would drown myself for the love of a guinea-hen,
I would change my humanity with a baboon. 310

RODERIGO What should I do? I confess it is my shame to be so fond,
but it is not in my virtue to amend it.

IAGO Virtue? A fig! 'Tis in ourselves that we are thus or thus. Our
bodies are our gardens, to the which our wills are gardeners. So
that if we will plant nettles or sow lettuce, set hyssop and weed 315
up thyme, supply it with one gender of herbs or distract it
with many, either to have it sterile with idleness or manured with
industry, why the power and corrigible authority of this lies in
our wills. If the balance of our lives had not one scale of reason
to poise another of sensuality, the blood and baseness of our 320
natures would conduct us to most preposterous conclusions. But
we have reason to cool our raging motions, our carnal stings,
our unbitted lusts; whereof I take this, that you call love, to be
a sect or scion.

RODERIGO It cannot be. 325

Iago continues to persuade Roderigo that Desdemona and Othello will soon tire of one another. He tells of his hatred for Othello and urges Roderigo to join him in seeking revenge.

The dialogue in lines 297–364 has all been in prose. Discuss as a class why Shakespeare might have chosen to do this and what difference it makes. Think about the situation, the content of Iago's words, and his urging ten times that Roderigo get more money.

---

perdurable long-lasting
stead help
sequestration separation
locusts fruits of the carob tree

acerb bitter
coloquintida bitter apple
conjunctive allied
Traverse! About turn!

IAGO It is merely a lust of the blood and a permission of the will. Come, be a man. Drown thyself? Drown cats and blind puppies. I have professed me thy friend, and I confess me knit to thy deserving with cables of perdurable toughness. I could never better stead thee than now. Put money in thy purse. Follow 330 thou these wars; defeat thy favour with an usurped beard. I say, put money in thy purse. It cannot be that Desdemona should long continue her love to the Moor – put money in thy purse – nor he his to her. It was a violent commencement, and thou shalt see an answerable sequestration – put but money in thy 335 purse. These Moors are changeable in their wills – fill thy purse with money. The food that to him now is as luscious as locusts shall be to him shortly as acerb as the coloquintida. She must change for youth; when she is sated with his body she will find the error of her choice. Therefore put money in thy 340 purse. If thou wilt needs damn thyself, do it a more delicate way than drowning. Make all the money thou canst. If sanctimony and a frail vow betwixt an erring barbarian and a super-subtle Venetian be not too hard for my wits and all the tribe of hell, thou shalt enjoy her – therefore make money. A pox of drowning 345 thyself! It is clean out of the way. Seek thou rather to be hanged in compassing thy joy than to be drowned and go without her.

RODERIGO Wilt thou be fast to my hopes, if I depend on the issue?

IAGO Thou art sure of me. Go make money. I have told thee often, and I retell thee again and again, I hate the Moor. My cause is 350 hearted: thine hath no less reason. Let us be conjunctive in our revenge against him. If thou canst cuckold him, thou dost thyself a pleasure, me a sport. There are many events in the womb of time which will be delivered. Traverse! Go, provide thy money. We will have more of this tomorrow. Adieu. 355

RODERIGO Where shall we meet i'the morning?

IAGO At my lodging.

RODERIGO I'll be with thee betimes.

IAGO Go to; farewell. Do you hear, Roderigo?

RODERIGO What say you? 360

IAGO No more of drowning, do you hear?

RODERIGO I am changed.

IAGO Go to; farewell. Put money enough in your purse.

RODERIGO I'll sell all my land. *Exit*

Iago is left alone on stage. He reveals that he suspects his wife has been unfaithful with Othello. He begins to make plans to ruin Othello's marriage and to seek revenge on Cassio, by making Othello believe Cassio and Desdemona are lovers.

---

1 Iago's soliloquy (in pairs)

The **soliloquy** is a dramatic convention in which a character who is alone on stage speaks their own thoughts aloud. On the Elizabethan and Jacobean stage it is likely that the speech was addressed from the front of the stage directly to the audience.

Usually, the soliloquy reveals a character's thoughts, motives or state of mind at that point in the play.

This is the first time Iago has been alone on stage. It is the first time the audience has had the opportunity to hear his version of events. Three ways in which a director could present this speech are:

- directed towards the audience
- as if Iago is talking to himself
- as a voice-over, whilst the actor looks pensive and lost in thought.

All three methods have been used in film and television versions of Shakespeare plays.

Read the speech in each of the three ways listed above. Consider for each method:

- how the actor would speak the lines
- what movements would be required
- in what differing ways you wish the audience to react
- how it affects your interpretation of Iago's character. Is he sly, evil or manipulative? Does it draw the audience into colluding and sympathising with Iago?

Make notes on each version as you try it out. Report back to the rest of the class.

---

snipe a long-beaked bird (but here a derogatory term)
abroad generally
done my office slept with my wife

proper handsome
plume up my will have a bit of fun, or glorify myself
framed made
engendered formed, created

IAGO Thus do I ever make my fool my purse;   365
For I mine own gained knowledge should profane
If I would time expend with such a snipe
But for my sport and profit. I hate the Moor,
And it is thought abroad that 'twixt my sheets
He's done my office. I know not if't be true   370
Yet I, for mere suspicion in that kind,
Will do as if for surety. He holds me well:
The better shall my purpose work on him.
Cassio's a proper man: let me see now;
To get his place and to plume up my will   375
In double knavery. How? How? Let's see.
After some time, to abuse Othello's ear
That he is too familiar with his wife;
He hath a person and a smooth dispose
To be suspected, framed to make women false.   380
The Moor is of a free and open nature,
That thinks men honest that but seem to be so,
And will as tenderly be led by the nose
As asses are.
I have't. It is engendered. Hell and night   385
Must bring this monstrous birth to the world's light.   *Exit*

Looking back at Act 1
Activities for groups or individuals

1 Cast the play (in pairs)

Imagine you are a film director about to shoot a new version of *Othello*. Go through the cast list on page 1, noting down those characters you have encountered in Act 1. Decide which well-known film actors you would cast in each part. In each case, say what makes you believe they are right for the part.

2 Disputed stories

In Scene 3 it's clear that Brabantio believes that his daughter has been charmed by Othello, unnaturally lured away from her family by 'witchcraft'. Othello seems to believe that she was naturally enchanted by his heroic telling of stories that are a mixture of travellers' tales and action-man adventures. Desdemona does not reveal what actually happened during her courtship, but suggests to her father that she is in control of the situation. Reread the script on pages 27–39, then write three short pieces:

a Imagine that Brabantio makes a formal written complaint to the Senate, disputing the Duke's ruling.

b Othello writes a letter to the Duke, thanking him for his support.

c Desdemona writes to Brabantio, describing what happened to her and how she feels after hearing her father's abusive words in front of the Senate.

3 Tableaux (in groups of four)

Choose three of the following quotations (all taken from Act 1):

'Thus do I ever make my fool my purse'
'The robbed that smiles steals something from the thief'
'I am not what I am.'
'I must show out a flag and sign of love'
'trust not your daughters' minds / By what you see them act.'
'She loved me for the dangers I had passed'
'Hell and night / Must bring this monstrous birth to the world's light.'

For each quotation you have selected, devise a tableau (a still picture) or short series of tableaux that are suggested by the words. For this activity, you are not creating a freeze-frame of what's happening on stage at a given moment, but experimenting with ideas, symbols or concepts. Your tableaux are not meant to be naturalistic. Present your tableaux to the rest of the class – can they guess which quotation you are representing?

4 Public and private tensions

Why does Shakespeare set Act 1 in Venice?
One answer would be that Shakespeare's source story is set in Venice and Cyprus, and he simply copied it – but that's not the only answer. It's important to know something about sixteenth-century Venice and its social and economic significance in Europe, because places carry associations that may affect the way we interpret people or events.

So Venice carried certain associations?
For an English audience in 1604 (when the play was first performed), Venice was a byword for thriving capitalism. It was a republic where the wealthier merchant classes controlled the state, buying powerful military forces to protect their colonial exploits. In contrast, England had only just started increasing overseas trade in Africa, India and elsewhere, and was on the brink of massive colonial enterprise in the New World. English merchants would recognise in Venice the mercantile and colonial force that they would like to see England become.

And in the terms of the play . . .?
The Venetian state employed mercenary soldiers. It was a cosmopolitan state, so a black military leader would not be unusual. Othello, an ex-slave, is revered by the Venetian Senate simply because he very effectively defends their interests. He is, however, not entirely 'one of them' (as Brabantio makes clear) when it comes to marrying one of their daughters. Desdemona is described in terms of stolen jewellery precisely because Brabantio feels he has been robbed – by someone who was employed to *protect* his possessions! The non-feudal society of Venice confers *power* on Othello, but not *status*. This provides a rich source of dramatic tension.

In Act 1, Venetian law and order is seen to operate quickly and efficiently. Iago's trouble-making is easily dealt with, as is the Turkish threat to Venetian stability. But as you go into Act 2, remember we are moving to a disputed outpost on the edges of Venetian rule. Our introduction to Cyprus will be a violent storm where the natural boundaries between sea and sky are blurred.

Before you read on, use the information above and your knowledge of Act 1 to write several paragraphs on the tensions between 'private' and 'public' interests in the play so far.

Montano and two gentlemen discuss the terrible storm. A third gentleman brings news that the Turkish fleet has been destroyed. He reports that Cassio's ship has safely docked, but that Othello is still at sea.

1 Setting (in pairs)

As with most Elizabethan drama, there are no original stage directions for this scene specifying where it takes place. How would an audience know who these people are in this opening scene of Act 2? Read the dialogue opposite and pick out any clues as to setting and characters.

Imagine you are the directors of a production of *Othello*. Write notes on how you would stage this page of script, and what directions you would give the actors. Your aim is to help the audience to understand where they are and what is going on.

2 The storm – symbolic significance?

In the original story by Giraldi Cinthio, from which Shakespeare took his ideas for *Othello*, there is no storm at all, yet we have here a whole page of dialogue devoted to a description of it. You will also find that in the next few pages most of the characters will mention the storm several times. Presumably Shakespeare considered a storm at this point would have some dramatic or thematic use.

It certainly echoes the ominous mood established by Iago's couplet at the end of Act 1, and some commentators suggest that the storm has a symbolic function (as the calm before the storm, or as stormy emotions, and so on). Can you think of other similar sayings?

At the end of this act (see p. 90), you will be invited to look at this matter of the storm in more detail. As you read the rest of this scene, keep this stormy opening in mind, and reflect on its effect on what follows.

Descry   make out, see
ribs of oak   (of a boat)
hold the mortise   hold their joints together
banning   forbidding
chidden billow   waves hurled back

Bear, Pole   constellation of stars (Ursa Major) and the Pole Star
designment halts   enterprise is crippled
Veronesa   Italian ship

Act 2 Scene 1
Cyprus A quayside

Enter MONTANO *and two* GENTLEMEN.

MONTANO What from the cape can you discern at sea?
1 GENTLEMAN Nothing at all; it is a high-wrought flood.
    I cannot 'twixt the heaven and the main
    Descry a sail.
MONTANO Methinks the wind does speak aloud at land,   5
    A fuller blast ne'er shook our battlements.
    If it hath ruffianed so upon the sea,
    What ribs of oak, when mountains melt on them,
    Can hold the mortise? What shall we hear of this?
2 GENTLEMAN A segregation of the Turkish fleet: 10
    For do but stand upon the banning shore,
    The chidden billow seems to pelt the clouds;
    The wind-shaked surge, with high and monstrous mane,
    Seems to cast water on the burning Bear
    And quench the guards of th'ever-fixèd Pole.   15
    I never did like molestation view
    On the enchafèd flood.
MONTANO   If that the Turkish fleet
    Be not ensheltered and embayed, they are drowned:
    It is impossible they bear it out.

Enter a third GENTLEMAN.

3 GENTLEMAN News, lads! Our wars are done: 20
    The desperate tempest hath so banged the Turks
    That their designment halts. A noble ship of Venice
    Hath seen a grievous wrack and sufferance
    On most part of their fleet.
MONTANO How? Is this true?
3 GENTLEMAN   The ship is here put in,   25
    A Veronesa; Michael Cassio,
    Lieutenant to the warlike Moor Othello,
    Is come on shore; the Moor himself at sea,
    And is in full commission here for Cyprus.
MONTANO I am glad on't; 'tis a worthy governor.   30

Cassio lands safely, but he is worried that Othello's ship has not yet reached shore. A messenger reports another ship is sighted, and Cassio sends for news.

1 More views of Othello

Lines 1–59 contain several references to Othello. Collect them, and consider what aspects of Othello the comments refer to, and whether they are generally in praise or critical of him. What group of people might the commentators be seen to represent?

2 What is the dramatic purpose?

In the opening 171 lines, several characters ask the question 'Is Othello alive or dead?' What do you think is the dramatic purpose of this delay before Othello's triumphant entrance, fresh from the storm? It may be helpful to reflect on how Othello's entrance in Act 1 was also delayed.

3 *Venetian Chronicle* (in small groups)

Imagine you are a newspaper journalist reporting on the destruction of the Turkish fleet and on Othello's expected triumphant return. Compile the front page of your newspaper. It might contain news of the routing of the Turkish fleet, the storm, the fears for Othello's safety, a profile of Othello, a report on his recent marriage and inter-views with witnesses/friends.

Remember, a Venetian paper would be very supportive of Othello and his exploits, whereas a Cyprus-owned newspaper might view the events differently. Produce a large-format front page for your classroom wall and compare it with other groups' versions.

main sea		**allowance** reputation	
aerial blue sky		**surfeited to death** excessive	
An indistinct regard indistinguishable		**in bold cure** healthy	

3 GENTLEMAN But this same Cassio, though he speak of comfort
    Touching the Turkish loss, yet he looks sadly
    And prays the Moor be safe; for they were parted
    With foul and violent tempest.
MONTANO   Pray heaven he be;
    For I have served him, and the man commands   35
    Like a full soldier. Let's to the seaside, ho!
    As well to see the vessel that's come in
    As to throw out our eyes for brave Othello,
    Even till we make the main and th'aerial blue
    An indistinct regard.
3 GENTLEMAN   Come, let's do so;   40
    For every minute is expectancy
    Of more arrivance.

Enter CASSIO.

CASSIO Thanks, you the valiant of this warlike isle
    That so approve the Moor. O, let the heavens
    Give him defence against the elements,   45
    For I have lost him on a dangerous sea.
MONTANO Is he well shipped?
CASSIO His bark is stoutly timbered, and his pilot
    Of very expert and approved allowance;
    Therefore my hopes, not surfeited to death,   50
    Stand in bold cure.
    [*A shout*] *within, 'A sail, a sail, a sail!'*

Enter a MESSENGER.

CASSIO What noise?
MESSENGER The town is empty; on the brow o'the sea
    Stand ranks of people and they cry, 'A sail!'
CASSIO My hopes do shape him for the governor.   55
    A shot [*is heard within*].
2 GENTLEMAN They do discharge their shot of courtesy;
    Our friends at least.
CASSIO   I pray you, sir, go forth,
    And give us truth who 'tis that is arrived.
2 GENTLEMAN I shall.   *Exit*

Cassio describes to Montano the virtues of Desdemona. Iago is reported to have come ashore. Desdemona, Iago, Emilia and Roderigo are greeted by Cassio, but there is still no news of Othello.

1 Cassio's descriptions of Desdemona (in pairs)

In the script opposite, Cassio uses at least four different ways of referring to Desdemona. For example, the 'riches of the ship' is his description of Desdemona as she comes ashore.

a Pick out four different descriptions of Desdemona and write them down.

b Comment on the language used (e.g. Is she compared to anything? Do you think the praise is exaggerated?).

c Two other characters have already compared Desdemona to treasure (in Act 1). Identify them, and locate the references. What do you think is the effect of these comparisons?

2 What is your impression of Cassio? (in groups of three)

Spend about five minutes discussing how Cassio's personality is emerging in this scene. Find quotations to support your opinions.

What advice would you give an actor playing Cassio? Go through the script and make decisions about your advice on each of Cassio's speeches so far.

Finally, look back at Act 1 Scene 1, lines 19–27, and Act 1 Scene 3, lines 374–80, and then make a list of the qualities you think Cassio possesses. Find a photograph in a newspaper or magazine that represents 'your' imagined impression of Cassio.

---

paragons excels
blazoning praising
essential vesture perfect beauty
ingener designer

enscarped drawn up into ridges
footing landing
se'nnight week
let her have your knees kneel to her

MONTANO But, good lieutenant, is your general wived?   60
CASSIO Most fortunately: he hath achieved a maid
   That paragons description and wild fame;
   One that excels the quirks of blazoning pens
   And in th'essential vesture of creation
   Does tire the ingener.

     Enter Second Gentleman.

     How now? Who's put in?   65
2 GENTLEMAN 'Tis one Iago, ancient to the general.
CASSIO He's had most favourable and happy speed:
   Tempests themselves, high seas, and howling winds,
   The guttered rocks and congregated sands,
   Traitors enscarped to clog the guiltless keel,   70
   As having sense of beauty do omit
   Their mortal natures, letting go safely by
   The divine Desdemona.
MONTANO   What is she?
CASSIO She that I spake of, our great captain's captain,
   Left in the conduct of the bold Iago,   75
   Whose footing here anticipates our thoughts
   A se'nnight's speed. Great Jove Othello guard
   And swell his sail with thine own powerful breath,
   That he may bless this bay with his tall ship,
   Make love's quick pants in Desdemona's arms,   80
   Give renewed fire to our extincted spirits,
   And bring all Cyprus comfort.

  Enter DESDEMONA, IAGO, EMILIA *and* RODERIGO.

      O, behold,
   The riches of the ship is come on shore!
   You men of Cyprus, let her have your knees.
   Hail to thee, lady! And the grace of heaven,   85
   Before, behind thee, and on every hand,
   Enwheel thee round.
DESDEMONA   I thank you, valiant Cassio.
   What tidings can you tell me of my lord?
CASSIO He is not yet arrived; nor know I aught
   But that he's well, and will be shortly here.   90

While waiting for news of Othello's ship, Iago, Emilia and Desdemona pass the time in conversation. Iago makes provocative comments about wives and women.

1 Cassio's kiss – dramatic possibilities

Cassio has greeted Desdemona with a flourish and a bow (see lines 84–5); now he kisses Emilia – but he apologises first to Iago for his 'bold show of courtesy' and puts it down to his good 'breeding' and 'manners'. It's potentially a dramatically fascinating moment on stage, open to a very wide range of acting possibilities.

a How would *you* interpret Cassio's behaviour?
  - He's a macho flirt with a reputation to keep up.
  - He's a naturally courteous man.
  - He's deliberately winding Iago up.
  - He's aware of Iago's jealous nature.
  - He's trying to be nice to everyone at a difficult moment.
  - He's not very confident in social situations.
  - He's deliberately patronising Emilia.
  - Some other interpretation.

b How many different ways could you direct Cassio and Emilia at this point in the script? For example, is Cassio's kiss a courteous peck – or is he taking liberties? How does Emilia react (for instance, embarrassed, flattered, irritated or . . .)?

c In the video version of Trevor Nunn's 1990 production, Iago is clearly jealous. He swiftly moves across to take hold of Emilia, as if reclaiming his property. Decide how *you* would like Iago to react.

---

gall annoy
have list want
puts her tongue . . . heart holds her
  tongue
chides with thinking keeps her
  thoughts to herself

pictures silent
bells noisy
assay try

DESDEMONA O, but I fear – how lost you company?

CASSIO The great contention of the sea and skies
   Parted our fellowship.
   [A shout] within, 'A sail, a sail!' [A shot is heard.]
      But hark, a sail!

2 GENTLEMAN They give their greeting to the citadel:
   This likewise is a friend.

CASSIO   See for the news.   95
          [Exit Second Gentleman]
   Good ancient, you are welcome. *[To Emilia]* Welcome,
    mistress.
   Let it not gall your patience, good Iago,
   That I extend my manners. 'Tis my breeding
   That gives me this bold show of courtesy.
      [He kisses Emilia.]

IAGO Sir, would she give you so much of her lips 100
   As of her tongue she oft bestows on me
   You would have enough.

DESDEMONA Alas, she has no speech.

IAGO   In faith, too much:
   I find it still when I have list to sleep.
   Marry, before your ladyship, I grant   105
   She puts her tongue a little in her heart
   And chides with thinking.

EMILIA   You've little cause to say so.

IAGO Come on, come on; you are pictures out of doors, bells in
  your parlours, wild-cats in your kitchens, saints in your injuries,
  devils being offended, players in your housewifery, and 110
  housewives in your beds.

DESDEMONA O fie upon thee, slanderer!

IAGO Nay, it is true, or else I am a Turk:
   You rise to play and go to bed to work.

EMILIA You shall not write my praise.

IAGO   No, let me not.   115

DESDEMONA What wouldst thou write of me, if thou shouldst
   praise me?

IAGO O, gentle lady, do not put me to't,
   For I am nothing if not critical.

DESDEMONA Come on, assay. There's one gone to the harbour?

IAGO Ay, madam.   120

Desdemona reveals that she is deliberately joining in the conversation to take her mind off waiting for Othello. Iago continues to joke about women.

___

1 Friendly banter or pointed comments? (in small groups)

How should this part of the scene be played? Is it light-hearted banter, the only tension being that of Desdemona awaiting news that her husband is safe? Or is there bitterness and tension arising out of Iago's pointed comments about women in general, and about his wife in particular? Some commentators have further suggested there is an underlying class conflict between the courtly, educated Cassio and the uneducated, lower-class Iago.

Discuss whether you think it is an episode of friendly chatter, or one tinged with misogyny (hatred of women), domestic strife and class-based tension.

2 Puns, paradoxes and epigrams (in pairs)

Shakespeare's audiences were amused and fascinated by all types of language play. Find examples of each of the following:

a **Puns**   Words that sound the same but have quite different meanings. Puns were a highly fashionable form of wordplay. In *Romeo and Juliet*, Mercutio, fatally stabbed, makes a pun: 'ask for me tomorrow and you shall find me a grave man'. Here, Iago puns on the words 'white' (meaning colour, wit or cleverness) and 'wight' (an old word for person or lover). The words 'fair' and 'black' are used repeatedly in this play. They are used to denote the actual physical colouring of Othello and Desdemona, and also carry certain connotative meanings (associations), which Iago is keen to exploit.

b **Epigrams**   Also very popular. An epigram is a concise, witty poem which often ends on a surprising turn of thought. Sardonic generalisations were commonly put into the mouths of down-to-earth, 'honest' characters.

c **Paradoxes**   A kind of riddle, containing ideas which are self-contradictory.

___

birdlime   sticky substance to catch birds
frieze   woollen cloth
muse   goddess of poetry

fond   foolish
One that . . . itself   a good woman that even malice would praise
wight   lover

DESDEMONA [*Aside*] I am not merry, but I do beguile
    The thing I am by seeming otherwise –
    Come, how wouldst thou praise me?
IAGO I am about it, but indeed my invention
    Comes from my pate as birdlime does from frieze –   125
    It plucks out brains and all. But my muse labours,
    And thus she is delivered:
    'If she be fair and wise, fairness and wit,
    The one's for use, the other useth it.'
DESDEMONA Well praised! How if she be black and witty?   130
IAGO 'If she be black, and thereto have a wit,
    She'll find a white that shall her blackness fit.'
DESDEMONA Worse and worse.
EMILIA   How if fair and foolish?
IAGO 'She never yet was foolish that was fair,
    For even her folly helped her to an heir.'   135
DESDEMONA These are old fond paradoxes to make fools laugh
    i'th'alehouse. What miserable praise hast thou for her that's foul
    and foolish?
IAGO 'There's none so foul and foolish thereunto,
    But does foul pranks which fair and wise ones do.'   140
DESDEMONA O heavy ignorance! Thou praisest the worst best. But
    what praise couldst thou bestow on a deserving woman indeed? One
    that in the authority of her merit did justly put on the vouch of
    very malice itself?
IAGO 'She that was ever fair, and never proud,   145
    Had tongue at will, and yet was never loud;
    Never lacked gold, and yet went never gay;
    Fled from her wish, and yet said "Now I may";
    She that being angered, her revenge being nigh,
    Bade her wrong stay, and her displeasure fly;   150
    She that in wisdom never was so frail
    To change the cod's head for the salmon's tail;
    She that could think and ne'er disclose her mind,
    See suitors following and not look behind;
    She was a wight, if ever such wight were –'   155
DESDEMONA To do what?
IAGO 'To suckle fools and chronicle small beer.'
DESDEMONA O, most lame and impotent conclusion! Do not learn of
    him, Emilia, though he be thy husband. How say you, Cassio, is
    he not a most profane and liberal counsellor?   160

Iago revels in Cassio's attention to Desdemona, seeing in it a way in which he can ruin Cassio. Othello arrives safely. He and Desdemona greet each other, speaking of happiness and love.

---

1 '. . . an excellent courtesy!' (in groups of three or four)

Read Iago's Aside to the audience (lines 163–71) and then act it out, matching the movements of Cassio and Desdemona to Iago's commentary. Where should Iago stand, and how should he say the words? Iago uses several images in his speech, in turn: a spider's web, a snare ('gyve') and, lastly, tubes for inserting enemas into the rectum ('clyster-pipes')!

If you have enough people in your group, you could also include either Roderigo or Emilia, and show what they might be engaged in at this point.

2 Another kiss (in small groups)

a How do Othello and Desdemona kiss? In Oliver Parker's 1995 film version it is an intensely passionate embrace, the lovers oblivious of the public gaze. In Trevor Nunn's 1990 Royal Shakespeare Company production it is restrained and gives little away of the private life of the couple.

b Spend about five minutes discussing how you would differentiate between the three different kisses contained in this scene so far (one is mentioned in Iago's Aside opposite). You could show them in frozen picture form and get the rest of the class to identify each. Don't forget to include Iago; consider his position, actions, facial expressions and so on.

c Now write three separate paragraphs in role as Iago, speaking about how he reacts to each kiss. Think about what Iago has revealed about his attitudes, feelings and jealousies in his soliloquies so far.

---

home plainly
bark ship
Olympus (mountain home of the gods in classical mythology)

If it were now to die if I were to die now

CASSIO He speaks home, madam; you may relish him more in the
soldier than in the scholar.

IAGO [*Aside*] He takes her by the palm. Ay, well said; whisper.
With as little a web as this will I ensnare as great a fly as Cassio.
Ay, smile upon her, do. I will gyve thee in thine own courtship.   165
You say true, 'tis so indeed. If such tricks as these strip you out
of your lieutenantry, it had been better you had not kissed your
three fingers so oft, which now again you are most apt to play the
sir in. Very good, well kissed, an excellent courtesy! 'Tis so
indeed. Yet again your fingers to your lips? Would they were   170
clyster-pipes for your sake!

Trumpets within.

The Moor! I know his trumpet.

CASSIO   'Tis truly so.

DESDEMONA Let's meet him and receive him.

CASSIO   Lo, where he comes!

Enter OTHELLO *and* ATTENDANTS.

OTHELLO O, my fair warrior!

DESDEMONA   My dear Othello!

OTHELLO It gives me wonder great as my content   175
To see you here before me. O, my soul's joy,
If after every tempest come such calms,
May the winds blow till they have wakened death,
And let the labouring bark climb hills of seas,
Olympus-high, and duck again as low   180
As hell's from heaven. If it were now to die,
'Twere now to be most happy; for I fear
My soul hath her content so absolute
That not another comfort like to this
Succeeds in unknown fate.

DESDEMONA   The heavens forbid   185
But that our loves and comforts should increase,
Even as our days do grow.

OTHELLO   Amen to that, sweet powers!
I cannot speak enough of this content;
It stops me here; it is too much of joy.

They kiss.

And this, and this, the greatest discords be   190
That e'er our hearts shall make.

Othello and Desdemona go off together, leaving Iago alone with Roderigo. Iago tells him that Desdemona is in love with Cassio, because she must necessarily tire of Othello.

1 Making sweet music together

Iago's comment (line 191) that Othello and his wife 'are well tuned' is followed by his vow to 'set down the pegs' (to slacken the strings of an instrument). The metaphor uses the harmony of music to indicate the current harmony of Othello's marriage, and Iago's intention to disrupt that harmony. (For an activity on imagery, see p. 229.)

2 Othello's voyage

Write Othello's ship's log for his journey to Cyprus. You might include some of the following:

- thoughts on setting out
- plans to defend Cyprus
- any possible encounters with the Turkish ships
- thoughts about Desdemona
- a description of the storm
- fears for Desdemona's safety
- feelings on reaching harbour safely.

3 Iago's argument – how convincing? (in pairs)

According to Iago, Othello is defective in 'loveliness in / favour, sympathy in years, manners and beauties . . .'. He assures Roderigo that Desdemona will quickly tire of her husband 'When the blood / is made dull with the act of sport', and that she had only been attracted to his 'bragging' and 'fantastical lies'.

Read lines 212–35 to each other, taking turns to read small sections.

On what evidence is Iago basing his version of Othello and Desdemona's relationship? How convincing a case does Iago manage to put together for Roderigo's sake?

I dote I'm not making sense
master captain of the ship
list me listen to me

Lay thy finger thus put your finger to your lips (Ssshh!)
compassing achieving
salt lecherous

IAGO [*Aside*]   O, you are well tuned now!
    But I'll set down the pegs that make this music,
    As honest as I am.
OTHELLO   Come, let us to the castle.
    News, friends; our wars are done; the Turks are drowned.
    How does my old acquaintance of this isle?   195
    Honey, you shall be well desired in Cyprus;
    I have found great love amongst them. O my sweet,
    I prattle out of fashion and I dote
    In mine own comforts. I prithee, good Iago,
    Go to the bay and disembark my coffers;   200
    Bring thou the master to the citadel;
    He is a good one, and his worthiness
    Does challenge much respect. Come, Desdemona,
    Once more well met at Cyprus!
                   Exeunt [all except Iago and Roderigo]
IAGO [*To a departing Attendant*] Do thou meet me presently at the   205
harbour. [*To Roderigo*] Come hither. If thou be'st valiant – as
they say base men being in love have then a nobility in their
natures more than is native to them – list me. The lieutenant
tonight watches on the court of guard. First, I must tell thee this:
Desdemona is directly in love with him.   210
RODERIGO With him? Why, 'tis not possible!
IAGO Lay thy finger thus, and let thy soul be instructed. Mark me
with what violence she first loved the Moor but for bragging and
telling her fantastical lies. And will she love him still for prating?
Let not thy discreet heart think it. Her eye must be fed. And   215
what delight shall she have to look on the devil? When the blood
is made dull with the act of sport, there should be, again to
inflame it and to give satiety a fresh appetite, loveliness in
favour, sympathy in years, manners and beauties: all which the
Moor is defective in. Now for want of these required conveniences,   220
her delicate tenderness will find itself abused, begin to heave the
gorge, disrelish and abhor the Moor. Very nature will instruct
her in it, and compel her to some second choice. Now, sir, this
granted – as it is a most pregnant and unforced position – who
stands so eminent in the degree of this fortune as Cassio does? – a   225
knave very voluble; no further conscionable than in putting on
the mere form of civil and humane seeming for the better
compassing of his salt and most hidden loose affection.

Iago assures Roderigo that Desdemona has tired of Othello, and has her eye
on other men. Iago tells his plan. He urges Roderigo to provoke Cassio to
anger that night. The resulting riot will ruin Cassio's prospects.

1 '. . . a slipper and subtle knave' (in pairs)

Read Iago's description of Cassio (lines 229–35). Pick out features
that you agree to be an accurate portrait of Cassio, and those that
you think are deliberately false.

2 Prediction (in pairs)

Iago's plot to provoke Cassio into a fight with Roderigo is in lines
248–62. He makes two practical suggestions, then adds 'or from what
other course you please'. From what you know of both characters,
improvise the situation. What comments might Roderigo make to
aggravate Cassio?

3 A romantic image

Iago says of Cassio and Desdemona: 'They met so near with their
lips / that their breaths embraced together' (lines 244–5). Coming
from Iago, this is scornful (and a distortion of the truth). But in
another situation it would be a highly romantic image. Either make a
design based on the words, or write a paragraph or two in the genre
of a love story, ending with the quotation.

4 Roderigo – the gull

Roderigo seems remarkably gullible. His protests about Iago's
descriptions suggest he is besotted with Desdemona. Yet he quickly
agrees to Iago's plan. Advise him how he might react as Iago speaks
lines 248–65.

---

slipper slippery
stamp and counterfeit make a
 forgery of

fig's end rubbish
in choler when angry
qualification pacifying

Why none; why none – a slipper and subtle knave, a finder out of occasions, that has an eye can stamp and counterfeit advantages, though true advantage never present itself; a devilish knave! Besides, the knave is handsome, young, and hath all those requisites in him that folly and green minds look after. A pestilent complete knave; and the woman hath found him already.

RODERIGO I cannot believe that in her; she's full of most blest condition.

IAGO Blest fig's end! The wine she drinks is made of grapes. If she had been blest she would never have loved the Moor. Blest pudding! Didst thou not see her paddle with the palm of his hand? Didst not mark that?

RODERIGO Yes, that I did; but that was but courtesy.

IAGO Lechery, by this hand: an index and obscure prologue to the history of lust and foul thoughts. They met so near with their lips that their breaths embraced together – villainous thoughts, Roderigo! When these mutualities so marshal the way, hard at hand comes the master and main exercise, the incorporate conclusion. Pish! But, sir, be you ruled by me. I have brought you from Venice; watch you tonight; for the command, I'll lay't upon you. Cassio knows you not; I'll not be far from you. Do you find some occasion to anger Cassio, either by speaking too loud or tainting his discipline, or from what other course you please, which the time shall more favourably minister.

RODERIGO Well.

IAGO Sir, he's rash and very sudden in choler, and haply with his truncheon may strike at you: provoke him that he may; for even out of that will I cause these of Cyprus to mutiny, whose qualification shall come into no true taste again but by the displanting of Cassio. So shall you have a shorter journey to your desires by the means I shall then have to prefer them, and the impediment most profitably removed without the which there were no expectation of our prosperity.

RODERIGO I will do this, if you can bring it to any opportunity.

IAGO I warrant thee. Meet me by and by at the citadel. I must fetch his necessaries ashore. Farewell.

RODERIGO Adieu.   *Exit*

Iago again says that he is seeking revenge because he suspects that Othello has slept with Emilia. He plans to use Roderigo to ensure the downfall of Cassio, whom he also suspects has made love to Emilia.

1 Direct the actor

a Identify in lines 267–93 all the words associated with love; then pick out words to do with sex. Summarise what Iago appears to be saying in this speech.

b How might Iago say key words (e.g. 'love', 'the Moor', 'Michael Cassio', 'revenge')?

c Write two or three paragraphs of advice for an actor playing Iago. It will help if you are able to watch two different film/video versions of this soliloquy and discuss differences, including movement and props.

2 Hot-seat Iago (whole class)

What questions would you *really* like to ask Iago?

One volunteer steps into role as Iago and the class questions them about any matters they wish.

Frank Finlay as Iago, National Theatre, 1964.

---

howbeit   even though
peradventure   perhaps
accountant   accountable
leaped into my seat   made love to my wife
inwards   innards, guts
trace   follow after (hunting term)

on the hip   at my mercy (hunting metaphor)
rank garb   foul manner
with my night-cap   in my bed
egregiously   extraordinarily, outstandingly
practising upon   plotting against

IAGO That Cassio loves her, I do well believe't;
        That she loves him, 'tis apt and of great credit.
        The Moor, howbeit that I endure him not,
        Is of a constant, loving, noble nature;   270
        And I dare think he'll prove to Desdemona
        A most dear husband. Now, I do love her too,
        Not out of absolute lust – though peradventure
        I stand accountant for as great a sin –
        But partly led to diet my revenge,   275
        For that I do suspect the lusty Moor
        Hath leaped into my seat, the thought whereof
        Doth like a poisonous mineral gnaw my inwards;
        And nothing can or shall content my soul
        Till I am evened with him, wife for wife;   280
        Or failing so, yet that I put the Moor
        At least into a jealousy so strong
        That judgement cannot cure. Which thing to do,
        If this poor trash of Venice, whom I trace
        For his quick hunting, stand the putting on,   285
        I'll have our Michael Cassio on the hip,
        Abuse him to the Moor in the rank garb –
        For I fear Cassio with my night-cap too –
        Make the Moor thank me, love me, and reward me,
        For making him egregiously an ass,   290
        And practising upon his peace and quiet
        Even to madness. 'Tis here, but yet confused;
        Knavery's plain face is never seen till used.   *Exit*

A Herald publicly announces celebrations to mark the destruction of the Turkish fleet. They also honour Othello's wedding. Scene 3 opens with Othello's bidding Cassio to inspect the guard at night.

1 The proclamation (in small groups)

a Read the Herald's proclamation aloud. Talk together about whether, if you were directing the play, you would cut this or keep it in. Give your reasons.

b Decide how the scene might be performed: straight to the audience; spoken to a crowd on stage, with the Herald mingling in the audience; or in some other dramatically effective way.

c Imagine three or four ordinary Cypriot field workers pausing from their labours to listen to the proclamation. Improvise *their* particular reaction to each section of it.

d Suggest how the proclamation identifies both Othello's public role and his private role.

2 'Iago is most honest'

The fairly obvious piece of dramatic irony in line 6 of Scene 3 comes very soon after Iago's vow in Scene 1 to drive Othello 'Even to madness'. What effect do you think Othello's comment would have on an audience in the theatre?

If this were a pantomime, such a misguided comment by the hero would invite the audience to shout out to warn him! Write down what you would want to say to Othello at this moment, if you had the chance to step out of the audience onto the stage with the characters.

---

mere perdition   total destruction
offices   kitchens, food stores
full liberty of   free
stop   restraint

out-sport discretion   celebrate to excess
with your earliest   at your earliest convenience

Act 2 Scene 2
Cyprus   A street

Enter Othello's HERALD *with a proclamation.*

HERALD It is Othello's pleasure, our noble and valiant general, that
upon certain tidings now arrived importing the mere perdition
of the Turkish fleet, every man put himself into triumph: some
to dance, some to make bonfires, each man to what sport and revels
his addiction leads him; for besides these beneficial news, it is   5
the celebration of his nuptial. So much was his pleasure should
be proclaimed. All offices are open, and there is full liberty of
feasting from this present hour of five till the bell have told
eleven. Heaven bless the isle of Cyprus and our noble general
Othello!   *Exit*   10

Act 2 Scene 3
Cyprus   A room in the castle

Enter OTHELLO, DESDEMONA, CASSIO *and* ATTENDANTS.

OTHELLO Good Michael, look you to the guard tonight.
    Let's teach ourselves that honourable stop,
    Not to out-sport discretion.
CASSIO Iago hath direction what to do;
    But notwithstanding with my personal eye   5
    Will I look to't.
OTHELLO   Iago is most honest.
    Michael, good night; tomorrow with your earliest
    Let me have speech with you – Come, my dear love,
    The purchase made, the fruits are to ensue;
    That profit's yet to come 'tween me and you.   10
    Good night.

Exeunt Othello, Desdemona [and Attendants]

Iago persuades Cassio to join in the celebrations with various male friends. Cassio reveals he has a poor head for alcohol, and declines to drink further. Iago plans to make Cassio drunk and quarrelsome.

---

1 Men's talk (in pairs)

Read the dialogue between Iago and Cassio. What differences can you detect between the two speakers in their attitudes towards Desdemona in particular or women in general?

a Act out the dialogue up to line 39 in such a way as to highlight any significant differences between the two men and the nature of their remarks. Experiment with playing Cassio in more than one way. For example, do you think that he is ill at ease with the way Iago directs the conversation?

b After you have experimented with speaking the lines, talk together about how Iago takes control of the dialogue. Do this by considering each interchange between the two men. For example, Cassio begins by stressing 'we must to the watch', implying that they must ensure quiet and restraint among the public while Othello and Desdemona consummate their love. How does Iago avoid that order? And so on.

2 Iago's plan (in groups of four)

Read through Iago's soliloquy (lines 40–55), taking turns to read up to each full stop. Now reduce the information contained within each sentence to a key phrase or group of words. Present your abbreviated version of the soliloquy to the rest of the class.

---

cast dismissed
Jove (king of the gods, known for his sexual prowess)
game sexual tricks
parley summons, invitation

stoup jug
craftily / qualified carefully diluted
Potations pottle-deep many mugs or tankards of drink

Enter IAGO.

CASSIO Welcome, Iago; we must to the watch.

IAGO Not this hour, lieutenant; 'tis not yet ten o'th'clock. Our general cast us thus early for the love of his Desdemona; who let us not therefore blame: he hath not yet made wanton the night with her, and she is sport for Jove.   15

CASSIO She's a most exquisite lady.

IAGO And I'll warrant her full of game.

CASSIO Indeed she is a most fresh and delicate creature.

IAGO What an eye she has! Methinks it sounds a parley to provocation.   20

CASSIO An inviting eye, and yet methinks right modest.

IAGO And when she speaks, is it not an alarum to love?

CASSIO She is indeed perfection.

IAGO Well, happiness to their sheets! Come, lieutenant, I have a stoup of wine, and here without are a brace of Cyprus gallants, that would fain have a measure to the health of the black Othello.   25

CASSIO Not tonight, good Iago; I have very poor and unhappy brains for drinking. I could well wish courtesy would invent some other custom of entertainment.   30

IAGO O, they are our friends – but one cup; I'll drink for you.

CASSIO I have drunk but one cup tonight, and that was craftily qualified too; and behold what innovation it makes here. I am unfortunate in the infirmity and dare not task my weakness with any more.   35

IAGO What, man! 'Tis a night of revels; the gallants desire it.

CASSIO Where are they?

IAGO Here at the door; I pray you call them in.

CASSIO I'll do't, but it dislikes me.   *Exit*

IAGO If I can fasten but one cup upon him,   40
       With that which he hath drunk tonight already,
       He'll be as full of quarrel and offence
       As my young mistress' dog. Now my sick fool Roderigo,
       Whom love hath turned almost the wrong side out,
       To Desdemona hath tonight caroused   45
       Potations pottle-deep, and he's to watch.

Iago gets the party going, singing drinking songs.

---

1 'My boat sails freely' (in pairs)

Iago's metaphor 'My boat sails freely, both with wind and stream' (line 55) echoes earlier imagery. Work out what Iago means by this image and talk together about whether you think it is appropriate, and why.

Iago (3rd left) is a man of many parts. Here he entertains the party, and demonstrates a sociable side; he is someone it is fun to be with. Make a list of other parts or roles Iago has played so far.

That hold their honours in a wary distance quick to protect their honour
flustered confused
rouse drink

cannikin drinking can, tankard
potent in / potting heavy drinkers
Almain German

Three lads of Cyprus, noble swelling spirits,
That hold their honours in a wary distance,
The very elements of this warlike isle,
Have I tonight flustered with flowing cups;   50
And they watch too. Now, 'mongst this flock of
    drunkards,
Am I to put our Cassio in some action
That may offend the isle. But here they come.

    Enter Cassio, MONTANO *and* GENTLEMEN.

If consequence do but approve my dream,
My boat sails freely, both with wind and stream.   55
CASSIO 'Fore God, they have given me a rouse already.
MONTANO Good faith, a little one; not past a pint, as I am a soldier.
IAGO Some wine, ho!
    [*Sings*]
    And let me the cannikin clink, clink,
    And let me the cannikin clink;   60
      A soldier's a man,
      O, man's life's but a span,
    Why then, let a soldier drink.
  Some wine, boys!
CASSIO 'Fore God, an excellent song.   65
IAGO I learned it in England, where indeed they are most potent in
    potting. Your Dane, your German, and your swag-bellied
    Hollander – drink, ho! – are nothing to your English.
CASSIO Is your Englishman so exquisite in his drinking?
IAGO Why, he drinks you with facility your Dane dead drunk; he sweats 70
    not to overthrow your Almain; he gives your Hollander a vomit
    ere the next pottle can be filled.
CASSIO To the health of our general!
MONTANO I am for it, lieutenant, and I'll do you justice.

The party continues and Cassio becomes drunk very quickly. Cassio goes off to take his turn on guard, and Iago comments on his dangerous 'vice': his weakness for alcohol.

1 The drinking song

Iago sings two verses of a rousing drinking song, 'King Stephen was and a worthy peer' (lines 76–83). Exactly imitating the rhythm and the rhyme pattern, compose an appropriate third verse. If you can, find a tune to fit the words and then accompany yourself and others in your class.

2 Party photograph (in groups of four to six)

Take line 97, 'Do not think, gentlemen, I am drunk', and imagine freezing the action on stage. Create this photograph or freeze-frame, each person making it clear from the way they are positioned whom they represent.

The rest of the class guesses the characters in each photograph.

3 Acting the drunk (in pairs)

a Acting a drunk is one of the most difficult tasks for any actor. But in lines 85–102, Shakespeare provides a script for Cassio that really does catch the rhythms of drunken speech. Take parts and read the lines, using any actions you think appropriate. Experiment!

b After your experiments, talk together about whether you think Cassio is displaying a less attractive side of his character here. He has let Othello down as a good commander, and he emphasises his social superiority when he asserts 'the lieutenant is to be / saved before the ancient'.

---

lown rogue
wight man
degree status
platform gun ramparts

set the watch mount the guard
just equinox exact equivalent or
  counterbalance

IAGO O sweet England!   75
    [*Sings*]
    King Stephen was and a worthy peer,
      His breeches cost him but a crown;
    He held them sixpence all too dear,
      With that he called the tailor lown.

    He was a wight of high renown,   80
      And thou art but of low degree;
    'Tis pride that pulls the country down;
      Then take thine auld cloak about thee.
    Some wine, ho!
CASSIO 'Fore God, this is a more exquisite song than the other.   85
IAGO Will you hear't again?
CASSIO No, for I hold him to be unworthy of his place that does those
    things. Well, God's above all, and there be souls must be
    saved, and there be souls must not be saved.
IAGO It's true, good lieutenant.   90
CASSIO For mine own part – no offence to the general, nor any man of
    quality – I hope to be saved.
IAGO And so do I too, lieutenant.
CASSIO Ay, but by your leave, not before me; the lieutenant is to be
    saved before the ancient. Let's have no more of this; let's to our   95
    affairs. God forgive us our sins! Gentlemen, let's look to our
    business. Do not think, gentlemen, I am drunk; this is my ancient,
    this is my right hand, and this is my left hand. I am not drunk
    now, I can stand well enough, and I speak well enough.
ALL Excellent well.   100
CASSIO Why, very well then; you must not think then that I am
    drunk.   *Exit*
MONTANO To the platform, masters. Come, let's set the watch.
IAGO You see this fellow that is gone before,
    He is a soldier fit to stand by Caesar   105
    And give direction. And do but see his vice –
    'Tis to his virtue a just equinox,
    The one as long as th'other. 'Tis pity of him.
    I fear the trust Othello puts him in,
    On some odd time of his infirmity,   110
    Will shake this island.

Montano thinks that Othello should be told of Cassio's weakness for drink. Iago sends Roderigo after Cassio, and the two re-enter fighting. Montano tries to stop Cassio striking Roderigo.

1 Appearance versus reality

Iago continues to paint a very negative picture of Cassio, alleging that his 'vice' of drunkenness occurs every night. Montano is concerned that Othello should be advised of Cassio's 'evils', and that Othello's good nature sees only 'virtue' in his lieutenant.

Write a paragraph that explains how Montano's response to Iago's lies is yet another aspect of the theme of appearance versus reality that runs through the play.

2 '. . . an honest action' (in small groups)

Iago is constantly associated with the word 'honest' in the play. Discuss how appropriate you think this is, and what effect it might have on an audience. Flick back through the play so far and find any other moments where 'honest' has been applied to Iago. Jot down the line references and the speakers, then compare your findings with those of other groups. Now turn over the page and look at Activity 2, in which you will be asked to continue to gather all references to Iago's honesty as you work through this scene. (At the end of the play you will need to consider why it's important that so many people have been taken in by Iago.)

3 What did Roderigo do? (in pairs)

So, what happened outside? What *did* Roderigo do or say to annoy Cassio so much? Take line 130 as a clue, then improvise the incident.

---

horologe a double set   twice round the clock
put in mind   told
hazard   risk

ingraft   deep-rooted
twiggen bottle   bottle encased in wicker-work
mazzard   head, skull

MONTANO   But is he often thus?

IAGO 'Tis evermore the prologue to his sleep:
       He'll watch the horologe a double set,
       If drink rock not his cradle.

MONTANO   It were well
       The general were put in mind of it.   115
       Perhaps he sees it not, or his good nature
       Prizes the virtue that appears in Cassio
       And looks not on his evils: is not this true?

Enter RODERIGO.

IAGO [*Aside to Roderigo*] How now, Roderigo?
       I pray you after the lieutenant, go.   120

                                  Exit Roderigo

MONTANO And 'tis great pity that the noble Moor
       Should hazard such a place as his own second
       With one of an ingraft infirmity;
       It were an honest action to say so
       To the Moor.

IAGO   Not I, for this fair island: 125
       I do love Cassio well, and would do much
       To cure him of this evil.
             [*A cry of*] '*Help, help!' within.*
       But hark! what noise?

Enter Cassio, pursuing Roderigo.

CASSIO Zounds, you rogue, you rascal!

MONTANO What's the matter, lieutenant?

CASSIO A knave teach me my duty! I'll beat the knave into a   130
twiggen bottle.

RODERIGO Beat me?

CASSIO Dost thou prate, rogue?
             [*He strikes Roderigo.*]

MONTANO Nay, good lieutenant, I pray you, sir, hold your hand.

CASSIO Let me go, sir; or I'll knock you o'er the mazzard.   135

MONTANO Come, come, you're drunk.

Cassio, incensed by Montano's accusation of drunkenness, fights him. The alarm is sounded. Othello enters to restore order and demand an explanation. Iago denies he knows who began the brawl.

---

1 The fight (in groups of five or six)

Create a slow-motion, silent version of the scene from line 128, 'Enter Cassio, pursuing Roderigo' to line 150, 'From whence ariseth this?' Make each character visibly recognisable and each stage of the action clearly defined. Remember: slow motion, safety and clarity of action are your guides.

2 Honest Iago (in pairs)

There's that description again (line 158). Take a large sheet of paper and design a graphic presentation of all the uses of 'honest' in the script so far.

Leave room for further additions to the list – you'll find that examples come thick and fast in the rest of this scene. Add to your diagram as you read the rest of the play.

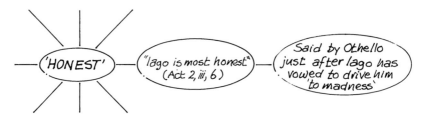

3 Iago's language

Iago chooses his words to suit his listeners. In lines 160–8, find three or four expressions that Iago knows will appeal to Othello. Give reasons for your choice.

Diabolo the devil
rise riot
carve for his own rage stab someone in anger

Holds his soul light doesn't value his life
quarter friendship

76

CASSIO Drunk?

They fight.

IAGO [*Aside to Roderigo*] Away I say, go out and cry a mutiny.
[*Exit Roderigo*]

Nay, good lieutenant; God's will, gentlemen!   140
Help ho! Lieutenant, sir! Montano, sir!
Help, masters, here's a goodly watch indeed!
A bell rings.
Who's that which rings the bell? Diabolo, ho!
The town will rise. God's will, lieutenant, hold!
You will be shamed forever.

Enter Othello, and GENTLEMEN with weapons.

OTHELLO What is the matter here?
MONTANO   Zounds, I bleed still.   145
I am hurt to th'death.
OTHELLO   Hold for your lives!
IAGO Hold ho, lieutenant, sir, Montano, gentlemen,
Have you forgot all place of sense and duty?
Hold! the general speaks to you, hold, for shame!
OTHELLO Why, how now, ho! From whence ariseth this?   150
Are we turned Turks, and to ourselves do that
Which heaven hath forbid the Ottomites?
For Christian shame, put by this barbarous brawl.
He that stirs next to carve for his own rage
Holds his soul light: he dies upon his motion.   155
Silence that dreadful bell: it frights the isle
From her propriety. What is the matter, masters?
Honest Iago, that looks dead with grieving,
Speak. Who began this? On thy love, I charge thee.
IAGO I do not know. Friends all but now, even now,   160
In quarter and in terms like bride and groom,
Divesting them for bed; and then but now —
As if some planet had unwitted men —
Swords out and tilting one at other's breasts
In opposition bloody. I cannot speak   165
Any beginning to this peevish odds:
And would in action glorious I had lost
Those legs that brought me to a part of it.

Othello

Othello tries to discover who started the fight. Cassio gives no explanation.
Montano pleads self-defence, and says Iago knows as much as he does.
Othello orders Iago to speak.

1 Cassio's silence (in pairs)

At the beginning of this scene, Othello had twice called Cassio
'Michael'. Once again he uses 'Michael' as he asks Cassio to explain.
It denotes friendship and trust that will soon be lost. But why, when
questioned, does Cassio choose to say nothing? Do you think that is
the right course of action? If not, what should he have said? Spend
about five minutes creating a possible reply for Cassio.

2 Why is Othello so angry? (in small groups)

Go back over the scene from the point of Othello's entrance at
line 144 to line 198. Suggest at least four factors that contribute
to Othello's rage: why his 'passion . . . Assays to lead the way.'

3 '. . . collied'

Othello becomes impatient and indicates that he is on the verge of
losing his temper with the brawlers. At line 187 he exclaims:

passion having my best judgement collied,
Assays to lead the way.

He is saying that his passion or rage is about to take over from his
better ('best') judgement. The word 'collied' is usually defined as
'blackened', with its links with the word 'coal' ('collier', 'colliery').
What do you think is meant by 'collied' here? What other associations
might it carry?

censure judgement   self-charity self-defence   Assays attempts

partially affined taking sides   leagued in office intimidated by being   of inferior rank

OTHELLO How comes it, Michael, you are thus forgot?

CASSIO I pray you pardon me, I cannot speak. 170

OTHELLO Worthy Montano, you were wont be civil:
The gravity and stillness of your youth
The world hath noted; and your name is great
In mouths of wisest censure. What's the matter
That you unlace your reputation thus, 175
And spend your rich opinion for the name
Of a night-brawler? Give me answer to it.

MONTANO Worthy Othello, I am hurt to danger;
Your officer Iago can inform you –
While I spare speech, which something now offends me – 180
Of all that I do know; nor know I aught
By me that's said or done amiss this night,
Unless self-charity be sometimes a vice,
And to defend ourselves it be a sin
When violence assails us. 185

OTHELLO   Now by heaven
My blood begins my safer guides to rule,
And passion having my best judgement collied,
Assays to lead the way. Zounds, if I stir,
Or do but lift this arm, the best of you 190
Shall sink in my rebuke. Give me to know
How this foul rout began, who set it on,
And he that is approved in this offence,
Though he had twinned with me, both at a birth,
Shall lose me. What, in a town of war, 195
Yet wild, the people's hearts brimful of fear,
To manage private and domestic quarrel,
In night, and on the court and guard of safety?
'Tis monstrous. Iago, who began't?

MONTANO If partially affined or leagued in office,
Thou dost deliver more or less than truth, 200
Thou art no soldier.

IAGO   Touch me not so near.
I had rather have this tongue cut from my mouth
Than it should do offence to Michael Cassio.

Iago gives an account of how Cassio started the affray. Saying Iago's honesty has made him play down Cassio's offence, Othello immediately dismisses Cassio from office.

1 Gossip column (in pairs)

Write an account of the barrack-room party and its outcome, as if for the gossip column of the local *Cyprus Mail*. Whose version of events might be reflected and what other gossip might be contained in the column?

2 Iago's diary

Consider how well Iago has orchestrated the whole incident of the brawl. Do you think Iago would feel pleased with the way he has played his part as a loyal friend to Cassio, yet been obliged to tell the truth to his commanding officer, Othello?

Write Iago's diary entry for that day's events. Pay attention to the kind of language he is likely to use, and try to incorporate quotations where possible in your account. Have Iago think back over all he said to Othello in lines 201–27, and comment on his own words. At the end, indicate how successfully Iago considers he has set things up for his future plans.

3 Personal feelings, public judgement, making 'an example'

Iago gives a falsely sympathetic account of Cassio's behaviour. Othello is taken in by Iago's cunning, and confirms that his 'honesty and love' have made it 'light to Cassio'. In dismissing Cassio, Othello distinguishes between his private feelings for his friend and his public judgement of his lieutenant. Suggest how both those aspects are implied in Othello's line 231, 'Look if my gentle love be not raised up!'

entreats his pause begs him to stop **indignity** insult **mince this matter** tone it down

fall in fright become alarmed

I returned . . . that I thought it best to turn back because

Yet, I persuade myself, to speak the truth
Shall nothing wrong him. This it is, general: 205
Montano and myself being in speech,
There comes a fellow crying out for help,
And Cassio following him with determined sword
To execute upon him. Sir, this gentleman
Steps in to Cassio and entreats his pause;   210
Myself the crying fellow did pursue,
Lest by his clamour – as it so fell out –
The town might fall in fright. He, swift of foot,
Outran my purpose and I returned the rather
For that I heard the clink and fall of swords   215
And Cassio high in oath, which till tonight
I ne'er might say before. When I came back –
For this was brief – I found them close together
At blow and thrust, even as again they were
When you yourself did part them.   220
More of this matter can I not report;
But men are men; the best sometimes forget.
Though Cassio did some little wrong to him,
As men in rage strike those that wish them best,
Yet surely Cassio, I believe, received   225
From him that fled some strange indignity
Which patience could not pass.
OTHELLO   I know, Iago,
Thy honesty and love doth mince this matter,
Making it light to Cassio. Cassio, I love thee,
But never more be officer of mine.   230

Enter Desdemona attended.

Look if my gentle love be not raised up!
I'll make thee an example.
DESDEMONA   What's the matter, dear?
OTHELLO All's well now, sweeting; come away to bed.
Sir, for your hurts myself will be your surgeon.
                                        [*Montano is led off*]

After Othello has gone back to bed, Cassio bemoans the loss of his reputation to Iago. Iago tells him to make an appeal. Cassio curses what drink does to men.

1 From verse to prose

After Othello and Desdemona's exit (line 238), the script changes from verse to prose for this dialogue between Cassio and Iago. Write a paragraph suggesting why. Page 228 will help you.

2 Reputation (in pairs)

Read lines 242–9 to each other several times. Cassio uses the word 'reputation' six times in three lines, and defines it as 'the immortal part of myself', without which 'what / remains is bestial'. In contrast, Iago defines reputation as 'an idle and most false imposition, oft got without / merit and lost without deserving'.

Talk together and make notes, outlining how far you consider these two conflicting definitions to have significance for each of the two speakers.

3 Campaign against alcohol (in small groups)

Imagine that Cassio has been employed by the Venetian Health Education Council to make a series of advertisements outlining the dangers of alcohol abuse.

Design the campaign, complete with a suitable logo, a slogan (taken from the script, if possible) and other techniques or gimmicks. Improvise a three-minute television commercial featuring Cassio's account of his own personal experiences at the hands of the 'invisible spirit of wine'.

---

cast / in his mood dismissed in anger
Sue appeal

fustian rubbish, bombastic nonsense
nothing wherefore not what it was about

Iago, look with care about the town, 235
And silence those whom this vile brawl distracted.
Come, Desdemona, 'tis the soldier's life
To have their balmy slumbers waked with strife.

Exeunt [all but Iago and Cassio]

IAGO What, are you hurt, lieutenant?

CASSIO Ay, past all surgery. 240

IAGO Marry, God forbid!

CASSIO Reputation, reputation, reputation! O, I have lost my reputation! I have lost the immortal part of myself, and what remains is bestial. My reputation, Iago, my reputation!

IAGO As I am an honest man, I thought you had received some bodily 245 wound: there is more of sense in that than in reputation. Reputation is an idle and most false imposition, oft got without merit and lost without deserving. You have lost no reputation at all, unless you repute yourself such a loser. What, man! There are ways to recover the general again. You are but now cast 250 in his mood, a punishment more in policy than in malice, even so as one would beat his offenceless dog to affright an imperious lion. Sue to him again, and he's yours.

CASSIO I will rather sue to be despised than to deceive so good a commander with so light, so drunken, and so indiscreet an 255 officer. Drunk! And speak parrot! And squabble! Swagger! Swear! And discourse fustian with one's own shadow! O thou invisible spirit of wine, if thou hast no name to be known by, let us call thee devil!

IAGO What was he that you followed with your sword? What had he 260 done to you?

CASSIO I know not.

IAGO Is't possible?

CASSIO I remember a mass of things, but nothing distinctly: a quarrel, but nothing wherefore. O God, that men should put an enemy 265 in their mouths to steal away their brains! That we should with joy, pleasance, revel and applause transform ourselves into beasts!

IAGO Why, but you are now well enough. How came you thus recovered?

CASSIO It hath pleased the devil drunkenness to give place to the devil 270 wrath; one unperfectness shows me another, to make me frankly despise myself.

Iago suggests that Cassio should approach Desdemona about his reinstatement. Her good nature and her influence over Othello will restore Cassio to office. Cassio accepts the advice, and promises he will approach Desdemona the next morning.

1 'Had I as many mouths as Hydra'

Hydra (see line 277), a many-headed monster of Greek mythology. New heads grew to replace those that were cut off. Even Cassio uses bestial imagery.

2 What's in Iago's mind? (in pairs)

Iago deceitfully advises Cassio to ask Desdemona for help. Stand back to back and read Iago's speeches from line 281 to line 301. At the end of every phrase or sentence, punctuate Iago's actual words with what he really means. Show what is going on in his mind, his unrevealed thoughts.

---

inordinate superfluous
familiar creature friendly spirit
approved it tested it out

splinter mend (apply a splint)
betimes early

IAGO Come, you are too severe a moraler. As the time, the place, and the condition of this country stands, I could heartily wish this had not befallen; but since it is as it is, mend it for your own good.   275

CASSIO I will ask him for my place again; he shall tell me I am a drunkard. Had I as many mouths as Hydra, such an answer would stop them all. To be now a sensible man, by and by a fool, and presently a beast! O strange! Every inordinate cup is unblessed, and the ingredience is a devil.   280

IAGO Come, come, good wine is a good familiar creature, if it be well used; exclaim no more against it. And, good lieutenant, I think you think I love you.

CASSIO I have well approved it, sir. I drunk!

IAGO You or any man living may be drunk at a time, man. I'll   285
tell you what you shall do. Our general's wife is now the general. I may say so in this respect, for that he hath devoted and given up himself to the contemplation, mark, and denotement of her parts and graces. Confess yourself freely to her, importune her help to put you in your place again. She is of so free, so kind,   290
so apt, so blest a disposition, that she holds it a vice in her goodness not to do more than she is requested. This broken joint between you and her husband entreat her to splinter; and my fortunes against any lay worth naming, this crack of your love shall grow stronger than it was before.   295

CASSIO You advise me well.

IAGO I protest, in the sincerity of love and honest kindness.

CASSIO I think it freely; and betimes in the morning I will beseech the virtuous Desdemona to undertake for me. I am desperate of my fortunes if they check me here.   300

IAGO You are in the right. Good night, lieutenant, I must to the watch.

CASSIO Good night, honest Iago.   *Exit*

Left alone, Iago reveals his plan to lie to Othello about Desdemona and Cassio having an affair. When Desdemona pleads for Cassio's reinstatement it will only make things worse for all three of them. Roderigo tells Iago that he's fed up.

1 Iago's soliloquy – bare bones (in groups of three)

Read through Iago's soliloquy opposite (lines 303–29) in order to get the general sense. It shows how acutely aware he is that appearances can be deceptive, and uses antitheses (opposing words) that culminate in 'virtue' versus 'pitch' (line 327). Then, in your group, take one line at a time and agree what you consider to be the *key* word. Write down that key word (one word only per line). When you have done this for the whole speech, you will have a 'bare bones' script of twenty-seven words.

Keeping the words in their original order, present this new script in any ways that seem appropriate (e.g. movement, mime, choral speech, sound effects, echoing individual words). Share your presentation with the rest of the class.

2 Roderigo interrupts

Roderigo enters at line 329, just as Iago is revealing the destructive nature of his plans. Iago then resumes his soliloquy (over the page) after he has sent Roderigo off again.

a How might Iago react to Roderigo's sudden entrance? How does his tone change from the words 'enmesh them all' to 'How now, Roderigo?'

b What complaints does Roderigo make (lines 330–4)?

Probal reasonable
inclining sympathetic
baptism Christian faith
seals and symbols for example, the
sign of the cross

Divinity study of religion
suggest tempt, seduce
repeals him tries to get him reinstated
cudgelled beaten

IAGO And what's he then that says I play the villain,
        When this advice is free I give, and honest,
        Probal to thinking, and indeed the course   305
        To win the Moor again? For 'tis most easy
        Th'inclining Desdemona to subdue
        In any honest suit. She's framed as fruitful
        As the free elements; and then for her
        To win the Moor, were't to renounce his baptism,   310
        All seals and symbols of redeemèd sin,
        His soul is so enfettered to her love,
        That she may make, unmake, do what she list,
        Even as her appetite shall play the god
        With his weak function. How am I then a villain   315
        To counsel Cassio to this parallel course
        Directly to his good? Divinity of hell!
        When devils will the blackest sins put on,
        They do suggest at first with heavenly shows
        As I do now. For whiles this honest fool   320
        Plies Desdemona to repair his fortunes,
        And she for him pleads strongly to the Moor,
        I'll pour this pestilence into his ear:
        That she repeals him for her body's lust;
        And by how much she strives to do him good,   325
        She shall undo her credit with the Moor.
        So will I turn her virtue into pitch,
        And out of her own goodness make the net
        That shall enmesh them all.

                        Enter Roderigo.

                        How now, Roderigo?
RODERIGO I do follow here in the chase, not like a hound that hunts, 330
        but one that fills up the cry. My money is almost spent; I have
        been tonight exceedingly well cudgelled; and I think the issue will
        be, I shall have so much experience for my pains; and so, with
        no money at all, and a little more wit, return again to Venice.

Iago bids Roderigo to be patient, and tells him they have already succeeded in disgracing Cassio. Left alone, Iago plans to make Emilia urge Desdemona to help Cassio, then to ensure that Othello sees his wife and Cassio together.

1 Director's notes

For this activity you are going to work on both parts of Iago's soliloquy, from the previous page to this (lines 303–29) and lines 347–53. Imagine you are directing a new production of *Othello*. You need to prepare this key speech in detail before working with the actor who is playing Iago. Annotate the speech, indicating:

- how you want Iago to speak and to move;
- what facial expressions and gestures he should employ;
- where there might be pauses and silences;
- what Iago might be thinking/feeling.

You may wish to work with an enlarged photocopy of the speech. An example to get you started is given below:

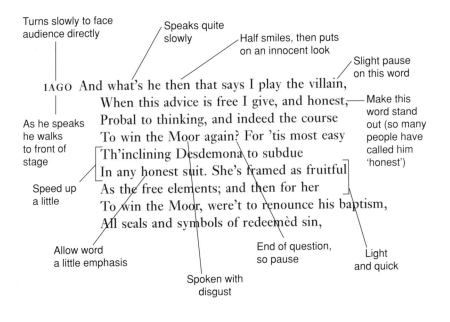

Turns slowly to face audience directly

Speaks quite slowly

Half smiles, then puts on an innocent look

Slight pause on this word

IAGO And what's he then that says I play the villain,
        When this advice is free I give, and honest,
        Probal to thinking, and indeed the course
        To win the Moor again? For 'tis most easy
        Th'inclining Desdemona to subdue
        In any honest suit. She's framed as fruitful
        As the free elements; and then for her
        To win the Moor, were't to renounce his baptism,
        All seals and symbols of redeemèd sin,

As he speaks he walks to front of stage

Make this word stand out (so many people have called him 'honest')

Speed up a little

Allow word a little emphasis

Spoken with disgust

End of question, so pause

Light and quick

---

dilatory dragging, slow
cashiered Cassio got Cassio dismissed
move plead

the while meanwhile
jump at the very moment
device plot

IAGO How poor are they that have no patience!   335
        What wound did ever heal but by degrees?
        Thou know'st we work by wit and not by witchcraft,
        And wit depends on dilatory time.
        Does't not go well? Cassio hath beaten thee,
        And thou by that small hurt hath cashiered Cassio.   340
        Though other things grow fair against the sun,
        Yet fruits that blossom first will first be ripe.
        Content thyself awhile. By th'mass, 'tis morning:
        Pleasure and action make the hours seem short.
        Retire thee, go where thou art billeted.   345
        Away, I say, thou shalt know more hereafter –
        Nay, get thee gone.

                                    Exit Roderigo
                    Two things are to be done.
        My wife must move for Cassio to her mistress –
        I'll set her on.
        Myself the while to draw the Moor apart,   350
        And bring him jump when he may Cassio find
        Soliciting his wife. Ay, that's the way:
        Dull not device by coldness and delay.   *Exit*

Looking back at Act 2
Activities for groups or individuals

1 The storm

The opening scene of Act 2 is dominated by the severe storm threatening the shores of Cyprus. However, in the Italian story by Giraldi Cinthio (from which Shakespeare took the basic idea for his play), the main characters sail to Cyprus on 'a sea of the utmost tranquillity'.

a Write about Shakespeare's dramatic use of the storm, carefully considering its relevance to all that has gone on in Act 2.

b A director of the play has decided to take the storm as a central image for their production. They have asked you to make a design for a backdrop that will be visible throughout the performance. Using Act 2 Scene 1 as your inspiration (particularly lines 12–17), produce two or three possible designs which could be used. Can you account for the director's choice of image; why do they regard the storm at sea to be so important?

2 Epithets (in pairs)

An **epithet** is an adjective or describing phrase added before a name or noun which defines the person or thing; for example, 'honest Iago'. In Act 2 there have been several examples of epithets applied to various characters. First, identify who said each of the following; then discuss how appropriate the description is:

the warlike Moor	brave Othello
valiant Cassio	divine Desdemona
bold Iago	the lusty Moor
the virtuous Desdemona	honest Iago.

3 Headlines – what's happened so far?

There are three scenes in Act 1 and three scenes in Act 2. Imagine you are a newspaper sub-editor. Decide what type of paper you work for ('serious' or 'popular'). Your job is to write brief, memorable headlines for each of the six scenes so far. Make your headlines as accurate as possible; but, remember, they must be short.

4 Judgements and justice (in pairs)

In both Act 1 and Act 2, a crucial judgement is made and 'justice' publicly dispensed. With a partner, locate each judgement, and the participants in each case. Identify the motive, the 'evidence' presented and the consequences of the ruling made. What key similarities and/or differences are there?

Devise a graphic way of recording your findings on a large sheet of display paper.

5 Metaphors

Cassio refers to Desdemona as 'The riches of the ship' in Scene 1 (line 83). In this image, essential qualities which Cassio attributes to Desdemona are pictured graphically for us. Create your own metaphors to describe a particular attribute of Othello, Cassio and Iago.

6 A production photograph

Below is a photograph taken from John Barton's 1971 Royal Shakespeare Company production of *Othello*. It shows Iago photographing the wedding party. Suggest where this moment fitted into Act 2. Why do you think the director wanted to include a wedding photograph in the production?

Cassio's hired Musicians play for Othello and Desdemona. A Clown jokes with a Musician. Cassio sends the Clown to Emilia, to ask her to come out and speak with him.

___

1 The Clown and the Musicians (in groups of three)

Elizabethan and Jacobean acting companies always employed a comic actor, or clown. His main role was to play funny parts in plays, possibly embellishing the given script with 'off-the-cuff' jokes. Playwrights would create a specific role in order to accommodate the clown, even in tragic plays. One effect (e.g. in *Macbeth*) may be to relieve growing tension in the drama.

a Read the page of script aloud. Discuss what you think of the humour here; for instance, the Clown's punning on the word 'Naples', a joke on the nasal sound of a Neapolitan accent and 'Neapolitan disease', a venereal disease. Some critics argue that the dramatic function of the Clown's punning is to foreshadow the misunderstandings that are shortly to come. Consider that argument in your discussion. It may help if you speculate on a popular stage or television comic you would cast in the role.

b It was an Elizabethan custom to wake newly-weds with music outside their bedchamber. Talk together about whether you would open the scene with musicians actually playing music on stage, and, in a modern production, what music you would choose and why. You might be able to think of a particular piece of music or song which has significant meaning for the characters at this point.

2 Make a director's decision

Lines 1–27 are often cut from productions of the play. Decide whether you would include them. Try to state at least two reasons both *for* and *against* their inclusion. Your discussion in the activity above will help.

___

content your pains   pay you for your trouble   **quillets**   puns and wordplays

Act 3 Scene 1
Cyprus   Outside Desdemona's bedchamber

Enter CASSIO, MUSICIANS *and* CLOWN.

CASSIO Masters, play here; I will content your pains.
　　　　Something that's brief, and bid 'Good morrow, general.'
　　　　　　　　　　　　[*They play.*]

CLOWN Why, masters, have your instruments been in Naples, that
　　　they speak i'th'nose thus?

I MUSICIAN How, sir, how?　　　　　　　　　　　　　　　　　　　　5

CLOWN Are these, I pray you, wind instruments?

I MUSICIAN Ay, marry are they, sir.

CLOWN O, thereby hangs a tail.

I MUSICIAN Whereby hangs a tale, sir?

CLOWN Marry, sir, by many a wind instrument that I know. But,　　10
　　　masters, here's money for you; and the general so likes your music
　　　that he desires you, for love's sake, to make no more noise with
　　　it.

I MUSICIAN Well sir, we will not.

CLOWN If you have any music that may not be heard, to't again; but,　　15
　　　as they say, to hear music the general does not greatly care.

I MUSICIAN We have none such, sir.

CLOWN Then put up your pipes in your bag, for I'll away. Go,
　　　vanish into air, away!

　　　　　　　　　　　　　　　　　　　　Exeunt Musicians

CASSIO Dost thou hear, mine honest friend?　　　　　　　　　　　　20

CLOWN No, I hear not your honest friend; I hear you.

CASSIO Prithee keep up thy quillets – there's a poor piece of gold for
　　　thee. If the gentlewoman that attends the general's wife be
　　　stirring, tell her there's one Cassio entreats her a little favour of
　　　speech. Wilt thou do this?　　　　　　　　　　　　　　　　25

CLOWN She is stirring, sir; if she will stir hither, I shall seem to notify
　　　unto her.

CASSIO Do, good my friend.

　　　　　　　　　　　　　　　　　　　　Exit Clown

Iago promises Cassio he will take Othello out of the way for a while, so that Cassio and Emilia can talk freely. Emilia tells Cassio that Othello feels obliged to make an example of him, but intends to reinstate him at a convenient moment.

1 Time-scale of the play (in pairs)

Iago's opening comment, 'You have not been abed then?' suggests that this is the very next morning after the drunken party. The dramatic function might be:

- to give the impression that Cassio is too upset to sleep
- to make the action seem to happen very quickly
- to give the play continuity
- to give a sense of urgency to the events
- to keep the party fresh in the audience's mind
- to heighten tension
- to illustrate how astute or cunning Iago is.

Discuss each of the above options and rank them in order, with the most important reason at the top. Compare your ideas with the rest of the class.

As you read through the rest of the play, pay attention to the passage of time and consider what sense you get of the speed of events happening.

2 Emilia: character and relationships

Emilia, in the dual role of Desdemona's companion and Iago's wife, becomes an increasingly important character in the play. Read all that Emilia says opposite. Write a paragraph outlining what impression it gives you of her. Then write a second paragraph saying what her lines suggest to you about her relationships with Iago, Cassio, Othello and Desdemona.

---

presently at once
stoutly loyally
great affinity important relations

refuse dismiss
bosom mind, feelings

Enter IAGO.

      In happy time, Iago.
IAGO You have not been abed then?
CASSIO Why, no; the day had broke before we parted.   30
    I have made bold, Iago,
    To send in to your wife. My suit to her
    Is that she will to virtuous Desdemona
    Procure me some access.
IAGO   I'll send her to you presently;
    And I'll devise a mean to draw the Moor   35
    Out of the way, that your converse and business
    May be more free.
CASSIO   I humbly thank you for't.

            Exit [Iago]

    I never knew a Florentine more kind and honest.

Enter EMILIA.

EMILIA Good morrow, good lieutenant; I am sorry
    For your displeasure; but all will sure be well.   40
    The general and his wife are talking of it,
    And she speaks for you stoutly. The Moor replies
    That he you hurt is of great fame in Cyprus
    And great affinity, and that in wholesome wisdom
    He might not but refuse you; but he protests he loves you, 45
    And needs no other suitor but his likings
    To take the safest occasion by the front
    To bring you in again.
CASSIO   Yet I beseech you,
    If you think fit, or that it may be done,
    Give me advantage of some brief discourse   50
    With Desdemon alone.
EMILIA   Pray you, come in;
    I will bestow you where you shall have time
    To speak your bosom freely.
CASSIO   I am much bound to you.

            Exeunt

Othello goes off to inspect the fortifications. In Scene 3 Desdemona assures Cassio that she will help him. Cassio expresses his gratitude.

1 Write Othello's official report

Othello has written an official report ('letters') to the Duke of Venice. Write his report, thinking carefully about the tone and the appropriate language. He will tell of the sea journey, happenings in Cyprus, and his personnel changes. How will Othello explain these?

2 The dramatic function of Scene 2 (in pairs)

As you can see at a glance, Scene 2 is extremely short. What dramatic purpose does this scene serve? You will need to look back at the previous scene, and glance forward to the beginning of the next. Copy out the diagram below and fill in the relevant information:

	Scene 1	Scene 2	Scene 3
Characters			
Where does it take place?			
What happens?			
How is the plot taken forward?			

What can you deduce about the function of Scene 2? Consider the following issues in your discussions:

- Othello's role as a military leader
- Iago's relationship with Othello
- Desdemona's whereabouts
- the time scheme
- Cassio's whereabouts
- Cyprus as a colonial outpost.

---

works ramparts, fortifications
Repair return

He shall . . . distance he will distance himself from you only whilst it is politically necessary

Act 3 Scene 2
Cyprus   Outside the castle

Enter OTHELLO, IAGO *and* GENTLEMEN.

OTHELLO These letters give, Iago, to the pilot,
    And by him do my duties to the senate.
    That done, I will be walking on the works;
    Repair there to me.
IAGO   Well, my good lord, I'll do't.   [*Exit*]
OTHELLO This fortification, gentlemen, shall we see't?   5
GENTLEMEN We'll wait upon your lordship.

                                   Exeunt

Act 3 Scene 3
Cyprus   A room in the castle

Enter DESDEMONA, CASSIO *and* EMILIA.

DESDEMONA Be thou assured, good Cassio, I will do
    All my abilities in thy behalf.
EMILIA Good madam, do; I warrant it grieves my husband
    As if the case were his.
DESDEMONA O, that's an honest fellow. Do not doubt, Cassio,   5
    But I will have my lord and you again
    As friendly as you were.
CASSIO   Bounteous madam,
    Whatever shall become of Michael Cassio,
    He's never anything but your true servant.
DESDEMONA I know't; I thank you. You do love my lord,   10
    You have known him long, and be you well assured
    He shall in strangeness stand no farther off
    Than in a politic distance.

Cassio fears that Othello may not relent, but Desdemona again pledges her support. Othello sees them in conversation, and Iago draws attention to Cassio's hurried departure, implying furtiveness and guilt.

1 Desdemona's 'warrant' (in pairs)

Desdemona promises Cassio: 'I give thee warrant of thy place.' She will help him back to his military position on the grounds of personal friendship. Spend about five minutes discussing Desdemona's role here, as friend, wife, woman and civilian. Compare your ideas with the rest of the class.

2 Exits, entrances and movement (in small groups)

The manner and timing of characters' entrances and exits in this moment of the play are crucial to the dramatic development. The Elizabethan or Jacobean stage had a deep acting area with two entrance/exit doors at the back. The size of the acting area would make it possible for Othello and Iago to enter and pass by Cassio at a distance, allowing the remaining dialogue (notably, Iago's 'Ha! I like not that') to work theatrically.

Turn to the picture of an Elizabethan stage on page 186. It is similar in shape to the Globe Theatre, where *Othello* was performed. Try 'blocking' the moves of all the characters involved between line 25 and line 51. Match the characters' movements and precise entrances and exits with lines of script. Decide how many lines of script it takes, for example, for Cassio to make his exit, and where Othello and Iago might be during those lines.

3 'Ha! I like not that'

Write notes on how Iago shapes what Othello thinks he sees in lines 35–40. Then write about how chance yet again plays into Iago's hands in lines 41–51.

warrant promise	**board** dinner table, meals
watch him keep him awake (a way of taming hawks)	**shrift** confessional, place for penance
	solicitor advocate, helper

CASSIO   Ay, but, lady,
   That policy may either last so long
   Or feed upon such nice and waterish diet,   15
   Or breed itself so out of circumstance,
   That I being absent and my place supplied,
   My general will forget my love and service.
DESDEMONA Do not doubt that. Before Emilia here,
   I give thee warrant of thy place. Assure thee   20
   If I do vow a friendship, I'll perform it
   To the last article. My lord shall never rest,
   I'll watch him tame and talk him out of patience;
   His bed shall seem a school, his board a shrift;
   I'll intermingle every thing he does   25
   With Cassio's suit. Therefore be merry, Cassio;
   Thy solicitor shall rather die
   Than give thy cause away.

Enter OTHELLO *and* IAGO.

EMILIA Madam, here comes my lord.
CASSIO Madam, I'll take my leave.   30
DESDEMONA Why, stay and hear me speak.
CASSIO Madam, not now: I am very ill at ease,
   Unfit for mine own purposes.
DESDEMONA Well, do your discretion.

Exit Cassio

IAGO Ha! I like not that.
OTHELLO   What dost thou say?   35
IAGO Nothing, my lord; or if – I know not what.
OTHELLO Was not that Cassio parted from my wife?
IAGO Cassio, my lord? No, sure I cannot think it
   That he would steal away so guilty-like,
   Seeing you coming.
OTHELLO   I do believe 'twas he.   40
DESDEMONA How now, my lord?
   I have been talking with a suitor here,
   A man that languishes in your displeasure.
OTHELLO Who is't you mean?

Desdemona playfully lobbies Othello about Cassio's reinstatement. She reminds him that Cassio accompanied Othello during their courtship. Othello agrees Cassio may come to see him at any time.

1 Desdemona pleads for a friend (in pairs)

Several readers of the play have commented that Desdemona shows little understanding of the responsibilities of her husband's position. She confuses personal feelings with official duties, and believes that Cassio should be pardoned for a military offence simply because he has been their good friend. Discuss how far you believe Desdemona is justified to plead on Cassio's behalf.

2 Othello's response

Othello says, 'I will deny thee nothing' (line 76). What do you think is his manner? Consider the following suggestions in turn. Othello's mood is:

- weary
- condescending
- impatient with Desdemona
- loving and indulgent
- anxious
- angry
- surprised that Desdemona is so assertive.

Write a paragraph outlining what might be going on in Othello's mind, and how he should utter these words.

3 A private conversation? (in groups of four)

When you read the script on the page, it is possible to forget that characters who have fallen silent are still on stage. Step into roles as each character present and create a freeze-frame of the line 'I shall not dine at home.' Then, in turn, bring your character to life and express their thoughts at this moment in the play.

---

sooth in truth
trespass misdeed

check rebuke
mammering on stuttering

DESDEMONA Why, your lieutenant, Cassio. Good my lord,   45
   If I have any grace or power to move you,
   His present reconciliation take.
   For if he be not one that truly loves you,
   That errs in ignorance, and not in cunning,
   I have no judgement in an honest face.   50
   I prithee call him back.
OTHELLO   Went he hence now?
DESDEMONA Ay, sooth; so humbled
   That he hath left part of his grief with me
   To suffer with him. Good love, call him back.
OTHELLO Not now, sweet Desdemon; some other time.   55
DESDEMONA But shall't be shortly?
OTHELLO   The sooner, sweet, for you.
DESDEMONA Shall't be tonight at supper?
OTHELLO   No, not tonight.
DESDEMONA Tomorrow dinner then?
OTHELLO   I shall not dine at home.
   I meet the captains at the citadel.
DESDEMONA Why, then, tomorrow night, or Tuesday morn,   60
   On Tuesday noon, or night; on Wednesday morn.
   I prithee name the time, but let it not
   Exceed three days. In faith, he's penitent;
   And yet his trespass, in our common reason –
   Save that, they say, the wars must make example   65
   Out of their best – is not almost a fault
   T'incur a private check. When shall he come?
   Tell me, Othello. I wonder in my soul
   What you would ask me that I should deny,
   Or stand so mammering on. What! Michael Cassio,   70
   That came a-wooing with you, and so many a time
   When I have spoke of you dispraisingly
   Hath tane your part, to have so much to do
   To bring him in? By'r Lady, I could do much –
OTHELLO Prithee no more. Let him come when he will;   75
   I will deny thee nothing.

Othello dismisses Desdemona, promising to grant her requests. Iago continues to drop deceptive hints about Cassio. Othello tries to find out what's on Iago's mind.

1 Sowing the seeds of doubt (in small groups)

Right from Cassio's exit and Iago's accompanying 'I like not that' at line 35, Iago manages to plant ideas in Othello's mind without saying very much. Understatement is highly effective and suggestive. Share out the following quotations between the groups and work out a dramatic presentation of them. Bring out the insidious way in which Iago works, probing, asking questions, vaguely hinting.

Ha! I like not that.	My lord, for aught I know.
No further harm.	Honest, my lord?
Nothing, my lord;	Think, my lord?
. . . or if	Cassio, my lord?
Indeed?	

2 'Chaos is come again' – imagery, or a memory?

For Othello, falling out of love with Desdemona will be 'the end of the world'. Some Elizabethans believed that a state of Chaos existed before the creation, and that when the world ended, Chaos would return. It was something to be feared, in the same way that even in the twenty-first century some people fear that a catastrophe (like a comet strike) will destroy the world.

But consider Othello's comment at a personal level. It might mean that the effects of falling out of love will be personally catastrophic (using cosmic imagery) – or that personal chaos will literally return ('come again'), implying that he has experienced such a state of personal disorder once before. Which interpretation do you think is more likely? Are both equally likely?

---

boon personal favour
peculiar personal
touch your love put your love to the
  test

Whereon at this point
Perdition damnation

DESDEMONA   Why, this is not a boon;
          'Tis as I should entreat you wear your gloves,
          Or feed on nourishing dishes, or keep you warm,
          Or sue to you to do a peculiar profit
          To your own person. Nay, when I have a suit   80
          Wherein I mean to touch your love indeed,
          It shall be full of poise and difficult weight,
          And fearful to be granted.
OTHELLO   I will deny thee nothing.
          Whereon, I do beseech thee, grant me this,
          To leave me but a little to myself.   85
DESDEMONA Shall I deny you? No; farewell, my lord.
OTHELLO Farewell, my Desdemona, I'll come to thee straight.
DESDEMONA Emilia, come. Be as your fancies teach you;
          Whate'er you be, I am obedient.
                              Exeunt Desdemona and Emilia
OTHELLO Excellent wretch! Perdition catch my soul   90
          But I do love thee; and when I love thee not,
          Chaos is come again.
IAGO   My noble lord –
OTHELLO What dost thou say, Iago?
IAGO   Did Michael Cassio,
          When you wooed my lady, know of your love?
OTHELLO He did from first to last. Why dost thou ask?   95
IAGO But for a satisfaction of my thought;
          No further harm.
OTHELLO   Why of thy thought, Iago?
IAGO I did not think he had been acquainted with her.
OTHELLO O yes, and went between us very oft.
IAGO Indeed?   100
OTHELLO Indeed? Ay, indeed. Discern'st thou aught in that?
          Is he not honest?
IAGO Honest, my lord?
OTHELLO Honest? Ay, honest.
IAGO My lord, for aught I know.
OTHELLO   What dost thou think?   105
IAGO Think, my lord?
OTHELLO Think, my lord! By heaven, he echoes me,
          As if there were some monster in his thought
          Too hideous to be shown. Thou dost mean something.

Othello presses Iago to reveal his thoughts, assuring him that he knows him to be an honest and faithful man. Iago says he believes Cassio to be honest, but asks to be excused from telling his inner thoughts.

1 Qualified praise (in groups of three)

At line 126, Iago appears to be asserting his confidence in Cassio's honesty. Yet if you look carefully at the exact words he uses, he is cleverly and subtly suggesting the opposite. Start with the basic statement 'he is honest' and see how Iago doubly modifies it with phrases which signal doubt.

Take the following three statements and experiment with ways of presenting them to bring out Iago's qualified praise:

he is honest
I think that he is honest
I dare be sworn I think that he is honest.

2 The false and the just (in small groups)

Shortly before Iago's breathtakingly hypocritical 'Men should be what they seem', in lines 118–25, Othello talks of the 'just' man and the 'false' man. He says both can speak in the same style or manner, but from different causes. For a 'false disloyal knave', hesitation in speech is a customary habit. For a 'just' man it arises because he is carefully weighing his words. It is ironic that Othello thinks Iago's 'stops' (hesitations) are a mark of honesty.

But how *do* you know when someone is telling the truth? Talk together about whether you think you can distinguish between a truthful person and a liar by the way they speak.

---

conceit idea
tricks of custom familiar deceptions
close dilations involuntary delays
  (note that there is much disagreement
  about the meaning of this phrase)

ruminate think
leets local courts
law-days days on which courts are in
  session

I heard thee say even now thou lik'st not that,   110
When Cassio left my wife. What didst not like?
And when I told thee he was of my counsel
In my whole course of wooing, thou cried'st 'Indeed?'
And didst contract and purse thy brow together,
As if thou then hadst shut up in thy brain   115
Some horrible conceit. If thou dost love me,
Show me thy thought.

IAGO My lord, you know I love you.

OTHELLO   I think thou dost;
    And for I know thou'rt full of love and honesty,
    And weigh'st thy words before thou giv'st them breath,   120
    Therefore these stops of thine fright me the more;
    For such things in a false disloyal knave
    Are tricks of custom; but in a man that's just,
    They're close dilations, working from the heart,
    That passion cannot rule.

IAGO   For Michael Cassio,   125
    I dare be sworn I think that he is honest.

OTHELLO I think so too.

IAGO   Men should be what they seem;
    Or those that be not, would they might seem none!

OTHELLO Certain, men should be what they seem.

IAGO Why then, I think Cassio's an honest man.   130

OTHELLO Nay, yet there's more in this.
    I prithee speak to me as to thy thinkings,
    As thou dost ruminate, and give thy worst of thoughts
    The worst of words.

IAGO   Good my lord, pardon me;
    Though I am bound to every act of duty,   135
    I am not bound to that all slaves are free to.
    Utter my thoughts! Why, say they are vile and false?
    As where's that palace, whereinto foul things
    Sometimes intrude not? Who has a breast so pure,
    But some uncleanly apprehensions   140
    Keep leets and law-days, and in session sit
    With meditations lawful?

Iago continues to seem reluctant to reveal what he claims to know about Cassio and Desdemona. He strongly defends the importance of a man's or woman's reputation, and warns Othello to beware of jealousy.

---

1 Metaphors (in groups of three or four)

Iago had earlier dismissed Cassio's lament about loss of 'reputation'. But now he describes 'Good name' or reputation in a man or woman as 'the immediate jewel of their souls' (lines 156–7). He uses another visual image to describe jealousy: 'the green-eyed monster which doth mock / The meat it feeds on.'

Choose one of these metaphors and create a tableau, a physical representation of the line (remember you are not showing a picture of what is happening on stage). For the other line, create a drawing or collage which seems to you to best illuminate the words. Share both with the rest of the class.

Afterwards talk together about how Iago develops each of these images through practical examples in the lines that follow (158–62, 168–72).

2 Game tactics (in groups of three)

Iago tactically approaches his task of heightening Othello's anxiety. It is as intriguing following his verbal 'moves' as it can be monitoring a game of football, chess or snooker, where each individual move is part of a much wider game strategy.

One of you becomes a commentator on the game and the other two take the parts of Iago and Othello. Read aloud lines 143–78. Present the dialogue as if it were a game being watched by a radio or television presenter who comments throughout on the tactics Iago uses against Othello, and Othello's responses.

---

it is my nature's plague I can't help it
conceits imagines
scattering and unsure observance
  random and uncertain perceptions

quiet peace of mind
cuckold wronged husband
dotes loves

OTHELLO Thou dost conspire against thy friend, Iago,
          If thou but think'st him wronged, and mak'st his ear
          A stranger to thy thoughts.
IAGO   I do beseech you,   145
          Though I perchance am vicious in my guess –
          As I confess it is my nature's plague
          To spy into abuses, and oft my jealousy
          Shapes faults that are not – that your wisdom then,
          From one that so imperfectly conceits,   150
          Would take no notice, nor build yourself a trouble
          Out of his scattering and unsure observance.
          It were not for your quiet, nor your good,
          Nor for my manhood, honesty, and wisdom,
          To let you know my thoughts.
OTHELLO   What dost thou mean?   155
IAGO Good name in man and woman, dear my lord,
          Is the immediate jewel of their souls.
          Who steals my purse, steals trash; 'tis something,
              nothing,
          'Twas mine, 'tis his, and has been slave to thousands:
          But he that filches from me my good name   160
          Robs me of that which not enriches him
          And makes me poor indeed.
OTHELLO By heaven, I'll know thy thoughts.
IAGO You cannot, if my heart were in your hand,
          Nor shall not, while 'tis in my custody.   165
OTHELLO Ha!
IAGO O beware, my lord, of jealousy:
          It is the green-eyed monster which doth mock
          The meat it feeds on. That cuckold lives in bliss
          Who certain of his fate loves not his wronger;   170
          But O, what damnèd minutes tells he o'er
          Who dotes, yet doubts, suspects, yet fondly loves?
OTHELLO O misery!

Othello assures Iago he's not a naturally jealous man. He says he is confident of his wife's virtue. Iago warns him to watch Desdemona with Cassio; she is capable of deception.

---

1 Key words and phrases (in groups of three)

Read lines 178–206. Between you, agree on what seems to be a key word or phrase in each line. Now, working only with those words or phrases you have chosen, experiment with ways of presenting the exchange between Iago and Othello to express Othello's apparent confidence but underlying uncertainty, and Iago's insinuations and warning.

You could 'intercut' (interweave) the two sets of key words, for example, if you feel that contributes to an understanding of the dynamics of the dialogue. Make use of the dramatic approach that seems to be most appropriate. Compare your presentation with those of other groups and discuss similarities or differences.

At what moment in the script opposite do you think this photograph was taken?

---

fineless   endless
goat   (goats were supposed to be particularly lecherous)
exsufflicate   exaggerated
surmises   suspicions
Matching thy inference   equal to your interpretation

Wear your eyes thus   (What gesture might Iago make?)
self-bounty   natural generosity and kindness
pranks   sexual exploits

IAGO Poor and content is rich, and rich enough;
　　　　　But riches fineless is as poor as winter　　　　175
　　　　　To him that ever fears he shall be poor.
　　　　　Good God, the souls of all my tribe defend
　　　　　From jealousy.
OTHELLO　　　　　　　Why, why is this?
　　　　　Think'st thou I'd make a life of jealousy,
　　　　　To follow still the changes of the moon　　　　180
　　　　　With fresh suspicions? No, to be once in doubt
　　　　　Is once to be resolved. Exchange me for a goat
　　　　　When I shall turn the business of my soul
　　　　　To such exsufflicate and blown surmises
　　　　　Matching thy inference. 'Tis not to make me jealous　　185
　　　　　To say my wife is fair, feeds well, loves company,
　　　　　Is free of speech, sings, plays, and dances well:
　　　　　Where virtue is, these are more virtuous.
　　　　　Nor from mine own weak merits will I draw
　　　　　The smallest fear or doubt of her revolt,　　　　190
　　　　　For she had eyes and chose me. No, Iago,
　　　　　I'll see before I doubt; when I doubt, prove;
　　　　　And on the proof, there is no more but this:
　　　　　Away at once with love or jealousy!
IAGO I am glad of this; for now I shall have reason　　　195
　　　　　To show the love and duty that I bear you
　　　　　With franker spirit. Therefore, as I am bound,
　　　　　Receive it from me. I speak not yet of proof.
　　　　　Look to your wife, observe her well with Cassio;
　　　　　Wear your eyes thus: not jealous, nor secure.　　　200
　　　　　I would not have your free and noble nature,
　　　　　Out of self-bounty, be abused. Look to't.
　　　　　I know our country disposition well:
　　　　　In Venice they do let God see the pranks
　　　　　They dare not show their husbands. Their best
　　　　　　　conscience　　　　　　　　　　　　　　　205
　　　　　Is not to leave't undone, but keep't unknown.

Iago reminds Othello that Desdemona has already deceived her father. He professes his love for Othello, but continues to drop hints about Desdemona's lack of fidelity, and to heighten Othello's unease.

1 Iago the manipulator (in pairs)

Iago continues to undermine Othello, using further cunning strategies to heighten Othello's doubts. Each of Iago's speeches opposite employs a different technique of insidious persuasion. Consider each speech in turn and trace the way Iago puts words into Othello's mouth and thoughts into his head to create suspicion of Desdemona.

2 Who's deceiving whom?

Iago has already commented (lines 203–6) on Venetian women's ability to deceive. Now, his 'She did deceive her father, marrying you' closely echoes Brabantio's parting words in Act 1 Scene 3, lines 288–9. See if you can devise a diagrammatic way of representing which characters are being (or have been) deceived by Iago at this point, and who believes they are being deceived by others. For each 'strand' of your diagram, find a relevant quotation and include that in your design.

3 'I am bound to thee for ever'

Does Othello speak more truly than he knows in line 215? Write a paragraph advising the two actors how they might bring out the meanings of this line to make the greatest impact on the audience.

---

seel   stitch up
close as oak   like the close grain of an oak tree
bound   indebted

strain   push further
larger reach   go beyond
success   result

OTHELLO Dost thou say so?

IAGO She did deceive her father, marrying you;
   And when she seemed to shake and fear your looks
   She loved them most.

OTHELLO   And so she did.

IAGO   Why, go to then!   210
   She that so young could give out such a seeming
   To seel her father's eyes up close as oak
   He thought 'twas witchcraft – but I am much to blame,
   I humbly do beseech you of your pardon
   For too much loving you.

OTHELLO   I am bound to thee for ever.   215

IAGO I see this hath a little dashed your spirits.

OTHELLO Not a jot, not a jot.

IAGO   I'faith, I fear it has.
   I hope you will consider what is spoke
   Comes from my love. But I do see you're moved.
   I am to pray you not to strain my speech   220
   To grosser issues nor to larger reach
   Than to suspicion.

OTHELLO I will not.

IAGO   Should you do so, my lord,
   My speech should fall into such vile success
   As my thoughts aimed not at. Cassio's my worthy
     friend –   225
   My lord, I see you're moved.

OTHELLO   No, not much moved.
   I do not think but Desdemona's honest.

IAGO Long live she so, and long live you to think so!

OTHELLO And yet how nature erring from itself –

Iago implies the unnaturalness of Desdemona in preferring a black man over someone of her own colour and society. Othello orders Iago to set Emilia to watch Desdemona. Iago advises Othello to see how Desdemona pleads for Cassio's reinstatement.

1 Stage directions: '*Going*' and '*Returning*'

Iago skilfully plays his victim and even pretends to leave the stage, only to come straight back as if having a spontaneous second thought. Give advice to the actor playing Iago – how should he go and return?

2 Natural – then and now? (in small groups)

Iago's 'in all things nature tends' (line 233) echoes Othello's 'And yet how nature erring from itself' (line 229). But is Desdemona's marriage to Othello unnatural? Talk together about whether you feel that people's views on 'mixed race' marriage have changed since Shakespeare's time.

Contrast the relationship between Othello and Iago as shown here with that shown in the picture on page 108.

affect like	**means** methods
clime country	**strain his entertainment** urges his
disproportion impropriety	reinstatement
fall to match come to compare	**importunity** pleading
country forms own countrymen	**government** self-control
happily perhaps	

IAGO Ay, there's the point: as, to be bold with you,   230
        Not to affect many proposèd matches
        Of her own clime, complexion, and degree,
        Whereto we see in all things nature tends –
        Foh! one may smell, in such, a will most rank,
        Foul disproportion, thoughts unnatural.   235
        But pardon me: I do not in position
        Distinctly speak of her; though I may fear
        Her will, recoiling to her better judgement,
        May fall to match you with her country forms,
        And happily repent.
OTHELLO   Farewell, farewell.   240
        If more thou dost perceive, let me know more;
        Set on thy wife to observe. Leave me, Iago.
IAGO [*Going.*] My lord, I take my leave.
OTHELLO Why did I marry? This honest creature doubtless
        Sees and knows more, much more, than he unfolds.   245
IAGO [*Returning.*] My lord, I would I might entreat your honour
        To scan this thing no farther. Leave it to time.
        Although 'tis fit that Cassio have his place –
        For sure he fills it up with great ability –
        Yet if you please to hold him off awhile,   250
        You shall by that perceive him and his means.
        Note if your lady strain his entertainment
        With any strong or vehement importunity –
        Much will be seen in that. In the mean time,
        Let me be thought too busy in my fears –   255
        As worthy cause I have to fear I am –
        And hold her free, I do beseech your honour.
OTHELLO Fear not my government.
IAGO I once more take my leave.   *Exit*

Othello reflects that his colour, speech and age may have lost him Desdemona. He sees women's unfaithfulness as the curse of marriage. But the sight of Desdemona seems to make him reject his suspicions.

1 Othello's soliloquy: Iago's influence (in pairs)

Iago's success in troubling Othello's mind is evident. He even affects the language that Othello now begins to use. Read Othello's soliloquy opposite and identify the ways in which it is reminiscent of Iago's language and attitudes. For example, how does his choice of image reflect Iago's growing influence over him? Look particularly at any references to creatures or animals – what kind of animals are they, and what are they used in reference to?

2 Hawking imagery

Using trained hawks for hunting small prey was a courtly pursuit in Elizabethan and Jacobean times. Othello uses a number of hawking images in his soliloquy about Desdemona. He wonders if she will prove to be a 'haggard' (a wild, untrained hawk), in which case he will set her free ('whistle her off') and untie the 'jesses' (the straps tied round the hawk's legs). He will 'let her down the wind / To prey at fortune' – in other words, let her go to look after herself.

Write a paragraph explaining how appropriate you find this image to be. Show if you think it is effective, given the character and mood of Othello and Desdemona. Suggest whether it reveals anything about the way Othello regards marriage. (See p. 229 for more information about imagery in *Othello*.)

Haply for   perhaps because
chamberers   gallants, young men
vapour   stinking air
Prerogatived   privileged

forkèd plague   cuckold's horns (the mark of deceived husbands)
do quicken   are born

OTHELLO This fellow's of exceeding honesty   260
      And knows all qualities, with a learnèd spirit,
      Of human dealings. If I do prove her haggard,
      Though that her jesses were my dear heart-strings,
      I'd whistle her off and let her down the wind
      To prey at fortune. Haply for I am black,   265
      And have not those soft parts of conversation
      That chamberers have, or for I am declined
      Into the vale of years – yet that's not much –
      She's gone, I am abused, and my relief
      Must be to loathe her. O curse of marriage,   270
      That we can call these delicate creatures ours
      And not their appetites! I had rather be a toad
      And live upon the vapour of a dungeon
      Than keep a corner in the thing I love
      For others' uses. Yet 'tis the plague of great ones,   275
      Prerogatived are they less than the base;
      'Tis destiny unshunnable, like death:
      Even then this forkèd plague is fated to us
      When we do quicken. Look where she comes.

Enter Desdemona and Emilia.

If she be false, O then heaven mocks itself;   280
I'll not believe it.

Desdemona greets Othello, who claims he has a headache. She tries to bind his head with her handkerchief, but he pushes it aside. Emilia picks it up, remembering that Iago has urged her to steal it.

1 'I am to blame' (in pairs)

Discuss what reasons Othello might have to claim that he is to blame (line 284) – and to blame for what?

2 Why does Iago want the handkerchief?

As Emilia holds the handkerchief ('napkin'), she reflects that Iago 'hath a hundred times / Wooed me to steal it'. Why?

Predict what Iago might want to do with Desdemona's handkerchief. What indications are there that this seemingly insignificant object will prove to be of great importance later on?

Decide where, in lines 302–20, this production photo was taken.

---

watching lack of sleep, being on duty
remembrance keepsake

conjured her made her swear
work tane out the embroidery copied

DESDEMONA   How now, my dear Othello?
    Your dinner and the generous islanders,
    By you invited, do attend your presence.
OTHELLO I am to blame.
DESDEMONA   Why do you speak so faintly?
    Are you not well?   285
OTHELLO I have a pain upon my forehead here.
DESDEMONA Faith, that's with watching; 'twill away again.
    Let me but bind it hard, within this hour
    It will be well.
OTHELLO   Your napkin is too little.
    [*He puts the handkerchief from him, and she drops it.*]
    Let it alone. Come, I'll go in with you.   290
DESDEMONA I am very sorry that you are not well.
                      Exeunt Othello and Desdemona
EMILIA I am glad I have found this napkin:
    This was her first remembrance from the Moor.
    My wayward husband hath a hundred times
    Wooed me to steal it; but she so loves the token,   295
    For he conjured her she should ever keep it,
    That she reserves it evermore about her
    To kiss and talk to. I'll have the work tane out
    And give't Iago.
    What he will do with it, heaven knows, not I: 300
    I nothing but to please his fantasy.

Emilia hands the handkerchief over to her husband. Iago reveals to the audience what he intends to do with it.

---

1 Iago and Emilia: what relationship? (in groups of three)

Lines 302–21 present an exchange between husband and wife. It is possible to direct it so as to bring out very different interpretations of the relationship between Iago and Emilia. You could even make an important statement about the institution of marriage as it's presented in the play.

One person directs the other two, who take the two acting parts. You will have to make decisions about Iago's attitude to his wife, and Emilia's mood and the way she approaches her husband. For example, Emilia may be:

- nervous of Iago
- cheerful
- confident
- desperate for her husband's attention
- frustrated
- playfully coquettish
- resentful and moody.

You may find it useful to know that 'thing' in Elizabethan slang was used for the female sexual organ. Does Emilia knowingly use it in this sense (line 303) or is Iago introducing the obscene meaning (line 304)? Decide at precisely what point she would reveal the handkerchief to Iago. Consider how Emilia would relinquish the handkerchief according to your interpretation of the mood of the exchange. How does she leave the stage at line 321?

Afterwards, write three separate paragraphs interpreting this dialogue in three separate ways (see the brief explanations of these approaches on p. 222):

- a feminist interpretation
- a psychoanalytical interpretation
- an interpretation which deconstructs the way power operates in this episode, both through the roles of Iago and Emilia and in a wider context.

Be not acknown on't say you know nothing about it

holy writ the Bible
conceits imaginings

Enter Iago.

IAGO   How now? What do you here alone?
EMILIA   Do not you chide; I have a thing for you.
IAGO   You have a thing for me? It is a common thing –
EMILIA   Ha!   305
IAGO   To have a foolish wife.
EMILIA   O, is that all? What will you give me now
              For that same handkerchief?
IAGO   What handkerchief?
EMILIA   What handkerchief!
              Why, that the Moor first gave to Desdemona,   310
              That which so often you did bid me steal.
IAGO   Hast stolen it from her?
EMILIA   No, faith; she let it drop by negligence,
              And to th'advantage I being here took't up.
              Look, here it is.
IAGO   A good wench! Give it me.   315
EMILIA   What will you do with't, that you have been so earnest
              To have me filch it?
IAGO [*Snatching it.*]   Why, what's that to you?
EMILIA   If it be not for some purpose of import,
              Give't me again. Poor lady, she'll run mad
              When she shall lack it.
IAGO   Be not acknown on't: 320
              I have use for it. Go, leave me.
                                                            Exit Emilia

              I will in Cassio's lodging lose this napkin
              And let him find it. Trifles light as air
              Are to the jealous confirmations strong
              As proofs of holy writ. This may do something.   325
              The Moor already changes with my poison:
              Dangerous conceits are in their natures poisons,
              Which at the first are scarce found to distaste
              But, with a little act upon the blood,
              Burn like the mines of sulphur. I did say so.   330

Othello is convinced of Desdemona's infidelity. He wishes he were ignorant of it and declares he has lost interest in his life as a professional soldier. He demands that Iago provide him with hard evidence.

1 Othello's 'general camp' speech (in large groups)

Othello laments his loss of content, reputation and occupation.

a One member of the group reads lines 346–58 aloud. The rest of the group listen carefully and echo any words to do with military activity.

b Divide the speech (from line 349) between group members. Each person takes one or two lines or meaningful phrases. Learn your respective chunks of text, and work out a choral version, using actions, to present your group's delivery of the speech, entitled 'Othello's occupation's gone'.

c Use your experience of a and b to discuss what the speech suggests to you about Othello at this point in the play.

2 '. . . ocular proof' (in pairs)

a Decide what kind of things Othello could mean by 'ocular proof' in line 361 (ocular = to do with eyes). Can you detect any inconsistencies in the way Othello is thinking? Spend three or four minutes comparing your ideas.

b On page 122 there is a picture showing one director's interpretation of how Othello played this speech. Discuss what is happening here in the relationship between Iago and Othello and how you think this piece of dialogue should be played.

3 'Is't come to this?' (in pairs)

In your own words say what you think the situation has 'come to' (line 364) from your own perspective. Next, each partner should take the role of either Iago or Othello and briefly explain what they believe or hope the situation has 'come to'.

---

poppy, mandragora sleep-inducing
 drugs from plants
thou owed'st was yours
general camp the whole army
Pioners men of lowest rank

trump trumpet
circumstance ceremony
engines cannons
clamours thunder

Enter Othello.

Look where he comes! Not poppy nor mandragora,
Nor all the drowsy syrups of the world,
Shall ever medicine thee to that sweet sleep
Which thou owed'st yesterday.

OTHELLO   Ha, ha, false to me!

IAGO Why, how now, general! No more of that.   335

OTHELLO Avaunt, be gone! Thou hast set me on the rack.
I swear 'tis better to be much abused
Than but to know't a little.

IAGO   How now, my lord!

OTHELLO What sense had I of her stolen hours of lust?
I saw't not, thought it not, it harmed not me.   340
I slept the next night well, fed well, was free and merry;
I found not Cassio's kisses on her lips.
He that is robbed, not wanting what is stolen,
Let him not know't and he's not robbed at all.

IAGO I am sorry to hear this.   345

OTHELLO I had been happy if the general camp,
Pioners and all, had tasted her sweet body
So I had nothing known. O, now for ever
Farewell the tranquil mind! Farewell content!
Farewell the plumèd troops, and the big wars   350
That makes ambition virtue – O farewell!
Farewell the neighing steed and the shrill trump,
The spirit-stirring drum, th'ear-piercing fife,
The royal banner, and all quality,
Pride, pomp, and circumstance of glorious war!   355
And, O you mortal engines, whose rude throats
Th'immortal Jove's dread clamours counterfeit,
Farewell! Othello's occupation's gone.

IAGO Is't possible, my lord?

OTHELLO Villain, be sure thou prove my love a whore;   360
Be sure of it. Give me the ocular proof,
Or by the worth of mine eternal soul,
Thou hadst been better have been born a dog
Than answer my waked wrath!

IAGO   Is't come to this?

Othello curses Iago if his suspicions are without foundation. Iago protests that he was only acting as a friend and asks what proof Othello requires of his wife's infidelity.

1 In two minds (in pairs)

To experience Othello's tortured, contradictory emotions, share lines 384–91 between you, speaking them as an argument between two people.

2 '. . . honesty's a fool'

Consider how far Iago's phrase (line 383) could be regarded as central to the play as a whole so far. Write a paragraph outlining your views, supported by evidence from the script.

Identify from the script opposite what line you think Othello is saying here.

probation proof
office job, appointment
profit lesson
sith since

Dian (goddess of virginity)
satisfied certain
topped with a man on top of
her

OTHELLO Make me to see't; or, at the least, so prove it   365
       That the probation bear no hinge nor loop
       To hang a doubt on – or woe upon thy life!
IAGO My noble lord –
OTHELLO If thou dost slander her and torture me,
       Never pray more; abandon all remorse;   370
       On horror's head horrors accumulate;
       Do deeds to make heaven weep, all earth amazed:
       For nothing canst thou to damnation add
       Greater than that.
IAGO   O grace! O heaven forgive me!
       Are you a man? Have you a soul? Or sense?   375
       God bu'y you; take mine office. O wretched fool,
       That lov'st to make thine honesty a vice!
       O monstrous world! Take note, take note, O world!
       To be direct and honest is not safe.
       I thank you for this profit, and from hence   380
       I'll love no friend, sith love breeds such offence.
OTHELLO Nay, stay: thou shouldst be honest.
IAGO I should be wise; for honesty's a fool
       And loses that it works for.
OTHELLO   By the world,
       I think my wife be honest, and think she is not;   385
       I think that thou art just, and think thou art not.
       I'll have some proof. Her name, that was as fresh
       As Dian's visage, is now begrimed and black
       As mine own face. If there be cords or knives,
       Poison or fire or suffocating streams,   390
       I'll not endure it. Would I were satisfied!
IAGO I see, sir, you are eaten up with passion.
       I do repent me that I put it to you.
       You would be satisfied?
OTHELLO   Would? Nay, I will.
IAGO And may. But how? How satisfied, my lord?   395
       Would you, the supervisor, grossly gape on?
       Behold her topped?
OTHELLO   Death and damnation! O!

Iago warns that it will be impossible to catch Desdemona and Cassio in the act of adultery. He reports that he has heard Cassio talk of Desdemona in his sleep. Othello threatens murder.

1 'I'll tear her all to pieces' (in pairs)

On page 115, at lines 280–1, Othello says:

> If she be false, O then heaven mocks itself;
> I'll not believe it.

Only 150 lines later, at line 432, he vows:

> I'll tear her all to pieces!

What has happened in the intervening five pages of script? Trace the stages of Iago's manipulation and record them and Othello's responses in the form of a flow diagram.

Also calculate how much time has elapsed in the time scheme of the play. Add this dimension to your diagram. Discuss the dramatic effect of this time-scale and write your conclusions on the diagram.

2 Animal instincts

What effect does Iago's talk of animals on heat (lines 404–5) have on you as a reader? Jot down brief notes about your responses. Then write some suggestions as to possible dramatic, emotional or verbal significances it might have in the context of the play.

---

bolster share a pillow
prime lecherous
salt lustful
in pride on heat

office task
sith since
gripe grasp

IAGO It were a tedious difficulty, I think,
　　　　To bring them to that prospect. Damn them then,
　　　　If ever mortal eyes do see them bolster　　　　　　　400
　　　　More than their own. What then? How then?
　　　　What shall I say? Where's satisfaction?
　　　　It is impossible you should see this,
　　　　Were they as prime as goats, as hot as monkeys,
　　　　As salt as wolves in pride, and fools as gross　　　405
　　　　As Ignorance made drunk. But yet, I say,
　　　　If imputation and strong circumstances,
　　　　Which lead directly to the door of truth,
　　　　Will give you satisfaction, you might have't.
OTHELLO Give me a living reason she's disloyal.　　　　410
IAGO I do not like the office;
　　　　But sith I am entered in this cause so far –
　　　　Pricked to't by foolish honesty and love –
　　　　I will go on. I lay with Cassio lately,
　　　　And being troubled with a raging tooth　　　　　　415
　　　　I could not sleep.
　　　　There are a kind of men so loose of soul
　　　　That in their sleeps will mutter their affairs.
　　　　One of this kind is Cassio.
　　　　In sleep I heard him say, 'Sweet Desdemona,　　　420
　　　　Let us be wary, let us hide our loves.'
　　　　And then, sir, he would gripe and wring my hand,
　　　　Cry, 'O sweet creature!' and then kiss me hard,
　　　　As if he plucked up kisses by the roots
　　　　That grew upon my lips; then laid his leg　　　　　425
　　　　Over my thigh, and sighed, and kissed, and then
　　　　Cried, 'Cursèd fate that gave thee to the Moor.'
OTHELLO O monstrous, monstrous!
IAGO　　　　　　　　　　　　　　Nay, this was but his dream.
OTHELLO But this denoted a foregone conclusion.
IAGO 'Tis a shrewd doubt, though it be but a dream;　　430
　　　　And this may help to thicken other proofs
　　　　That do demonstrate thinly.
OTHELLO　　　　　　　　　　　I'll tear her all to pieces!

Iago claims that Cassio has Desdemona's handkerchief. Othello is overcome with jealous grief and vows revenge. To Iago's call for patience, Othello replies his murderous thoughts will never change.

---

1 Proof (in pairs)

Othello greets Iago's comment about the handkerchief with the words, 'Now do I see 'tis true.' Yet Othello had asked for 'ocular proof'. Talk together about how Iago has managed to manipulate Othello to accept his *word*. Add this evidence to your diagram from Activity 1 on page 124.

2 Tableaux (in groups of three)

Express the following images through a series of two or three linked tableaux:

a 'Arise, black vengeance, from thy hollow cell!'

b 'Yield up, O love, thy crown and hearted throne / To tyrannous hate!'

3 The tidal wave of Othello's emotions (in large groups)

This activity (used by actors in rehearsal) will enable you to experience the relentless energy embodied in Othello's extended simile of the 'Baltic Sea' in lines 454–61 ('Swallow them up.'). You need to work in groups of around ten. It can be a lively and noisy exercise, so be warned! Divide up the lines into small, meaningful chunks (lines or phrases) and distribute them amongst your group members. Memorise your lines. Get into a long line, not necessarily facing the same way, and link arms securely. The two students on either end must tug and pull the line around the room in opposite directions. Try this out, shouting the lines you've learnt.

Afterwards, discuss what insights this activity has given you into Othello's state of mind at this point in the play, and how the style of his language (e.g. vocabulary, length of sentences, punctuation) reflects the intensity of his thoughts and feelings.

---

hearted in my heart
fraught burden, cargo
aspics venomous snakes
Pontic Sea (Black Sea)

Propontic (Sea of Marmora)
Hellespont (Dardanelles)
capable ample

IAGO Nay, yet be wise; yet we see nothing done,
   She may be honest yet. Tell me but this:
   Have you not sometimes seen a handkerchief   435
   Spotted with strawberries in your wife's hand?
OTHELLO I gave her such a one; 'twas my first gift.
IAGO I know not that; but such a handkerchief –
   I am sure it was your wife's – did I today
   See Cassio wipe his beard with.
OTHELLO   If it be that –   440
IAGO If it be that, or any that was hers,
   It speaks against her with the other proofs.
OTHELLO O that the slave had forty thousand lives!
   One is too poor, too weak, for my revenge.
   Now do I see 'tis true. Look here, Iago,   445
   All my fond love thus do I blow to heaven;
   'Tis gone.
   Arise, black vengeance, from thy hollow cell!
   Yield up, O love, thy crown and hearted throne
   To tyrannous hate! Swell, bosom, with thy fraught,   450
   For 'tis of aspics' tongues.
        He kneels.
IAGO   Yet be content.
OTHELLO O, blood, blood, blood!
IAGO Patience, I say; your mind perhaps may change.
OTHELLO Never, Iago. Like to the Pontic Sea,
   Whose icy current and compulsive course   455
   Ne'er feels retiring ebb but keeps due on
   To the Propontic and the Hellespont,
   Even so my bloody thoughts with violent pace
   Shall ne'er look back, ne'er ebb to humble love,
   Till that a capable and wide revenge   460
   Swallow them up. Now by yond marble heaven,
   In the due reverence of a sacred vow
   I here engage my words.

Iago swears to serve Othello, who instructs him to kill Cassio. Othello vows to kill Desdemona himself. He appoints Iago to be his lieutenant. Scene 4 opens with Desdemona sending a messenger to Cassio.

1 'But let her live' (in pairs)

Why do you think Iago tells Othello to let Desdemona live (line 475)? Consider the following possibilities:

- He has no quarrel with Desdemona, and/or fancies her.
- He seeks only Cassio's death.
- He's displaying old-fashioned courtesy towards women.
- He needs her alive to torment Othello further – and to torment her.
- He actually means the opposite – he's planting the idea deliberately in Othello's mind.
- It's all happening too quickly and easily.
- He wants to appear merciful to aid his deception.

Pool your ideas with the rest of the class. Are there other possibilities?

2 What does Iago mean?

Scene 3 ends on Iago's statement, 'I am your own for ever.' It could simply mean 'Thanks for the promotion, I'll serve you well.' But what other, more ominous meanings could his words carry at the end of the scene in which Iago has successfully stirred Othello to hatred, jealousy and determination to murder?

3 Scene changes: dramatic effect

An important feature of Shakespeare's stagecraft is how he contrasts scene with scene. If you were directing the play, what dramatic effect would you hope to achieve at the beginning of Scene 4? Think about: a swift or slow change of scene; Desdemona's mood; and how she and the Clown would speak. Write director's notes spanning Scene 3, line 480, and Scene 4, line 18.

---

clip enclose, embrace
execution activities
What bloody . . . ever however
 murderous it gets

acceptance bounteous generous
 reward
lies lodges

IAGO   Do not rise yet.
                                He kneels.
Witness you ever-burning lights above,
You elements that clip us round about,   465
Witness that here Iago doth give up
The execution of his wit, hands, heart,
To wronged Othello's service. Let him command,
And to obey shall be in me remorse,
What bloody business ever.
                           [*They rise.*]
OTHELLO   I greet thy love,   470
Not with vain thanks, but with acceptance bounteous;
And will upon the instant put thee to't.
Within these three days let me hear thee say
That Cassio's not alive.
IAGO   My friend is dead;
'Tis done at your request. But let her live.   475
OTHELLO Damn her, lewd minx! O, damn her, damn her!
Come, go with me apart. I will withdraw
To furnish me with some swift means of death
For the fair devil. Now art thou my lieutenant.
IAGO I am your own for ever.   480
                                    Exeunt

Act 3 Scene 4
Cyprus   A room in the castle

Enter DESDEMONA, EMILIA and CLOWN.

DESDEMONA Do you know, sirrah, where Lieutenant Cassio lies?
CLOWN I dare not say he lies anywhere.
DESDEMONA Why, man?
CLOWN He's a soldier, and for one to say a soldier lies is
    stabbing.   5

The Clown leaves to tell Cassio to visit Desdemona. She expresses concern about the loss of her handkerchief to Emilia. Othello greets Desdemona and comments on her hot hand.

---

1 Hot-seat Emilia (large groups or whole class)

When Emilia lies that she knows nothing about the loss of Desdemona's handkerchief ('I know not, madam', line 20), what might be going through her mind at that point?

A volunteer steps into role as Emilia. The group or class questions her, exploring her possible motives. Try to work out where her loyalties lie. How does Emilia see her position as wife, employee and confidante?

2 Sweaty palms (in small groups)

Othello takes Desdemona's hand and remarks that it is 'hot, and moist' – supposedly a sign of a lecherous nature. He goes on to tell Desdemona that instead of giving her 'hand' in marriage as a love match ('hearts of old gave hands') she has merely given her hand, not her heart as well (lines 41–3).

But in a different interpretation, some critics note that 'hands' occurs twice as many times as 'hearts'. They see this as signifying that Othello is rejecting love and emotion (represented by 'heart') and is giving priority to duty and his public office (represented by 'hand').

Read lines 28–43, then improvise a situation where you wrongly (and privately) suspect your girl/boyfriend of two-timing you, and all sorts of quite innocent conversation and behaviour become misinterpreted. After watching each other's improvisations, discuss how easily this kind of situation arises, and under what circumstances.

---

devise make up, invent	**crusadoes** gold coins
edified instructed	**humours** moods
catechise a method of religious instruction	**dissemble** hide one's true feelings
compass scope	**sequester** removal
	castigation discipline

DESDEMONA Go to. Where lodges he?

CLOWN To tell you where he lodges is to tell you where I lie.

DESDEMONA Can anything be made of this?

CLOWN I know not where he lodges, and for me to devise a lodging, and say he lies here, or he lies there, were to lie in mine own throat. 10

DESDEMONA Can you enquire him out, and be edified by report?

CLOWN I will catechise the world for him: that is, make questions, and by them answer.

DESDEMONA Seek him; bid him come hither; tell him I have moved my lord on his behalf and hope all will be well. 15

CLOWN To do this is within the compass of man's wit, and therefore I will attempt the doing of it.   *Exit*

DESDEMONA Where should I lose that handkerchief, Emilia?

EMILIA I know not, madam. 20

DESDEMONA Believe me, I had rather lose my purse
Full of crusadoes; and but my noble Moor
Is true of mind and made of no such baseness
As jealous creatures are, it were enough
To put him to ill thinking.

EMILIA   Is he not jealous? 25

DESDEMONA Who, he? I think the sun where he was born
Drew all such humours from him.

                   Enter OTHELLO.

EMILIA   Look where he comes.

DESDEMONA I will not leave him now; let Cassio
Be called to him. – How is't with you, my lord?

OTHELLO Well, my good lady. [*Aside*] O hardness to dissemble! 30
How do you, Desdemona?

DESDEMONA   Well, my good lord.

OTHELLO Give me your hand. This hand is moist, my lady.

DESDEMONA It yet hath felt no age, nor known no sorrow.

OTHELLO This argues fruitfulness and liberal heart.
Hot, hot, and moist. This hand of yours requires 35
A sequester from liberty, fasting and prayer,
Much castigation, exercise devout;
For here's a young and sweating devil here
That commonly rebels. 'Tis a good hand,
A frank one.

Othello asks for the handkerchief. When Desdemona denies she has lost it, Othello informs her of its magical powers and its great sentimental value. He claims it was magically made.

---

1 The myth of the handkerchief (in pairs)

Othello's description of the handkerchief's history (lines 51–71) is like a myth or folk tale. Read it dramatically, then experiment with retelling it as a fairy story for young children.

See page 221 for a consideration of the dramatic significance of this handkerchief in the play as a whole.

2 What if . . .? (in groups of three)

What if Desdemona had told Othello the truth at this point, that she had indeed accidentally lost the handkerchief? Each take a part (Desdemona, Emilia, Othello) and speculate how the scene might continue.

This photograph was not taken during the episode opposite, but has been interpreted as representing its underlying emotional mood. In what ways?

---

chuck (term of endearment)	**perdition** damnation
rheum cold	**sibyl** prophetess
charmer witch	**mummy** substance from mummified
amiable beloved	bodies
fancies lovers	

DESDEMONA You may indeed say so, 40
For 'twas that hand that gave away my heart.
OTHELLO A liberal hand! The hearts of old gave hands;
But our new heraldry is hands, not hearts.
DESDEMONA I cannot speak of this. Come now, your promise.
OTHELLO What promise, chuck? 45
DESDEMONA I have sent to bid Cassio come speak with you.
OTHELLO I have a salt and sorry rheum offends me;
Lend me thy handkerchief.
DESDEMONA Here, my lord.
OTHELLO That which I gave you.
DESDEMONA I have it not about me.
OTHELLO Not? 50
DESDEMONA No, faith, my lord.
OTHELLO That's a fault. That handkerchief
Did an Egyptian to my mother give:
She was a charmer and could almost read
The thoughts of people. She told her, while she kept it,
'Twould make her amiable and subdue my father 55
Entirely to her love; but if she lost it
Or made a gift of it, my father's eye
Should hold her loathèd and his spirits should hunt
After new fancies. She dying gave it me,
And bid me when my fate would have me wive, 60
To give it her. I did so, and take heed on't:
Make it a darling, like your precious eye.
To lose't or give't away were such perdition
As nothing else could match.
DESDEMONA Is't possible?
OTHELLO 'Tis true. There's magic in the web of it: 65
A sibyl, that had numbered in the world
The sun to course two hundred compasses,
In her prophetic fury sewed the work;
The worms were hallowed that did breed the silk,
And it was dyed in mummy, which the skilful 70
Conserved of maidens' hearts.

Othello orders Desdemona to bring him the handkerchief. She tries to divert his attention by reminding him of Cassio's unresolved plight, but he leaves, swearing. Emilia comments unflatteringly on men.

1 Desdemona's lie

Write a paragraph explaining what possible reasons there could be for Desdemona telling a very rare lie in the play: 'It is not lost . . .' (line 79).

2 Let's talk about Cassio! (in pairs)

Othello is clearly agitated about the lost handkerchief, yet Desdemona persists in pursuing a conversation about Cassio. Why do you think she does this? What advice would you give to the actor playing Desdemona? Is she, for instance:

- completely naive
- bemused by Othello's anger
- forceful and assertive
- irritated by Othello's behaviour
- deliberately provocative?

Try reading line 71 (from 'I'faith, is't true?') to line 93 in three or four different ways.

Emilia (right) expounds her philosophy concerning men in lines 97–100. She uses a food/appetite metaphor reminiscent of that used by Iago to talk about women in Act 2 Scene 1, lines 215–22. What do you think this suggests about Emilia and Iago's relationship?

---

suit original purpose
sufficient competent

Zounds! God's wounds!
(a curse)

DESDEMONA   I'faith, is't true?

OTHELLO Most veritable; therefore look to't well.

DESDEMONA Then would to God that I had never seen't!

OTHELLO Ha? Wherefore?

DESDEMONA Why do you speak so startingly and rash?   75

OTHELLO Is't lost? Is't gone? Speak; is't out of th'way?

DESDEMONA Heaven bless us!

OTHELLO Say you?

DESDEMONA It is not lost, but what and if it were?

OTHELLO How?   80

DESDEMONA I say it is not lost.

OTHELLO   Fetch't, let me see't.

DESDEMONA Why so I can, sir; but I will not now.
          This is a trick to put me from my suit.
          Pray you let Cassio be received again.

OTHELLO Fetch me the handkerchief. My mind misgives.   85

DESDEMONA Come, come;
          You'll never meet a more sufficient man.

OTHELLO The handkerchief!

DESDEMONA   I pray, talk me of Cassio.

OTHELLO The handkerchief!

DESDEMONA   A man that all his time
          Hath founded his good fortunes on your love,   90
          Shared dangers with you –

OTHELLO The handkerchief!

DESDEMONA   I'faith, you are to blame.

OTHELLO Zounds!   *Exit*

EMILIA Is not this man jealous?

DESDEMONA   I ne'er saw this before.
          Sure there's some wonder in this handkerchief;   95
          I am most unhappy in the loss of it.

EMILIA 'Tis not a year or two shows us a man.
          They are all but stomachs, and we all but food;
          They eat us hungerly, and when they are full,
          They belch us.

                    Enter IAGO *and* CASSIO.

                    Look you, Cassio and my husband.   100

IAGO There is no other way: 'tis she must do't.
          And lo, the happiness! Go, and importune her.

Cassio again asks Desdemona to plead with Othello on his behalf. She tells him he will have to be patient, since Othello seems to be behaving strangely. Iago leaves to find Othello.

---

1 'My lord is not my lord'

Desdemona states in line 118 that Othello is not himself. How far would you agree that this is more true than Desdemona realises, in that Othello's identity has been undermined by Iago, who is busily reconstructing a new one for him? Write one or two paragraphs exploring this idea.

2 Unspoken thoughts (in groups of three)

Look over Iago's short interchange with Emilia and Desdemona (lines 126–34). Both Emilia and Iago know more than they reveal, yet on the surface they appear innocent. Iago falsely expresses surprise at Othello's anger. He finds four different ways of using 'angry' as an emotion unfamiliar to Othello.

First, play with the script, experimenting with ways of acting it out and exploring the undercurrent of (partially) shared knowledge between Emilia and her husband.

Next, attempt to intercut (interweave) script with the unspoken thoughts and preoccupations of the three characters. If, in your initial explorations with acting out the script, you had actors exchanging significant looks, for example, explain in each character's words what is going through their mind at that point.

When you have an intercut script that you like, share it with other groups and discuss any similarities or differences.

---

suit purpose
office loyal service
shut myself up in confine myself to
To fortune's alms accepting whatever
  chance may put my way

favour appearance
blank centre of target
of moment momentous

DESDEMONA How now, good Cassio! What's the news with you?

CASSIO Madam, my former suit. I do beseech you
      That, by your virtuous means, I may again   105
      Exist and be a member of his love,
      Whom I, with all the office of my heart,
      Entirely honour. I would not be delayed.
      If my offence be of such mortal kind
      That nor my service past nor present sorrows,   110
      Nor purposed merit in futurity,
      Can ransom me into his love again,
      But to know so must be my benefit:
      So shall I clothe me in a forced content,
      And shut myself up in some other course   115
      To fortune's alms.

DESDEMONA   Alas, thrice-gentle Cassio,
      My advocation is not now in tune:
      My lord is not my lord; nor should I know him,
      Were he in favour as in humour altered.
      So help me every spirit sanctified,   120
      As I have spoken for you all my best,
      And stood within the blank of his displeasure
      For my free speech! You must awhile be patient.
      What I can do, I will; and more I will
      Than for myself I dare. Let that suffice you.   125

IAGO Is my lord angry?

EMILIA   He went hence but now
      And certainly in strange unquietness.

IAGO Can he be angry? I have seen the cannon
      When it hath blown his ranks into the air,
      And like the devil from his very arm   130
      Puffed his own brother – and is he angry?
      Something of moment then. I will go meet him.
      There's matter in't indeed if he be angry.

DESDEMONA I prithee do so.

Exit Iago

Desdemona reassures herself that Othello must be upset by some affair of state. Emilia hopes he is not growing jealous. Desdemona prays he has no such thought in mind and leaves to seek Othello. Bianca greets Cassio.

1 Public and private (in pairs)

In the scenes with Desdemona, it is easy to forget that Othello's primary role in Cyprus is to administer Venetian rule. In Desdemona's words about 'some unhatched practice' (secret plot), she draws attention to their position as quasi-colonial rulers once again. Keep this political dimension in mind as you grapple with the 'meaning' of the play.

2 '. . . men are not gods'

Desdemona assures Cassio and Emilia about this 'fact' – which to you may not seem a particularly earth-shattering revelation. Yet, if you think of gods as being in control of people's lives, as rulers, then might this have some deeper significance in terms of women's role in Venetian society? Is Desdemona's assertion here perhaps a sign that she might be ready to grasp some power and responsibility for herself in her relationship with her husband?

3 Secret thoughts (in groups of three)

Extend Activity 2 from page 136 to encompass lines 149–62. Try intercutting those lines with what might be the internalised dialogue of the three characters.

4 Jealousy: 'a monster / Begot upon itself, born on itself'

Again, Emilia's language is an unconscious echo of Iago's. Look back to page 107 and locate Iago's graphic jealousy metaphor. How are the two images similar?

---

endues   brings, leads (or infects)
observancy   loving attention
bridal   wedding night
Arraigning   accusing
suborned the witness   made the
  witness give false evidence

indicted   accused
toy   fancy
'Save you   God save you (a greeting
  like 'Good morning!')

                    Something sure of state,
          Either from Venice, or some unhatched practice   135
          Made demonstrable here in Cyprus to him,
          Hath puddled his clear spirit; and in such cases
          Men's natures wrangle with inferior things,
          Though great ones are their object. 'Tis even so;
          For let our finger ache, and it endues   140
          Our other healthful members even to a sense
          Of pain. Nay, we must think men are not gods,
          Nor of them look for such observancy
          As fits the bridal. Beshrew me much, Emilia,
          I was – unhandsome warrior as I am –   145
          Arraigning his unkindness with my soul;
          But now I find I had suborned the witness
          And he's indicted falsely.
EMILIA Pray heaven it be state matters, as you think,
          And no conception nor no jealous toy   150
          Concerning you.
DESDEMONA Alas the day, I never gave him cause.
EMILIA But jealous souls will not be answered so.
          They are not ever jealous for the cause,
          But jealous for they're jealous. 'Tis a monster   155
          Begot upon itself, born on itself.
DESDEMONA Heaven keep that monster from Othello's mind.
EMILIA Lady, amen!
DESDEMONA I will go seek him. Cassio, walk here about.
          If I do find him fit, I'll move your suit   160
          And seek to effect it to my uttermost.
CASSIO I humbly thank your ladyship.
                              Exeunt Desdemona and Emilia

                  Enter BIANCA.

BIANCA 'Save you, friend Cassio.
CASSIO   What make you from home?
          How is it with you, my most fair Bianca?
          I'faith, sweet love, I was coming to your house.   165

Bianca accuses Cassio of neglecting her. He pleads that worries have kept him away and gives Bianca the handkerchief, saying he found it in his bedroom. He asks Bianca to leave so that he may meet Othello.

1 Bianca: what's she like? (in groups of three)

What are your first impressions of Bianca, and what relationship do you think she has with Cassio? Explore this question by taking parts. Experiment with ways of playing the script, using your third group member as a director. Which interpretation of Bianca's personality do you prefer? (You will find further information about Bianca on p. 150.)

2 Bianca: dramatic purposes

What are the dramatic purposes of this little episode with Bianca? Write brief notes on plot, themes, dramatic tension, characterisation, politics and relationships. Present your views for whole-class discussion.

3 A puzzling time scheme (in pairs)

What is your impression of the amount of time that has elapsed from the beginning of Act 2? From Bianca's words at line 167 it would seem that a whole week has passed by since the Venetian fleet arrived at Cyprus, yet Othello wanted Cassio dead within three days at the end of Scene 3.

In performance, audiences tend not to notice or bother about this matter, but readers sometimes do. Many people have tried to sort out the seeming inconsistencies of timing within the play and have written much on the issue. From your experience as a reader or as a viewer, how important do you think such textual study to be?

Perhaps Shakespeare simply did not think about the time puzzle he was setting. But assume that he was being deliberately inconsistent, and suggest possible reasons why he created this time-scheme problem.

---

continuate   uninterrupted
Take me this work out   copy this
  embroidery for me

be circumstanced   put up with

BIANCA   And I was going to your lodging, Cassio.
          What! Keep a week away? Seven days and nights?
          Eight score eight hours? And lovers' absent hours
          More tedious than the dial eight score times!
          O weary reckoning!

CASSIO   Pardon me, Bianca.   170
          I have this while with leaden thoughts been pressed;
          But I shall in a more continuate time
          Strike off this score of absence. Sweet Bianca,
          Take me this work out.

BIANCA   O Cassio, whence came this?
          This is some token from a newer friend.   175
          To the felt absence now I feel a cause.
          Is't come to this? Well, well.

CASSIO   Go to, woman!
          Throw your vile guesses in the devil's teeth
          From whence you have them. You are jealous now
          That this is from some mistress, some remembrance.   180
          No, by my faith, Bianca.

BIANCA   Why, whose is it?

CASSIO I know not neither; I found it in my chamber.
          I like the work well. Ere it be demanded –
          As like enough it will – I'd have it copied.
          Take it and do't, and leave me for this time.   185

BIANCA Leave you? Wherefore?

CASSIO I do attend here on the general;
          And think it no addition, nor my wish,
          To have him see me womaned.

BIANCA   Why, I pray you?

CASSIO Not that I love you not.

BIANCA   But that you do not love me.   190
          I pray you, bring me on the way a little,
          And say if I shall see you soon at night.

CASSIO 'Tis but a little way that I can bring you,
          For I attend here; but I'll see you soon.

BIANCA 'Tis very good; I must be circumstanced.   195

                          Exeunt

Looking back at Act 3
Activities for groups or individuals

1 Iago's tempting (in large groups)

At the beginning of Scene 1, Othello is completely in control of himself; by the end of Scene 4, he seems to be verging on insanity. The following activity concentrates on the insidious way in which Iago goes to work on Othello's mind.

Each group member takes and learns one of the following lines:

'Ha! I like not that.'
'Cassio, my lord? . . . so guilty-like'
'Did Michael Cassio . . . know of your love?'
'Honest, my lord?'
'I dare be sworn I think that he is honest.'
'I think Cassio's an honest man.'
'I perchance am vicious in my guess'
'it is my nature's plague / To spy into abuses'
'O beware, my lord, of jealousy'
'cuckold'
'Who dotes, yet doubts, suspects, yet fondly loves?'
'the souls of all my tribe defend / From jealousy.'
'Look to your wife'
'observe her well with Cassio'
'She did deceive her father, marrying you'
'Foul disproportion'
'thoughts unnatural'
'Note if your lady strain his entertainment'
'Behold her topped'
'as prime as goats, as hot as monkeys'.

Move around the room, using all the available space. Speak your lines in different ways – for example as if you are all spies passing on secrets, small children telling tales, neighbours gossiping.

Next, form a large circle with one student in the centre, blindfolded. Those forming the circle hiss their lines at the central person (a volunteer), sometimes very close to them, sometimes at a distance from them, as the words are said. Experiment with different ways of presenting your lines, perhaps devising a way of demonstrating the progressive nature of the taunts.

Afterwards, talk together about this group experience. Each person then goes on to write a short essay entitled 'Honest Iago'.

2 Sculptures of trust and jealousy (in groups of three)

Issues of trust and jealousy are prominent throughout the act. One person takes on the job of sculptor, whilst two others become the raw material. The sculptor's task is to create, first, a statue entitled *Trust* and, second, one entitled *Jealousy*. Identify moments in the act that your statues might represent.

3 Caption the photographs

Here are four photographs, each taken from different stage productions during Act 3. Each shows Othello and Iago. Find an appropriate quotation for each picture.

Iago encourages Othello's jealousy with increasingly graphic references to Desdemona's supposed infidelity. He teases Othello with mention of the handkerchief.

1 Undermining Othello's self-control (in pairs)

Iago's opening words for the scene suggest that he and Othello are part-way through a conversation. Speculate about what Iago might have been saying before the opening line of script. Role-play the dialogue you create, then read through to line 46, in which Iago further stimulates Othello's imaginings of Desdemona's and Cassio's sexual relationship.

2 Iago's lies

Iago tells Othello four separate lies in the first thirty lines of this scene, some prompting Othello to echo his words. Identify each of the lies and write a quotation down for each. Now look closely at the punctuation and you will see that a number of Iago's comments are either in the form of a question, or an unfinished sentence, marked by a dash (–).

Talk with a partner about the effect of the way Iago uses language here, then write a paragraph recording your ideas.

3 The raven image

In describing his obsession with the lost handkerchief (lines 19–22), Othello uses a simile describing the belief that a croaking raven prophesied death to the inmates of a house, particularly in times of plague.

Try creating a graphic design incorporating this image of the bird of ill omen and the handkerchief. It doesn't matter if you don't consider yourself to be much good at art. Ideas are the most important element, not the artist's skills.

venial slip trivial misdeed
importunate suit persistent chatting-up, wooing

voluntary dotage willing infatuation
Convincèd or supplied overpowered or seduced

Act 4 Scene 1
Cyprus   A room in the castle

Enter OTHELLO *and* IAGO.

IAGO Will you think so?

OTHELLO   Think so, Iago?

IAGO   What,
    To kiss in private?

OTHELLO   An unauthorised kiss!

IAGO Or to be naked with her friend in bed
    An hour or more, not meaning any harm?

OTHELLO Naked in bed, Iago, and not mean harm?   5
    It is hypocrisy against the devil.
    They that mean virtuously and yet do so,
    The devil their virtue tempts, and they tempt heaven.

IAGO So they do nothing, 'tis a venial slip;
    But if I give my wife a handkerchief –   10

OTHELLO What then?

IAGO Why, then 'tis hers, my lord; and being hers,
    She may, I think, bestow't on any man.

OTHELLO She is protectress of her honour too.
    May she give that?   15

IAGO Her honour is an essence that's not seen:
    They have it very oft that have it not.
    But for the handkerchief –

OTHELLO By heaven, I would most gladly have forgot it.
    Thou said'st – O it comes o'er my memory,   20
    As doth the raven o'er the infected house,
    Boding to all! – he had my handkerchief.

IAGO Ay, what of that?

OTHELLO   That's not so good now.

IAGO   What
    If I had said I had seen him do you wrong?
    Or heard him say – as knaves be such abroad,   25
    Who having by their own importunate suit
    Or voluntary dotage of some mistress
    Convincèd or supplied them, cannot choose
    But they must blab –

Iago implies that Cassio has boasted about having sex with Desdemona. Othello is so upset that it appears to bring on an epileptic fit. Cassio enters but is persuaded by Iago to leave again.

1 Othello's breakdown (in pairs)

What is the effect of Othello's seizure on you as a reader or spectator? Discuss the following views in turn with your partner:

- It makes you wonder just what kind of man is in charge of law and order in Cyprus.
- It's pure melodrama.
- Your sympathy is increased for Othello.
- Iago knows exactly where his victim's weak points are.
- It shows you how much Othello loves Desdemona.
- It clearly demonstrates to you how insanely possessive Othello is towards women.
- Even though Othello is a tough and powerful military leader, it exposes how deeply insecure he is.
- So much for 'civilised' colonial forces!

2 Dramatic grammar

To discover something about the state of Othello's mind, read lines 35–41 aloud whilst walking around the room. Change direction sharply at every punctuation mark. You'll find it's dizzying, under-lining how Othello's tortured imaginings are not only signalled by the physical 'fit', but accompanied by a breakdown in his language.

Afterwards, write a paragraph about the way Shakespeare structures language to reflect a character's state of mind in a dramatic way. Consider such things as sentence structure, sentence length, types of sentence (e.g. questions, exclamations, statements), punctuation.

---

belie slander
fulsome revolting
shadowing overwhelming
instruction reason
lethargy loss of consciousness

have his quiet course follow its nature
savage madness (notice Iago's racial stereotyping)

OTHELLO   Hath he said anything?

IAGO He hath, my lord; but be you well assured   30
    No more than he'll unswear.

OTHELLO   What hath he said?

IAGO Faith, that he did – I know not what he did.

OTHELLO What, what?

IAGO Lie –

OTHELLO With her?

IAGO   With her, on her, what you will.

OTHELLO Lie with her? Lie on her? We say lie on her when they belie   35
    her. Lie with her! Zounds, that's fulsome! Handkerchief –
    confessions – handkerchief! To confess and be hanged for his
    labour. First to be hanged and then to confess. I tremble at it.
    Nature would not invest herself in such shadowing passion without
    some instruction. It is not words that shakes me thus. Pish! Noses,   40
    ears, and lips. Is't possible? – Confess? Handkerchief? O devil!

               [He] falls in a trance.

IAGO Work on,
    My medicine, work! Thus credulous fools are caught;
    And many worthy and chaste dames even thus,
    All guiltless, meet reproach. What ho, my lord!   45
    My lord, I say! Othello!

          Enter CASSIO.

          How now, Cassio!

CASSIO What's the matter?

IAGO My lord is fallen into an epilepsy.
    This is his second fit; he had one yesterday.

CASSIO Rub him about the temples.

IAGO   No, forbear.   50
    The lethargy must have his quiet course.
    If not, he foams at mouth and by and by
    Breaks out to savage madness. Look, he stirs.
    Do you withdraw yourself a little while;
    He will recover straight. When he is gone,   55
    I would on great occasion speak with you.

               [Exit Cassio]

Othello regains consciousness. Iago again assures him of the unfaithfulness of women, then instructs him to eavesdrop on a conversation in which Cassio will tell of his sexual intercourse with Desdemona.

---

1 '. . . be a man' (in pairs)

Iago makes four jibes at Othello's 'manhood' in the page of script opposite. Find the four references. Create an improvisation in which you may use only these four chunks of script. Your improvisation need not have anything to do with the plot of *Othello*.

Share your improvisation with other pairs. Afterwards, discuss why Iago chooses to employ such terms of criticism. What is there about Othello (and the society that has formed him) which might make it particularly appropriate?

2 'O, thou art wise; 'tis certain' (in groups of three)

Look carefully at Iago's five sentences in lines 63–71. Take each sentence in turn, and talk together about why Othello finds it so persuasive that he replies, 'O, thou art wise'.

3 Husbands and oxen

In lines 64–5, Iago compares husbands to oxen, yoked together to pull ('draw') heavy loads. Make a tableau of this image, or draw it.

4 Iago takes control (in pairs)

In lines 72–87 Iago swiftly sets out a course of action for Othello to follow. Earlier, he used insidious persuasive techniques, but now he is direct and unambiguous as he takes command of the situation. Take turns to speak the lines to bring out the urgency and seeming good sense of the plan he outlines. Emphasise words and phrases that will especially heighten Othello's fury.

A hornèd man a cuckold (a man thought to have an unfaithful wife was said to grow horns)
civil civilised
yoked 'hitched', married
peculiar their own

lip kiss
wanton lecherous person
a patient list the bounds of patience
ecstasy fit, trance
fleers mocks and jokes
cope copulate with

How is it, general? Have you not hurt your head?
OTHELLO Dost thou mock me?
IAGO   I mock you? No, by heaven!
    Would you would bear your fortune like a man!
OTHELLO A hornèd man's a monster and a beast.   60
IAGO There's many a beast then in a populous city,
    And many a civil monster.
OTHELLO Did he confess it?
IAGO   Good sir, be a man:
    Think every bearded fellow that's but yoked
    May draw with you. There's millions now alive   65
    That nightly lie in those unproper beds
    Which they dare swear peculiar. Your case is better.
    O, 'tis the spite of hell, the fiend's arch-mock,
    To lip a wanton in a secure couch
    And to suppose her chaste! No, let me know;   70
    And knowing what I am, I know what she shall be.
OTHELLO O, thou art wise; 'tis certain.
IAGO   Stand you awhile apart,
    Confine yourself but in a patient list.
    Whilst you were here, o'erwhelmèd with your grief –
    A passion most unsuiting such a man –   75
    Cassio came hither. I shifted him away
    And laid good scuse upon your ecstasy;
    Bade him anon return and here speak with me,
    The which he promised. Do but encave yourself,
    And mark the fleers, the gibes, and notable scorns   80
    That dwell in every region of his face;
    For I will make him tell the tale anew,
    Where, how, how oft, how long ago, and when
    He hath and is again to cope your wife.
    I say but mark his gesture. Marry, patience,   85
    Or I shall say you're all in all in spleen
    And nothing of a man.
OTHELLO   Dost thou hear, Iago?
    I will be found most cunning in my patience,
    But – dost thou hear – most bloody.

Othello hides and Iago reveals he will question Cassio about Bianca. Othello overhears part of their conversation about Cassio's love life. He wrongly thinks they speak of Desdemona.

1 Mime the 'eavesdropping' episode (in groups of three)

Lines 101–61 are often called the 'eavesdropping' episode because in them Othello overhears (and misinterprets) Cassio's responses to Iago's questions and statements. Gain a first impression by taking parts and speaking the lines, adding movements and gestures. Then prepare a version, imagining it to be taken from a silent movie. Ensure your gestures are broad and clear, and that characterisation is communicated through the way people move, stand or position themselves.

2 Versions of Bianca (individually, then in pairs)

According to Iago, Bianca is a 'housewife' (pronounced 'huzif') or hussy who sells her 'desires' to earn a living. He goes on to make his meaning clearer by calling her a 'strumpet' (a whore). Some editors of *Othello* assume that Bianca is a prostitute, and call her that in the list of characters at the beginning of the playscript. Yet how accurate is Iago as a judge of women? Can you take his description at face value? Flick back through the play, reminding yourself of what Iago has said about other women so far.

Next, turn to a partner and compare your findings on Iago's attitude to women. Talk together about what difference it makes to a production of the play if Bianca is unequivocally presented as a prostitute. Think about how it reflects on Cassio, and what general image of women is offered through the play, given that Bianca represents one third of the women in the cast.

unbookish ignorant	**Roman** like a victorious Roman
construe interpret	warrior
addition title	**customer** whore
Whose want the lack of which	**bear some / charity** give some
poor caitiff poor thing	credit

IAGO   That's not amiss.
            But yet keep time in all. Will you withdraw?   90
                        [*Othello withdraws.*]
            Now will I question Cassio of Bianca,
            A housewife that by selling her desires
            Buys herself bread and clothes. It is a creature
            That dotes on Cassio; as 'tis the strumpet's plague
            To beguile many and be beguiled by one.   95
            He, when he hears of her, cannot refrain
            From the excess of laughter. Here he comes.

                        Enter Cassio.

            As he shall smile, Othello shall go mad;
            And his unbookish jealousy must construe
            Poor Cassio's smiles, gestures, and light behaviours   100
            Quite in the wrong. How do you now, lieutenant?
CASSIO The worser that you give me the addition
            Whose want even kills me.
IAGO Ply Desdemona well and you are sure on't.
            Now if this suit lay in Bianca's power,   105
            How quickly should you speed!
CASSIO   Alas, poor caitiff!
OTHELLO [*Aside*] Look how he laughs already!
IAGO I never knew a woman love man so.
CASSIO Alas, poor rogue! I think, i'faith, she loves me.
OTHELLO [*Aside*] Now he denies it faintly, and laughs it out.   110
IAGO Do you hear, Cassio?
OTHELLO [*Aside*]   Now he importunes him
            To tell it o'er. Go to, well said, well said!
IAGO She gives it out that you shall marry her.
            Do you intend it?
CASSIO Ha, ha, ha!   115
OTHELLO [*Aside*] Do you triumph, Roman? Do you triumph?
CASSIO I marry her? What! A customer! I prithee, bear some
      charity to my wit. Do not think it so unwholesome. Ha, ha, ha!
OTHELLO [*Aside*] So, so, so, so: they laugh that wins.

Othello continues to believe, wrongly, that Cassio speaks of Desdemona. He watches as Bianca meets Cassio and flings the handkerchief back in his face, supposing it had been given to him by some other woman.

Is this how you imagine Bianca to look and dress? What alternative interpretations of Bianca can you suggest? Think of an actor or famous person you would cast in a film version of *Othello* and the costume you would have her wear.

scored wounded	**such another fitchew** none other
bauble pretty thing	than that polecat
hales tugs	**Marry** by Mary (a mild oath)
	hobby-horse whore

IAGO Faith, the cry goes that you shall marry her.   120

CASSIO Prithee, say true.

IAGO I am a very villain else.

OTHELLO [*Aside*] Have you scored me? Well.

CASSIO This is the monkey's own giving out. She is persuaded I will
marry her out of her own love and flattery, not out of my   125
promise.

OTHELLO [*Aside*] Iago beckons me. Now he begins the story.

CASSIO She was here even now. She haunts me in every place. I was
the other day talking on the sea-bank with certain Venetians, and
thither comes this bauble and, by this hand, falls me thus   130
about my neck.

OTHELLO [*Aside*] Crying 'O dear Cassio!' as it were. His gesture
imports it.

CASSIO So hangs and lolls and weeps upon me, so hales and pulls me.
Ha, ha, ha!   135

OTHELLO [*Aside*] Now he tells how she plucked him to my chamber.
O, I see that nose of yours, but not that dog I shall throw it
to!

CASSIO Well, I must leave her company.

IAGO Before me, look where she comes!   140

CASSIO 'Tis such another fitchew! Marry, a perfumed one.

Enter BIANCA.

What do you mean by this haunting of me?

BIANCA Let the devil and his dam haunt you! What did you mean
by that same handkerchief you gave me even now? I was a fine fool
to take it. I must take out the work? A likely piece of work   145
that you should find it in your chamber and not know who left
it there! This is some minx's token, and I must take out the work?
There, give it your hobby-horse, wheresoever you had it. I'll
take out no work on't.

CASSIO How now, my sweet Bianca! How now, how now!   150

OTHELLO [*Aside*] By heaven, that should be my handkerchief!

BIANCA If you'll come to supper tonight, you may. If you will not,
come when you are next prepared for.   *Exit*

Cassio leaves to prevent further outbursts by Bianca. Othello determines to kill both Cassio and Desdemona, but is torn between violent hatred and love for his wife. Iago persuades him to put aside any remaining affection.

---

1 'How shall I murder him . . .?'

Line 162 is Othello's immediate reaction to the dialogue he has just overheard. As a reader or spectator, are you shocked by the brutality of the words? Write a paragraph trying to account for Othello's response. For example, would you say it's understandable because Othello is a professional soldier, a man used to fighting?

2 In action (in groups of three)

Explore different ways of reading lines 162–200, in which Iago cunningly deepens Othello's murderous impulses. Try, for example, whispering, ranting, reasoning. You will find that Othello's feelings fluctuate, but that Iago ensures his hatred triumphs.

Experiment with movement and positioning:

- using two group members as Othello, and the third as Iago, sharing Othello's lines according to the mood and attitude they reflect
- standing back-to-back
- moving constantly around the room
- staying in the same place
- having Iago always behind Othello, whispering in his ear.

3 '. . . the pity of it, Iago!' (in pairs)

Discuss your response to the following two questions:

a Do you think Iago could ever feel pity?

b Do you think that Othello is being self-indulgent here?

---

rail shout
by this hand I swear it
a-killing dying a slow death

fond over foolish about
patent licence

IAGO After her, after her!

CASSIO Faith, I must. She'll rail in the streets else. 155

IAGO Will you sup there?

CASSIO Faith, I intend so.

IAGO Well, I may chance to see you; for I would very fain speak with you.

CASSIO Prithee, come; will you? 160

IAGO Go to; say no more.

Exit Cassio

OTHELLO [*Coming forward.*] How shall I murder him, Iago?

IAGO Did you perceive how he laughed at his vice?

OTHELLO O, Iago!

IAGO And did you see the handkerchief? 165

OTHELLO Was that mine?

IAGO Yours, by this hand. And to see how he prizes the foolish woman your wife: she gave it him, and he hath given it his whore.

OTHELLO I would have him nine years a-killing. A fine woman, a fair woman, a sweet woman! 170

IAGO Nay, you must forget that.

OTHELLO Ay, let her rot and perish, and be damned tonight, for she shall not live. No, my heart is turned to stone: I strike it and it hurts my hand. O, the world hath not a sweeter creature! She might lie by an emperor's side and command him tasks. 175

IAGO Nay, that's not your way.

OTHELLO Hang her, I do but say what she is: so delicate with her needle, an admirable musician – O, she will sing the savageness out of a bear – of so high and plenteous wit and invention –

IAGO She's the worse for all this. 180

OTHELLO O, a thousand, thousand times – and then of so gentle a condition!

IAGO Ay, too gentle.

OTHELLO Nay, that's certain; but yet the pity of it, Iago! O Iago, the pity of it, Iago! 185

IAGO If you are so fond over her iniquity, give her patent to offend; for if it touch not you, it comes near nobody.

OTHELLO I will chop her into messes. Cuckold me!

IAGO O, 'tis foul in her.

OTHELLO With mine officer! 190

IAGO That's fouler.

Othello determines to follow Iago's suggestion to strangle Desdemona in her bed. Iago promises to kill Cassio that night. Lodovico brings Othello a letter from Venice and asks about Cassio.

1 Justice redefined

According to Othello, to strangle his wife in bed represents 'justice' (line 197). Justice can, therefore, be added to a growing list of words which have been redefined in the course of the play. For an activity on redefined terms in the play as a whole, see page 230.

2 '*Enter* LODOVICO' (in pairs)

Step into role as director and write an outline of how you would stage Lodovico's entrance. Work out who would accompany Lodovico, and how they would be dressed. Detail the advice you would give an actor playing Lodovico regarding his tone, manner and general bearing. Add a justification for each of your decisions.

3 Two words (in small groups)

Tiny sections of a play can be highly charged with significance. At line 212, Iago says only 'Lives, sir.' But *how* does he say it, and how does Lodovico (and everyone else) react? Talk together about whether the remark is in character for Iago.

4 Innocent remarks – dire misunderstandings

Desdemona unwittingly provokes Othello's anger as she responds to Lodovico's questions. His comments echo those he made in the earlier 'eavesdropping' episode. Her 'the love I bear to Cassio' prompts Othello to 'Fire and brimstone!', and when you turn the page you will find an even more extreme reaction.

---

expostulate discuss
unprovide weaken

in the paper reading the letter

OTHELLO Get me some poison, Iago, this night. I'll not expostulate
with her, lest her body and beauty unprovide my mind again – this
night, Iago.

IAGO Do it not with poison; strangle her in her bed, even the bed she   195
hath contaminated.

OTHELLO Good, good! The justice of it pleases; very good!

IAGO And for Cassio, let me be his undertaker. You shall hear more
by midnight.

OTHELLO Excellent good!   200

A trumpet [sounds within].

What trumpet is that same?

IAGO I warrant something from Venice.

Enter LODOVICO, DESDEMONA *and* ATTENDANTS.

'Tis Lodovico. This comes from the duke. See, your wife's with
him.

LODOVICO God save you, worthy general!

OTHELLO   With all my heart, sir.   205

LODOVICO The duke and senators of Venice greet you.

[He gives Othello a letter.]

OTHELLO I kiss the instrument of their pleasures.

[He opens the letter and reads.]

DESDEMONA And what's the news, good cousin Lodovico?

IAGO I am very glad to see you, signior;
Welcome to Cyprus.   210

LODOVICO I thank you. How does Lieutenant Cassio?

IAGO Lives, sir.

DESDEMONA Cousin, there's fallen between him and my lord
An unkind breach; but you shall make all well.

OTHELLO Are you sure of that?   215

DESDEMONA My lord?

OTHELLO 'This fail you not to do, as you will –'

LODOVICO He did not call; he's busy in the paper.
Is there division 'twixt my lord and Cassio?

DESDEMONA A most unhappy one; I would do much   220
T'atone them, for the love I bear to Cassio.

OTHELLO Fire and brimstone!

DESDEMONA My lord?

Lodovico reveals that the letter orders Othello to be recalled to Venice and Cassio made governor of Cyprus. Desdemona says she is pleased. Othello strikes her in front of the Venetian delegation, and rages at her.

---

1 *'He strikes her'* (in pairs)

Othello striking Desdemona was thought by some nineteenth-century directors to be too shocking to show on stage, and consequently they omitted it. Talk together about what difference it would make to a production if that act of violence were missed out. Would you retain it? Give reasons for your decision.

2 Show the moment (in groups of five or six)

Create a freeze-frame of the action at line 231: 'I have not deserved this.' Make sure that characters are recognisable from their reactions, their spatial relationships and their frozen gestures. Show your freeze-frame to the rest of the class for them to guess who the different characters are. To add an extra layer of sophistication, ask individual characters to step out of the freeze-frame and explain what is going through their mind at that moment.

3 What is your view?

Some commentators suggest that Desdemona is deliberately provoking Othello here, in order to bring his increasingly disturbed behaviour out into the open. What do you think of that reading? Is there any evidence so far in the play that Desdemona is an assertive enough young woman to do this?

4 Othello's syntax (in groups of three)

Look carefully at Othello's syntax (sentence structure) in lines 243–54. What is different about his way of speaking here in comparison with his early speeches (e.g. Act 1 Scene 3, lines 127–69)? By exploring different ways of speaking the lines, discuss what they tell you about his state of mind. Write two paragraphs on Othello's changed language (Activity 2 on p. 146 may help).

Mistress   term used to address a prostitute in a brothel
mandate   command

avaunt   get out of my sight
Goats and monkeys   supposedly lecherous beasts

OTHELLO Are you wise?

DESDEMONA What, is he angry?

LODOVICO   Maybe the letter moved him;   225
    For as I think they do command him home,
    Deputing Cassio in his government.

DESDEMONA By my troth, I am glad on't.

OTHELLO   Indeed!

DESDEMONA   My lord?

OTHELLO I am glad to see you mad.

DESDEMONA   Why, sweet Othello?

OTHELLO Devil!   230

[*He strikes her.*]

DESDEMONA I have not deserved this.

LODOVICO My lord, this would not be believed in Venice,
    Though I should swear I saw't. 'Tis very much.
    Make her amends; she weeps.

OTHELLO   O devil, devil!
    If that the earth could teem with woman's tears,   235
    Each drop she falls would prove a crocodile.
    Out of my sight!

DESDEMONA   I will not stay to offend you.

LODOVICO Truly, an obedient lady.
    I do beseech your lordship, call her back.

OTHELLO Mistress!   240

DESDEMONA My lord?

OTHELLO What would you with her, sir?

LODOVICO   Who? I, my lord?

OTHELLO Ay, you did wish that I would make her turn.
    Sir, she can turn, and turn, and yet go on,
    And turn again. And she can weep, sir, weep.   245
    And she's obedient; as you say, obedient,
    Very obedient – proceed you in your tears –
    Concerning this, sir, – O, well-painted passion! –
    I am commanded home – get you away!
    I'll send for you anon. – Sir, I obey the mandate,   250
    And will return to Venice. – Hence, avaunt!

[*Exit Desdemona*]

    Cassio shall have my place. And, sir, tonight
    I do entreat that we may sup together.
    You are welcome, sir, to Cyprus. Goats and monkeys! *Exit*

Lodovico expresses his horror to Iago at what he has just seen. Iago remarks that Othello is greatly changed. The next scene opens with Othello questioning Emilia about his wife's infidelity.

1 The man 'Whom passion could not shake' (in pairs)

Lodovico comments on how the Venetians had always considered Othello to be a man with great self-control. Discuss whether you consider a lack of emotion in a man to be an admirable quality or not. Relate your discussion to Othello. What does it say about Venetian society that such a lack of emotional response was greatly valued in a leader?

2 Iago's persuasive skill

Some readers of the play have stressed Othello's stupidity and gullibility in being taken in by Iago. However, it is testimony to Iago's acting skill that he has succeeded in convincing everyone, including Lodovico at this point. Lodovico says with heavy (unconscious) irony: 'I am sorry that I am deceived in him' (meaning Othello, when it is in fact Iago who has deceived him).

Examine each of Iago's comments to Lodovico opposite and assess his skill in the way he imparts an opinion without seeming to do so. You will find it helpful to think about how Shakespeare often has characters speaking simple monosyllabic words when talking about identity (e.g. Iago's 'I am not what I am' at line 66 of the play's opening scene). Look for examples of that technique in Iago's responses here.

3 Imagine the scene (in groups of three)

Imagine Lodovico and two other members of his delegation later on that day, talking about what they had seen when they delivered the Duke's letter to Othello. Take roles and improvise the scene as they relax in a private room together.

---

all-in-all sufficient fully competent   **use** custom
censure judgement

LODOVICO Is this the noble Moor whom our full senate   255
        Call all-in-all sufficient? Is this the nature
        Whom passion could not shake? Whose solid virtue
        The shot of accident nor dart of chance
        Could neither graze nor pierce?
IAGO   He is much changed.
LODOVICO Are his wits safe? Is he not light of brain?   260
IAGO He's that he is; I may not breathe my censure
        What he might be. If what he might he is not,
        I would to heaven he were.
LODOVICO   What! Strike his wife!
IAGO Faith, that was not so well; yet would I knew
        That stroke would prove the worst.
LODOVICO   Is it his use?   265
        Or did the letters work upon his blood
        And new-create this fault?
IAGO   Alas, alas!
        It is not honesty in me to speak
        What I have seen and known. You shall observe him,
        And his own courses will denote him so,   270
        That I may save my speech. Do but go after,
        And mark how he continues.
LODOVICO I am sorry that I am deceived in him.
                           Exeunt

Act 4 Scene 2
Cyprus   Another room in the castle

Enter OTHELLO *and* EMILIA.

OTHELLO You have seen nothing then?
EMILIA Nor ever heard, nor ever did suspect.
OTHELLO Yes, you have seen Cassio and she together.
EMILIA But then I saw no harm, and then I heard
        Each syllable that breath made up between them.   5

Emilia states categorically that Desdemona is innocent. Othello sends for his wife. He dismisses Emilia, treating her as a brothel-keeper.

1 Terms used for women

Everyone who comes under Iago's influence begins to adopt offensively sexist language. Here, Othello refers to Emilia as a 'simple bawd' and Desdemona as a 'subtle whore'. He suggests that Emilia is a brothel-keeper and that Desdemona is a prostitute. Identify three or four ways in which that sexist image is used in lines 26–9. Then think of other characters who have had their views and language debased by Iago so far in the play.

2 Improvise an image (in a group or individually)

Othello uses the image of a 'closet lock and key of villainous secrets' (a cupboard securely locked) in reference to Desdemona.

Either, in groups of between three and five, build an improvisation around the image.

Or, on your own, create a design to illustrate the image. Make it poster sized for display on your classroom wall.

3 Desdemona's question (in pairs)

Only a little while earlier, Desdemona had been struck, then angrily dismissed by Othello. Now she has been sent for, she enters and asks a question. Decide how Desdemona would behave and sound as she speaks 'My lord, what is your will?' (line 23). Experiment, then make a directorial decision. Be prepared to justify it to the rest of the class. (You might like to refer back to Activity 3, p. 158.)

---

durst dare
bawd brothel-keeper
Some of your function get on with your job (as brothel-keeper)

procreants those engaged in sex
Your mystery get on with your trade

OTHELLO What! Did they never whisper?

EMILIA   Never, my lord.

OTHELLO Nor send you out o'th'way?

EMILIA   Never.

OTHELLO To fetch her fan, her gloves, her mask, nor nothing?

EMILIA Never, my lord.

OTHELLO That's strange.   10

EMILIA I durst, my lord, to wager she is honest,
        Lay down my soul at stake. If you think other,
        Remove your thought; it doth abuse your bosom.
        If any wretch have put this in your head,
        Let heaven requite it with the serpent's curse!   15
        For if she be not honest, chaste, and true,
        There's no man happy. The purest of their wives
        Is foul as slander.

OTHELLO   Bid her come hither; go!

Exit Emilia

        She says enough; yet she's a simple bawd
        That cannot say as much. This is a subtle whore,   20
        A closet lock and key of villainous secrets;
        And yet she'll kneel and pray. I have seen her do't.

Enter DESDEMONA *and Emilia.*

DESDEMONA My lord, what is your will?

OTHELLO   Pray, chuck, come hither.

DESDEMONA What is your pleasure?

OTHELLO   Let me see your eyes.
        Look in my face.

DESDEMONA   What horrible fancy's this?   25

OTHELLO [*To Emilia*] Some of your function, mistress:
        Leave procreants alone and shut the door;
        Cough or cry 'hem' if anybody come.
        Your mystery, your mystery! Nay, dispatch!

Exit Emilia

DESDEMONA Upon my knees, what doth your speech import?   30
        I understand a fury in your words,
        But not the words.

OTHELLO   Why? What art thou?

Othello accuses Desdemona of gross dishonesty. She doesn't understand what he is talking about, but thinks his anger may be because he has been recalled to Venice by Brabantio's plotting.

---

1 Why does he not reply? (in pairs)

Spend five minutes discussing why you think Othello avoids answering Desdemona's direct questions: 'To whom . . .? With whom? How . . . ?' (line 39). He merely responds to her three questions with 'away, away, away!'

2 Othello's language: soliloquy? (in groups of three)

Read through Othello's lines 46–68. Much of what he says is almost like a soliloquy. As one person reads, the other two echo any words or phrases connected with nature – for example, images of beauty or decay.

Next, go through the speeches in more detail, sentence by sentence, and talk together about to whom you think he speaks: the audience, himself, Desdemona or . . . Explore ways in which each section of the speeches might be spoken on stage to give the audience insight into Othello's thoughts and feelings from moment to moment.

Take turns to present a delivery to the class, explaining before or after your presentation the effects you would hope to achieve to show Othello's mental state and emotions.

3 Graphic imagery (in groups of three)

Look at lines 47–8, 53–4, 60–1 and 65–6. Each pair of lines contains a strongly visual image, all concerned in some way with the world of nature. Choose two and create either a tableau for each or a large collage for display.

Share your tableaux/collages with the rest of the class. Can they guess which images you've chosen?

---

lost him lost his favour
garnered up my heart stored up my
  love
gender breed
cherubin angel

shambles slaughterhouses
quicken even with blowing hatch as
  soon as the eggs are laid
ignorant unknowing

DESDEMONA Your wife, my lord; your true and loyal wife.

OTHELLO Come, swear it; damn thyself;
      Lest, being like one of heaven, the devils themselves 35
      Should fear to seize thee. Therefore be double-damned:
      Swear thou art honest.

DESDEMONA   Heaven doth truly know it.

OTHELLO Heaven truly knows that thou art false as hell.

DESDEMONA To whom, my lord? With whom? How am I false?

OTHELLO Ah, Desdemon, away, away, away! 40

DESDEMONA Alas, the heavy day! Why do you weep?
      Am I the motive of these tears, my lord?
      If haply you my father do suspect
      An instrument of this your calling back,
      Lay not your blame on me. If you have lost him, 45
      I have lost him too.

OTHELLO   Had it pleased heaven
      To try me with affliction, had they rained
      All kind of sores and shames on my bare head,
      Steeped me in poverty to the very lips,
      Given to captivity me and my utmost hopes, 50
      I should have found in some place of my soul
      A drop of patience. But, alas, to make me
      The fixèd figure for the time of scorn
      To point his slow unmoving finger at!
      Yet could I bear that too, well, very well; 55
      But there where I have garnered up my heart,
      Where either I must live or bear no life,
      The fountain from the which my current runs
      Or else dries up – to be discarded thence
      Or keep it as a cistern for foul toads 60
      To knot and gender in! Turn thy complexion there,
      Patience, thou young and rose-lipped cherubin;
      Ay, there look grim as hell!

DESDEMONA I hope my noble lord esteems me honest.

OTHELLO O ay: as summer flies are in the shambles, 65
      That quicken even with blowing. O, thou weed,
      Who art so lovely fair and smell'st so sweet
      That the sense aches at thee, would thou hadst ne'er been
         born!

DESDEMONA Alas, what ignorant sin have I committed?

Othello calls Desdemona a whore to her face. He ignores her pleas of innocence, and continues to treat Emilia and Desdemona as if they work in a brothel.

---

1 Cosmic images (in pairs)

Othello uses imagery of the heavens in his answer to Desdemona's innocent question, 'what ignorant sin have I committed?' (line 69). He harps on the word 'committed' and states that 'Heaven stops the nose at it' (the smell of Desdemona's sin), 'the moon winks' (the moon refuses to look) and 'The bawdy wind, that kisses all it meets, / Is hushed within the hollow mine of earth / And will not hear it' (lines 76–9). So, her sin is so revolting and so wide reaching that heaven, moon and wind are unable to bear it. This is a gross exaggeration if taken literally. But what does it indicate about Othello's state of mind and how he interprets his wife's behaviour? Discuss this with a partner after rereading lines 70–80.

2 Emilia's version (in pairs)

In his last two encounters with Emilia, Othello has persisted in addressing her as if she's a 'madam' and Desdemona is one of her working prostitutes. At line 92 he tells Emilia, 'We have done our course' (finished our business) and then proceeds to pay her! Imagine what Emilia might say about all of this to a friend amongst the other army wives. Build up an improvisation based on an imaginary scene in which Emilia confides in a friend and gives her version of all that has happened so far since their arrival in Cyprus.

3 Othello's questions, Desdemona's responses

Note all the questions Othello asks opposite. Match Desdemona's reply with each question, where appropriate. Compile a list of these questions and answers. There is a common element in each of Desdemona's four replies. Identify it and notice how it recurs in Othello's line 90. Write several sentences saying how important you feel it to be to Desdemona and to the play as a whole.

Saint Peter (the saint who guards the gates of heaven) **conceive** imagine

OTHELLO Was this fair paper, this most goodly book,   70
     Made to write 'whore' upon? What committed!
     Committed? O thou public commoner!
     I should make very forges of my cheeks
     That would to cinders burn up modesty
     Did I but speak thy deeds. What committed!   75
     Heaven stops the nose at it, and the moon winks;
     The bawdy wind, that kisses all it meets,
     Is hushed within the hollow mine of earth
     And will not hear it. What committed?
     Impudent strumpet!
DESDEMONA   By heaven, you do me wrong.   80
OTHELLO Are not you a strumpet?
DESDEMONA   No, as I am a Christian.
     If to preserve this vessel for my lord
     From any other foul unlawful touch
     Be not to be a strumpet, I am none.
OTHELLO What, not a whore?
DESDEMONA   No, as I shall be saved.   85
OTHELLO Is't possible?
DESDEMONA O, heaven forgive us!
OTHELLO   I cry you mercy then:
     I took you for that cunning whore of Venice
     That married with Othello. You, mistress,
     That have the office opposite to Saint Peter,   90
     And keeps the gate of hell! You, you, ay, you!

Enter Emilia.

     We have done our course; there's money for your pains.
     I pray you turn the key, and keep our counsel.   *Exit*
EMILIA Alas, what does this gentleman conceive?
     How do you, madam? How do you, my good lady?   95
DESDEMONA Faith, half-asleep.
EMILIA Good madam, what's the matter with my lord?
DESDEMONA With who?
EMILIA Why, with my lord, madam.
DESDEMONA Who is thy lord?
EMILIA   He that is yours, sweet lady.   100

Desdemona expresses her distress and bewilderment at Othello's treatment of her. She cannot speak the word 'whore'. Emilia speculates it is all the trick of a villain seeking promotion.

---

1 Desdemona's response (in small groups)

Many modern readers of the play have found Desdemona's utter submissiveness in the face of severe provocation rather frustrating. However, it is also argued that her behaviour might have been regarded by some people in the past as exemplary for a married woman.

a How would you act if you were a woman faced with similar circumstances? Put your 'wedding sheets' on the bed and hope for the best? Or pack your bags and slam a few doors on the way out? Discuss what courses of action you would take yourselves. Then talk together particularly about the precise social constraints operating on Desdemona. What options are realistically open to her in the society in which she lives?

b Lines 106–8 are Desdemona's only soliloquy in the play. The convention is that in soliloquy a character always speaks truthfully. What 'truths' does she utter in these three lines?

2 '. . . some eternal villain' (in pairs)

Emilia's guess that 'some eternal villain' is responsible for the 'slander' (lines 129–32) is extremely accurate. The dramatic irony is made even more acute by the fact that Iago is present. Has Emilia realised what the truth is? Do you believe her words contain a guarded warning, or is it just a case of unconscious irony? Discuss with your partner, then try to predict how Iago will react on stage, and what reply (if any) Iago might make – don't turn the page until you've both had a guess!

---

should go by water should be
  expressed in tears
meet fitting, appropriate
a child to chiding not used to being
  verbally abused

callet slut
cogging, cozening cheating,
  deceiving
office job

DESDEMONA I have none. Do not talk to me, Emilia.
    I cannot weep, nor answers have I none
    But what should go by water. Prithee tonight
    Lay on my bed my wedding sheets, remember;
    And call thy husband hither.
EMILIA   Here's a change indeed!   *Exit*   105
DESDEMONA 'Tis meet I should be used so, very meet!
    How have I been behaved that he might stick
    The smallest opinion on my least misuse?

     Enter IAGO *and Emilia.*

IAGO What is your pleasure, madam? How is't with you?
DESDEMONA I cannot tell. Those that do teach young babes   110
    Do it with gentle means and easy tasks.
    He might have chid me so; for, in good faith,
    I am a child to chiding.
IAGO   What is the matter, lady?
EMILIA Alas, Iago, my lord hath so bewhored her,
    Thrown such despite and heavy terms upon her   115
    As true hearts cannot bear.
DESDEMONA Am I that name, Iago?
IAGO   What name, fair lady?
DESDEMONA Such as she said my lord did say I was.
EMILIA He called her whore. A beggar in his drink
    Could not have laid such terms upon his callet.   120
IAGO Why did he so?
DESDEMONA I do not know; I am sure I am none such.
IAGO Do not weep, do not weep! Alas the day!
EMILIA Hath she forsook so many noble matches,
    Her father, and her country, and her friends,   125
    To be called whore? Would it not make one weep?
DESDEMONA It is my wretched fortune.
IAGO   Beshrew him for't!
    How comes this trick upon him?
DESDEMONA   Nay, heaven doth know.
EMILIA I will be hanged if some eternal villain,
    Some busy and insinuating rogue,   130
    Some cogging, cozening slave, to get some office,
    Have not devised this slander; I'll be hanged else.

Emilia continues to suggest that a villain has poisoned Othello's mind. She reminds Iago that he has suspected her of infidelity with Othello. Desdemona professes her undying love for Othello, whatever happens.

1 'Here I kneel': intercut two scenes (in groups of three)

At line 150 Desdemona kneels to Iago to enlist his help. Not only is this heavy with very obvious irony, but it also parallels the scene where Othello kneels before Iago to swear vengeance (Act 3 Scene 3, line 451).

Read both these two incidents and the relevant sections of surrounding script. Experiment to find a way of intercutting (interweaving) the two episodes where husband and wife both kneel unwittingly before their tormentor. The actions are similar, but what differences exist between the two 'kneelings'?

2 '. . . some most villainous knave' (in groups of three)

Emilia continues her railing against the 'scurvy fellow' who might be at the back of Othello's uncharacteristic behaviour. You may feel that it is a remarkably accurate character reference for Iago! What does he make of such a telling description? Look carefully at Iago's spoken replies. We can't tell from the words alone whether he is nervously alert, dangerously threatening towards Emilia, or confident that he remains undiscovered. Starting with Emilia's 'I will be hanged' (line 129), experiment with different ways of acting out the script down to line 147. How far do your experiments help you to decide whether Emilia suspects her husband?

3 Iago's secret thoughts (in pairs)

Work on Desdemona's lines 147–63. Break up the speech into meaningful units (phrases, lines, sentences) and punctuate Desdemona's words with Iago's undisclosed thoughts. Present your version of this 'intercutting' activity to the rest of the class.

---

halter noose
within door quietly
the seamy side without inside out

abhor horrify
chide with rebuke, criticise

IAGO Fie, there is no such man; it is impossible.

DESDEMONA If any such there be, heaven pardon him.

EMILIA A halter pardon him and hell gnaw his bones!   135
       Why should he call her whore? Who keeps her company?
       What place, what time, what form, what likelihood?
       The Moor's abused by some most villainous knave,
       Some base notorious knave, some scurvy fellow.
       O heaven, that such companions thou'dst unfold,   140
       And put in every honest hand a whip
       To lash the rascals naked through the world,
       Even from the east to th'west!

IAGO   Speak within door.

EMILIA O fie upon them! Some such squire he was
       That turned your wit the seamy side without   145
       And made you to suspect me with the Moor.

IAGO You are a fool, go to.

DESDEMONA   O good Iago,
       What shall I do to win my lord again?
       Good friend, go to him; for, by this light of heaven,
       I know not how I lost him. Here I kneel: 150
       If e'er my will did trespass 'gainst his love
       Either in discourse of thought or actual deed;
       Or that mine eyes, mine ears, or any sense
       Delighted them in any other form;
       Or that I do not yet, and ever did,   155
       And ever will – though he do shake me off
       To beggarly divorcement – love him dearly,
       Comfort forswear me! Unkindness may do much,
       And his unkindness may defeat my life,
       But never taint my love. I cannot say 'whore':   160
       It does abhor me now I speak the word;
       To do the act that might the addition earn
       Not the world's mass of vanity could make me.

IAGO I pray you be content; 'tis but his humour.
       The business of the state does him offence,   165
       And he does chide with you.

DESDEMONA If 'twere no other –

IAGO   It is but so, I warrant.

Emilia and Desdemona go off to dinner with the Venetian visitors. Roderigo is fed up with Iago, accusing him of tricking him out of jewellery which was meant to have been passed on to Desdemona. He threatens Iago.

1 What happened at dinner? (in groups of six or seven)

After the highly emotional episode of marital strife, Desdemona is called to a formal dinner to entertain her Venetian guests. This is not a scene which Shakespeare chose to stage, but there are strong dramatic possibilities in such an artificially polite and formal occasion, with its seething undercurrents of highly charged emotional discord. Improvise the imagined scene, giving due consideration to how Othello, Desdemona, Emilia and Lodovico might speak and behave towards one another in public.

2 How should it be played? (in pairs)

The final part of Scene 2 brings in Roderigo, who bitterly complains that he is being exploited and cheated by Iago, and has no prospect of winning Desdemona. Iago displays his usual quick-wittedness as his initially brief replies incite Roderigo's anger and a threat of a duel ('seek satisfaction'). On the next page of the script, Iago flatters Roderigo and devises a murderous plan to kill Cassio, so enabling Roderigo to win Desdemona.

This episode between Iago and Roderigo has been differently interpreted by readers and directors. Some see it as continuing to raise the tension. Others see it as having strong comic possibilities through the character of Roderigo, and thereby lowering the tension briefly. Take parts and read lines 171–235, then discuss how you would play the episode, giving your reasons.

---

stay the meat   await the meal
daff'st me   fob me off
votarist   nun
sudden respect   immediate attention

fopped   fooled
seek satisfaction of you   challenge
 you to a duel

[*Trumpets sound within.*]
Hark how these instruments summon to supper!
The messengers of Venice stay the meat.
Go in, and weep not; all things shall be well.   170

Exeunt Desdemona and Emilia

Enter RODERIGO.

How now, Roderigo?

RODERIGO I do not find that thou deal'st justly with me.

IAGO What in the contrary?

RODERIGO Every day thou daff'st me with some device, Iago, and
rather, as it seems to me now, keep'st from me all conveniency   175
than suppliest me with the least advantage of hope. I will indeed
no longer endure it. Nor am I yet persuaded to put up in peace
what already I have foolishly suffered.

IAGO Will you hear me, Roderigo?

RODERIGO Faith, I have heard too much; for your words and   180
performances are no kin together.

IAGO You charge me most unjustly.

RODERIGO With naught but truth. I have wasted myself out of my
means. The jewels you have had from me to deliver to Desdemona
would half have corrupted a votarist. You have told me she hath   185
received them, and returned me expectations and comforts of
sudden respect and acquaintance, but I find none.

IAGO Well, go to; very well.

RODERIGO Very well, go to! I cannot go to, man, nor 'tis not very
well. By this hand, I say 'tis very scurvy and begin to find myself   190
fopped in it.

IAGO Very well.

RODERIGO I tell you 'tis not very well. I will make myself known to
Desdemona. If she will return me my jewels, I will give over my
suit and repent my unlawful solicitation; if not, assure yourself I   195
will seek satisfaction of you.

IAGO You have said now?

Iago promises Roderigo that Desdemona will be available for him soon. He plots that Roderigo shall kill Cassio that night as Cassio leaves Bianca's house.

What information does Iago (left) pass on to Roderigo about Othello's next posting and about Cassio's forthcoming promotion? What reward is Roderigo (right) promised for 'knocking out [Cassio's] brains'?

engines for plots against	**second** support
Mauritania (a region of North Africa)	**necessity in** need for
abode be lingered stay be prolonged	**put it on him** kill him
harlotry harlot or 'tart'	

RODERIGO Ay, and said nothing but what I protest intendment of doing.

IAGO Why, now I see there's mettle in thee, and even from this instant   200
do build on thee a better opinion than ever before. Give me thy
hand, Roderigo. Thou hast taken against me a most just
exception; but yet I protest I have dealt most directly in thy
affair.

RODERIGO It hath not appeared.   205

IAGO I grant indeed it hath not appeared; and your suspicion is not
without wit and judgement. But, Roderigo, if thou hast that in
thee indeed, which I have greater reason to believe now than ever – I
mean purpose, courage, and valour – this night show it. If thou the
next night following enjoy not Desdemona, take me from this   210
world with treachery, and devise engines for my life.

RODERIGO Well, what is it? Is it within reason and compass?

IAGO Sir, there is especial commission come from Venice to depute
Cassio in Othello's place.

RODERIGO Is that true? Why, then Othello and Desdemona return again   215
to Venice.

IAGO O no, he goes into Mauritania and takes away with him the
fair Desdemona, unless his abode be lingered here by some
accident; wherein none can be so determinate as the removing of
Cassio.   220

RODERIGO How do you mean 'removing' of him?

IAGO Why, by making him uncapable of Othello's place – knocking out
his brains.

RODERIGO And that you would have me to do?

IAGO Ay, if you dare do yourself a profit and a right. He sups tonight   225
with a harlotry, and thither will I go to him. He knows not yet of
his honourable fortune. If you will watch his going thence – which
I will fashion to fall out between twelve and one – you may take
him at your pleasure. I will be near to second your attempt, and
he shall fall between us. Come, stand not amazed at it, but go along   230
with me. I will show you such a necessity in his death that you shall
think yourself bound to put it on him. It is now high supper-time
and the night grows to waste. About it!

RODERIGO I will hear further reason for this.

IAGO And you shall be satisfied.   235

Exeunt

Othello bids goodnight to Lodovico after their dinner, and orders Desdemona to go to bed to await him. She talks with Emilia of her love for Othello, of death, and of Barbary, her mother's maid.

---

1 Polite forms of address (in small groups)

In lines 1–9, the dialogue is peppered with polite forms of address: 'sir', 'Madam', and so on. The only person not to use such formality within every utterance is Othello. Can you suggest any reasons for that?

2 First impression (in pairs)

Scene 3 is often referred to as the 'willow' scene. To gain a first impression of what happens, take parts as Desdemona and Emilia, and read from line 10 to the end of the scene. As you read, think about the relationship between the two women: whether it is close friendship, or that of mistress and servant. Then work on some of the activities provided.

3 Foreboding

Read through the script opposite. There is a general sense of foreboding. Devise a diagram to show how each of the following contributes to the ominous atmosphere:

- sheets
- the order to dismiss Emilia
- Barbary's story
- the willow song
- Desdemona's complete obedience.

In each case add a quotation from the script. Your diagram should help others to understand what the dramatic effect of this part of the play might be.

4 Barbary's story

What happened to Barbary? Lines 25–9 show there's a story to be told! Write a tragi-romantic story, a ballad or a short play which narrates the tragic tale of *Barbary, a Woman Wronged*. You could experiment with a few ideas first by improvising in a small group.

---

incontinent straight away
approve value

willow (willow trees were traditionally symbolic of forsaken lovers)

Act 4 Scene 3
Cyprus   A room in the castle

Enter OTHELLO, LODOVICO, DESDEMONA,
EMILIA and ATTENDANTS.

LODOVICO I do beseech you, sir, trouble yourself no further.

OTHELLO O, pardon me; 'twill do me good to walk.

LODOVICO Madam, good night. I humbly thank your ladyship.

DESDEMONA Your honour is most welcome.

OTHELLO Will you walk, sir? O, Desdemona.   5

DESDEMONA My lord?

OTHELLO Get you to bed on th'instant. I will be returned forthwith.
    Dismiss your attendant there. Look't be done.

DESDEMONA I will, my lord.

       Exeunt [Othello, Lodovico and Attendants]

EMILIA How goes it now? He looks gentler than he did.   10

DESDEMONA He says he will return incontinent;
    He hath commanded me to go to bed
    And bade me to dismiss you.

EMILIA   Dismiss me?

DESDEMONA It was his bidding; therefore, good Emilia,
    Give me my nightly wearing, and adieu.   15
    We must not now displease him.

EMILIA I would you had never seen him.

DESDEMONA So would not I: my love doth so approve him
    That even his stubbornness, his checks, his frowns –
    Prithee, unpin me – have grace and favour in them.   20

EMILIA I have laid those sheets you bade me on the bed.

DESDEMONA All's one. Good faith, how foolish are our minds!
    If I do die before thee, prithee shroud me
    In one of those same sheets.

EMILIA   Come, come, you talk.

DESDEMONA My mother had a maid called Barbary: 25
    She was in love, and he she loved proved mad
    And did forsake her. She had a song of willow;
    An old thing 'twas but it expressed her fortune,
    And she died singing it. That song tonight
    Will not go from my mind. I have much to do   30
    But to go hang my head all at one side

Desdemona sings a sad song from her childhood as she prepares for bed. She and Emilia discuss their differing attitudes to marriage and fidelity.

1 '. . . a proper man' (in pairs)

Desdemona refers to Lodovico as being 'a proper man' (a good-looking man) and someone who 'speaks well'. Emilia agrees. Spend about five minutes discussing why Desdemona says this. What is in her mind?

2 Sing willow (in groups of five to ten)

Divide up the words of the Willow Song, lines 38–54 (excluding any inserted dialogue) between you. Memorise your line(s) on your own for a few minutes and make sure you know the correct order.

Next, explore ways of presenting the song so as to create a moving dramatic effect. Try whispering or wailing the words. You could experiment with making soft background noises, imitating the sound of wind through branches, or playing with ways of repeating the refrain. Dim the lights if that is possible. Think about how you move as a group, too. Aim at producing a complete theatrical experience, one that is both physical and emotional, expressing Desdemona's mood – and all done within your drama studio or classroom!

3 The Willow Song

The first edition of the play (published in 1622) omits the song altogether. Perhaps the boy actor who played Desdemona at that time couldn't sing. From your reading, or viewing, of either a live or videoed performance, what was your reaction to the song? What effect did it have on you? List what a performance would gain or lose if the song were omitted. Compare your feelings with other students.

---

dispatch hurry up
Lay by these put these (clothes) away
hie thee go away

moe more
bode foretell
in conscience honestly

And sing it like poor Barbary – prithee, dispatch.

EMILIA Shall I go fetch your nightgown?

DESDEMONA   No, unpin me here.
    This Lodovico is a proper man.

EMILIA A very handsome man.

DESDEMONA   He speaks well.   35

EMILIA I know a lady in Venice would have walked barefoot to Palestine
    for a touch of his nether lip.

DESDEMONA [*Sings*]
        The poor soul sat sighing by a sycamore tree,
            Sing all a green willow;
        Her hand on her bosom, her head on her knee,   40
            Sing willow, willow, willow;
        The fresh streams ran by her and murmured her moans;
            Sing willow, willow, willow.
        Her salt tears fell from her and softened the stones –
    Lay by these.   45
            Sing willow, willow, willow –
    Prithee, hie thee; he'll come anon.
            Sing all a green willow must be my garland.
        Let nobody blame him; his scorn I approve –
    Nay that's not next. Hark, who is't that knocks?   50

EMILIA It's the wind.

DESDEMONA [*Sings*]
        I called my love false love, but what said he then?
            Sing willow, willow, willow;
        If I court moe women, you'll couch with moe men –
    So get thee gone; good night. Mine eyes do itch –   55
    Does that bode weeping?

EMILIA   'Tis neither here nor there.

DESDEMONA I have heard it said so. O, these men, these men!
    Dost thou in conscience think – tell me, Emilia –
    That there be women do abuse their husbands
    In such gross kind?

EMILIA   There be some such, no question.   60

DESDEMONA Wouldst thou do such a deed for all the world?

EMILIA Why, would not you?

DESDEMONA   No, by this heavenly light.

EMILIA Nor I neither by this heavenly light;
    I might do't as well i'th'dark.

Emilia says she would commit adultery if it gained her husband the world. Desdemona can't believe this. Emilia asserts that husbands are to blame, and argues for equality and mutual respect in marriage.

Compare the two women's views of men and marriage. Would you agree that one is a romanticised view, whilst the other is much more practical? With a partner, discuss what the women say to each other in lines 57–101. What difference does their respective social position make to their separate views? It can be helpful to role-play Emilia and Desdemona justifying their views, making reference to their respective social positions, their own experience of men and married life and their hopes for the future.

joint-ring   a cheap ring
measures of lawn   lengths of fabric
exhibition   amount of money
Ud's   God's
venture purgatory   risk being
   condemned to the torture of purgatory

to th'advantage   in addition
store   populate
treasures   sexual favours
in despite   out of spite
galls   the guts to get revenge

DESDEMONA Wouldst thou do such a deed for all the world?   65

EMILIA The world's a huge thing; it is a great price
    For a small vice.

DESDEMONA   In troth, I think thou wouldst not.

EMILIA In troth, I think I should, and undo't when I had done it.
    Marry, I would not do such a thing for a joint-ring, nor for
    measures of lawn, nor for gowns, petticoats, nor caps, nor any   70
    petty exhibition. But for all the whole world! Ud's pity,
    who would not make her husband a cuckold, to make him a
    monarch? I should venture purgatory for't.

DESDEMONA Beshrew me, if I would do such a wrong for the whole
    world.   75

EMILIA Why, the wrong is but a wrong i'th'world; and having the world
    for your labour, 'tis a wrong in your own world, and you might
    quickly make it right.

DESDEMONA I do not think there is any such woman.

EMILIA Yes, a dozen; and as many to th'advantage as would store   80
    the world they played for.
        But I do think it is their husbands' faults
        If wives do fall. Say that they slack their duties
        And pour our treasures into foreign laps,
        Or else break out in peevish jealousies,   85
        Throwing restraint upon us; or say they strike us,
        Or scant our former having in despite –
        Why, we have galls, and though we have some grace,
        Yet have we some revenge. Let husbands know
        Their wives have sense like them: they see, and smell,   90
        And have their palates both for sweet and sour
        As husbands have. What is it that they do
        When they change us for others? Is it sport?
        I think it is. And doth affection breed it?
        I think it doth. Is't frailty that thus errs?   95
        It is so too. And have not we affections,
        Desires for sport, and frailty, as men have?
        Then let them use us well; else let them know
        The ills we do, their ills instruct us so.

DESDEMONA Good night, good night. God me such uses send,   100
    Not to pick bad from bad, but by bad mend!

                                      Exeunt

Looking back at Act 4
Activities for groups or individuals

---

1 Abuse of Desdemona (in groups of about ten)

This activity is an exploration both of Desdemona's experience and social position, and of Othello's use of increasingly crude and abusive language in Act 4. The following lines are all spoken by Othello directly to Desdemona's face:

'thou art false as hell'

'look grim as hell!'

'O, thou weed'

'Was this fair paper . . . Made to write "whore" upon?'

'O thou public commoner!'

'Impudent strumpet!'

'Are not you a strumpet?'

'What, not a whore?'

'I took you for that cunning whore of Venice'

'We have done our course'.

Take and learn one of the above lines each. Move around the room, and every time you encounter another student shout, hiss or sneer your line in their face.

Next, stand in a long line, all facing one way. Go swiftly down the row, spinning round one by one so that you are facing the next person, and snap out your lines. Then try standing in a tight circle with one student kneeling in the middle. Hurl your lines of abuse at them.

Try different ways of presenting the lines – perhaps you could form a 'speaking tableau' to suggest the roles and relationship of Othello and Desdemona. Experiment!

Use the physical experience of this activity to help you write a short essay that analyses Othello's motives for such language, and Desdemona's feelings in response to it.

2 Emilia (in groups of three)

In Act 4 Emilia begins to emerge as a fascinating character. She is in an ambiguous position in relation to Desdemona:

On the one hand, Emilia . . .	On the other, she . . .
is married to Iago	is employed by Desdemona and Othello
feels a sense of duty to her husband	feels a sense of duty to her mistress
is Desdemona's only female confidante in Cyprus	is Desdemona's maid/servant
tries to be sympathetic to Desdemona's situation	has led a less sheltered life than Desdemona and has a sceptical view of relationships

The four quotations below are all taken from scenes in which Desdemona and Emilia are together in Act 4 (Iago is present in one of them). For each, create a tableau or freeze-frame that makes the relationship between the two women clear. Think about the content of the words and the degree of intimacy the words suggest; then consider Emilia and Desdemona's relative positions, their respective 'personalities' and the dramatic context:

- Alas, what does this gentleman conceive? (Scene 2, line 94)
- I will be hanged if some eternal villain . . . Have not devised this slander (Scene 2, lines 129–32)
- No, unpin me here (Scene 3, line 33)
- Wouldst thou do such a deed for all the world? (Scene 3, line 65)

Use your practical experience to write about six paragraphs explaining how you see the relationship of Emilia and Desdemona.

Iago positions Roderigo for the murder. He hopes both Cassio and Roderigo will die. Roderigo fails to kill Cassio, who wounds him instead. Iago leaps out of hiding, strikes Cassio and runs off.

1 Count the commands

How many commands can you find in the opening five lines of Iago's conversation? What does this underline about the relationship between Iago and Roderigo?

2 Intrigue again

Act 5 opens in a very similar way to Act 1, with Iago and Roderigo plotting villainy in the streets, late at night. What other similarities are there with that opening scene – and what key differences?

3 Motiveless malignity? (in pairs)

Read through Iago's Aside, lines 11–22. The early nineteenth-century poet and writer Samuel Taylor Coleridge was intrigued by the character of Iago, whose activities he described as arising out of 'motiveless malignity'. Yet Iago himself has already given several reasons for his vendetta against Othello and Cassio, and in this Aside he adds to the list of possible reasons.

Discuss first what you think is meant by Iago's comment 'He hath a daily beauty in his life / That makes me ugly' (lines 19–20). Then talk together about Iago's motivation (or lack of it) to do harm to others and whether you think that Coleridge was right in his assessment. Coleridge's 'motiveless malignity' is often quoted when Iago is considered, so keep notes on your discussion.

4 Slow motion (in groups of four)

Show the action in slow motion (for the sake of safety) from line 22, 'But soft, I hear him coming' to Othello's entrance at line 27.

---

bulk projecting wall
straight immediately
quat spot or boil

Live Roderigo if Roderigo lives
bobbed conned, tricked
unfold expose

Act 5 Scene 1
Cyprus   A street at night

Enter IAGO *and* RODERIGO.

IAGO Here, stand behind this bulk, straight will he come.
Wear thy good rapier bare, and put it home.
Quick, quick, fear nothing; I'll be at thy elbow.
It makes us or it mars us; think on that,
And fix most firm thy resolution.   5
RODERIGO Be near at hand; I may miscarry in't.
IAGO Here, at thy hand; be bold, and take thy stand.
                          [*He retires.*]
RODERIGO I have no great devotion to the deed,
And yet he hath given me satisfying reasons.
'Tis but a man gone. Forth my sword! He dies!   10
IAGO [*Aside*] I have rubbed this young quat almost to the sense,
And he grows angry. Now, whether he kill Cassio,
Or Cassio him, or each do kill the other,
Every way makes my gain. Live Roderigo,
He calls me to a restitution large   15
Of gold and jewels that I bobbed from him
As gifts to Desdemona.
It must not be. If Cassio do remain,
He hath a daily beauty in his life
That makes me ugly; and besides, the Moor   20
May unfold me to him – there stand I in much peril.
No, he must die. But soft, I hear him coming.

Enter CASSIO.

RODERIGO I know his gait; 'tis he. Villain, thou diest!
                          [*He lunges at Cassio.*]
CASSIO That thrust had been mine enemy indeed
But that my coat is better than thou think'st.   25
I will make proof of thine.
                          [*He wounds Roderigo.*]
RODERIGO   O, I am slain!
                          [*Iago wounds Cassio in the leg and exit*]
CASSIO I am maimed forever. Help, ho! Murder, murder!

Enter OTHELLO.

Othello hears the scuffles and, satisfied Cassio is dead, goes off to kill Desdemona. Lodovico and Gratiano cautiously investigate the cries of the two wounded men. Iago arrives to help.

1 Who's doing what when? (in pairs)

There is much action in the first fifty-five lines of Scene 1. As you can imagine, on stage it is both quick moving and exciting. Below is one person's idea for staging it at Shakespeare's Globe Theatre (now rebuilt on London's Bankside). The drawing shows different characters at different moments and the events are numbered in the order in which they happen in the script.

Decide who each person in the drawing is and work out which moment in the script is being represented in each case. Find a suitable quotation for each one (five in all).

Minion darling (used contemptuously about Desdemona)	**watch** night patrol
	passage passers-by
hies is coming fast	**heavy** dark
blotted wiped out	**spoiled** wounded

186

OTHELLO [*Aside*] The voice of Cassio: Iago keeps his word.

RODERIGO O villain that I am!

OTHELLO [*Aside*]   It is even so.

CASSIO O help, ho! Light! A surgeon!   30

OTHELLO [*Aside*] 'Tis he. O brave Iago, honest and just,
    That hast such noble sense of thy friend's wrong!
    Thou teachest me. Minion, your dear lies dead,
    And your unblest fate hies. Strumpet, I come!
    Forth of my heart those charms, thine eyes, are blotted;   35
    Thy bed, lust-stained, shall with lust's blood be spotted.

Exit Othello

Enter LODOVICO *and* GRATIANO.

CASSIO What, ho! No watch? No passage? Murder, murder!

GRATIANO 'Tis some mischance; the cry is very direful.

CASSIO O, help!

LODOVICO Hark!   40

RODERIGO O, wretched villain!

LODOVICO Two or three groan. It is a heavy night.
    These may be counterfeits: let's think't unsafe
    To come in to the cry without more help.

RODERIGO Nobody come? Then I shall bleed to death.   45

LODOVICO Hark!

Enter Iago, with a light.

GRATIANO Here's one comes in his shirt, with light and weapons.

IAGO Who's there? Whose noise is this that cries on murder?

LODOVICO We do not know.

IAGO   Did you not hear a cry?

CASSIO Here, here; for heaven's sake, help me!

IAGO   What's the matter?   50

GRATIANO This is Othello's ancient, as I take it.

LODOVICO The same indeed, a very valiant fellow.

IAGO What are you here that cry so grievously?

CASSIO Iago? O, I am spoiled, undone by villains!
    Give me some help.   55

In pretending to investigate what has happened, Iago secretly stabs the wounded Roderigo. Cassio is discovered to have a severe leg wound. Bianca arrives to see what's happened and Iago insults her.

1 Darkness – and Iago's play-acting (in pairs)

In Shakespeare's time the play would have been acted at the Globe Theatre in broad daylight. So Shakespeare provides his actors with language and action to suggest that the scene takes place at night. The Jacobean audiences who watched the play were familiar with such dramatic presentations, and accepted them willingly, ready to suspend their disbelief.

Shakespeare also continues to present Iago as a cunning manipulator, ready to seize any opportunity to further his own interests. He plays the innocent, honest soldier yet again, calling in Lodovico and Gratiano to help, and even binding Cassio's wound with his shirt to show friendship. But he also takes the opportunity of darkness to stab Roderigo, whose words accurately describe him: 'O damned Iago! O inhuman dog!' One person speaks everything Iago says opposite, pausing after every sentence. In the pause the other person describes what impression Iago is attempting to create by his words.

2 Sentence structure: dramatic effect (in small groups)

The script is full of short, simple sentences. To catch the mood and the speed of the action, try these ways of reading lines 56–84:

a Read around the group, each person exclaiming a single sentence only before handing on.

b Repeat the exercise, but this time exclaim only one word – the one you think most important – in each sentence.

c Repeat both exercises, but as quickly as possible.

Identify which of these are questions, statements or exclamations. Afterwards, talk together about the speed at which you think the lines should be spoken, and why Shakespeare used so many short sentences here.

---

make away   escape

Marry   mild swearing (literally 'by the Virgin Mary')

IAGO O me, lieutenant! What villains have done this?

CASSIO I think that one of them is hereabout
  And cannot make away.

IAGO   O, treacherous villains!
  [*To Lodovico and Gratiano*] What are you there? Come in,
    and give some help.

RODERIGO O, help me here!   60

CASSIO That's one of them.

IAGO   O murderous slave! O villain!
  [*He stabs Roderigo.*]

RODERIGO O damned Iago! O inhuman dog!
  [*He faints.*]

IAGO Kill men i'th'dark? Where be these bloody thieves?
  How silent is this town! Ho, murder, murder!
    [*Lodovico and Gratiano come forward.*]
  What may you be? Are you of good or evil?   65

LODOVICO As you shall prove us, praise us.

IAGO Signior Lodovico?

LODOVICO He, sir.

IAGO I cry you mercy. Here's Cassio hurt by villains.

GRATIANO Cassio?   70

IAGO How is't, brother?

CASSIO My leg is cut in two.

IAGO   Marry, heaven forbid!
  Light, gentlemen. I'll bind it with my shirt.

Enter BIANCA.

BIANCA What is the matter, ho? Who is't that cried?

IAGO Who is't that cried?   75

BIANCA O, my dear Cassio, my sweet Cassio!
  O, Cassio, Cassio, Cassio!

IAGO O notable strumpet! Cassio, may you suspect
  Who they should be that have thus mangled you?

CASSIO No.   80

GRATIANO I am sorry to find you thus; I have been to seek you.

Iago accuses Bianca of involvement in the affray. He pretends to be surprised at identifying Roderigo as Cassio's attacker. He shows great concern for Cassio, and has him carried off to receive treatment.

1 Clever Iago? Or helped by chance?

Iago continues to play the role of concerned friendship. He bustles about, accusing Bianca, feigning innocent distress at discovering Roderigo, and calling for a chair for Cassio. Iago seems to have avoided personal disaster very narrowly, by a combination of mere chance and his own skill. However, if Lodovico and Gratiano had been more courageous and had immediately and properly investigated the screams from the street (line 37), the whole scene might have unfolded in a very different way.

Write down which aspects of this incident you think are down to Iago's skill (use Activity 1 on p. 188 to help you). Then write down how chance works in Iago's favour at this point. Try to think of another incident in the play so far where chance helps Iago out.

2 Bianca's statement

Iago is so confidently in his stride he doesn't hesitate to cast doubt on Bianca, calling her 'this trash'. He insinuates (lines 105–10) that she might be an accessory to the murder attempt. Over the page you will find that Bianca becomes an easy target for Emilia, too, who calls her a 'strumpet' (whilst Cassio is thought of as a poor victim!).

Imagine you are Bianca, and write a short statement defending yourself against Iago's charge. Practise reading it in role, and share it with the rest of the class.

---

trash rubbish (referring to Bianca)
To be a party in to have something to do with

a chair probably a sedan chair to carry off Cassio

IAGO Lend me a garter: so. O for a chair
    To bear him easily hence!
BIANCA   Alas, he faints!
    O, Cassio, Cassio, Cassio!
IAGO Gentlemen all, I do suspect this trash   85
    To be a party in this injury.
    Patience awhile, good Cassio. Come, come,
    Lend me a light. Know we this face or no?
    Alas, my friend and my dear countryman!
    Roderigo? No – yes, sure – O, heaven, Roderigo!   90
GRATIANO What, of Venice?
IAGO Even he, sir; did you know him?
GRATIANO   Know him? Ay.
IAGO Signior Gratiano! I cry your gentle pardon.
    These bloody accidents must excuse my manners
    That so neglected you.
GRATIANO   I am glad to see you.   95
IAGO How do you, Cassio? O, a chair, a chair!
GRATIANO Roderigo?
IAGO He, he, 'tis he.

        [*Enter* ATTENDANTS *with a chair.*]

    O, that's well said, the chair!
    Some good men bear him carefully from hence.
    I'll fetch the general's surgeon. [*To Bianca*] For you,
        mistress,   100
    Save you your labour. – He that lies slain here, Cassio,
    Was my dear friend. What malice was between you?
CASSIO None in the world, nor do I know the man.
IAGO [*To Bianca*] What, look you pale? – O, bear him out o'th'air.
        [*Cassio is carried off; Roderigo's body is removed*]

Iago accuses Bianca of looking guilty. He explains what's happened to Emilia, who verbally abuses Bianca. Iago sends Emilia to Othello with the news.

---

1 Guilty looks – and a wife's support (in pairs)

a Can you tell if a person is guilty by the way they look (lines 109–10)? Talk together about how Bianca probably looks at this moment and your views on whether guilt shows in a person's face.

b Why do you think Emilia supports her husband's view of Bianca, calling her 'strumpet'?

2 Fast forward (in groups of eight to ten)

For this activity you are going to need to work in a large, clear space because you'll be rushing around. So either clear a space in the classroom or use the drama studio or hall.

Think of old silent movies when the action gets ridiculously fast-moving, and is usually accompanied by breathlessly rapid music. Or think what happens when you hold down the 'fast forward' control on a video player and the action becomes comically frenetic. Try staging Act 5 Scene 1 as if it's being played like that. You will find the need for speed adds to your understanding of the sequence of events. If you do it properly, you should be completely out of breath at the end!

To make it more fun, find some suitable musical accompaniment: 'The Flight of the Bumble-Bee' or old silent movie chase music . . .

3 Afterwards . . .

While you are still catching your breath, sit in a circle and go immediately into a reading of the next scene. That way you will gain an appreciation of how Shakespeare effects a dramatic change in tone and pace between Scenes 1 and 2.

---

gastness terrified look
I therefore shake not I'm not afraid to say so

dressed have wounds treated
fordoes me quite ruins me completely

Stay you, good gentlemen. Look you pale, mistress?   105
Do you perceive the gastness of her eye?
[*To Bianca*] Nay, if you stare, we shall hear more anon.
Behold her well; I pray you, look upon her.
Do you see, gentlemen? Nay, guiltiness
Will speak, though tongues were out of use.   110

Enter EMILIA.

EMILIA 'Las, what's the matter? What's the matter, husband?
IAGO Cassio hath here been set on in the dark
        By Roderigo and fellows that are 'scaped.
        He's almost slain and Roderigo dead.
EMILIA Alas, good gentleman! Alas, good Cassio!   115
IAGO This is the fruits of whoring. Prithee, Emilia,
        Go know of Cassio where he supped tonight.
        [*To Bianca*] What, do you shake at that?
BIANCA He supped at my house, but I therefore shake not.
IAGO O, did he so? I charge you go with me.   120
EMILIA O, fie upon thee, strumpet!
BIANCA I am no strumpet, but of life as honest
        As you that thus abuse me.
EMILIA   As I? Foh! Fie upon thee!
IAGO Kind gentlemen, let's go see poor Cassio dressed.
        Come, mistress, you must tell's another tale.   125
        Emilia, run you to the citadel
        And tell my lord and lady what hath happed.
        Will you go on afore? [*Aside*] This is the night
        That either makes me, or fordoes me quite.
                                                        Exeunt

Othello reasons why Desdemona must die and that the dead cannot be restored to life. He kisses her and nearly abandons his intent to kill her, but resolves that she must die.

---

1 Two-handed soliloquy (in pairs)

Read through Othello's soliloquy opposite, with each person handing over the reading at each full stop, colon or semi-colon.

Now consider ways of performing this speech as if it's a conversation (and a soliloquy can be thought of, in a way, as an internal dialogue or developing argument). Experiment with ways of dividing up the speech, and ways of saying the words to create different effects. Decide how you might stand, move, use different levels and so on.

Use your experience of treating the soliloquy as a dialogue to work out how Othello might deliver the lines in performance. Then share your work with the rest of the class, either as a 'two-hander' or with a single person speaking the lines.

2 Othello's 'cause' (in groups of three or four)

Othello repeats the word 'cause' three times in the opening three lines of the scene. For the Elizabethans, 'cause' could carry several meanings:

- an action which prompts a reaction (Desdemona's infidelity)
- a morally justifiable end one is pursuing, 'all in a good cause' (Othello wishing to protect 'more men' and restore moral order)
- a legal usage meaning an accusation brought against someone in court (Othello sees himself as an agent of impartial justice – but at lines 16–17, as he kisses her, his emotions threaten to reject his role as a minister of 'justice').

Take the phrase 'It is the cause' and illustrate these three meanings in a way which relates to Othello's situation and state of mind at this point in the play. Use whatever dramatic method of presentation seems appropriate to you.

---

flaming minister burning torch
Promethean heat (in Greek mythology Prometheus stole fire from

the gods and used it to give life to mortals)
relume light again

Act 5 Scene 2
Cyprus   Desdemona's bedchamber

Enter OTHELLO, *with a light, and* DESDEMONA *in bed.*

OTHELLO It is the cause, it is the cause, my soul:
　　　　Let me not name it to you, you chaste stars.
　　　　It is the cause. Yet I'll not shed her blood,
　　　　Nor scar that whiter skin of hers than snow
　　　　And smooth as monumental alabaster –　　　　　　　　　5
　　　　Yet she must die, else she'll betray more men.
　　　　Put out the light, and then put out the light:
　　　　If I quench thee, thou flaming minister,
　　　　I can again thy former light restore,
　　　　Should I repent me; but once put out thy light,　　　　10
　　　　Thou cunning'st pattern of excelling nature,
　　　　I know not where is that Promethean heat
　　　　That can thy light relume. When I have plucked thy rose,
　　　　I cannot give it vital growth again;
　　　　It needs must wither. I'll smell it on the tree.　　　　15
　　　　　　　　　　　He kisses her.
　　　　O balmy breath, that dost almost persuade
　　　　Justice to break her sword! One more, one more!
　　　　Be thus when thou art dead, and I will kill thee
　　　　And love thee after. One more, and this the last.
　　　　So sweet was ne'er so fatal. I must weep.　　　　　　20
　　　　But they are cruel tears: this sorrow's heavenly –
　　　　It strikes where it doth love. She wakes.

Desdemona wakes. Othello orders her to confess her sins before her death. Desdemona, fearful, replies that her only sin is in loving him.

1 Read through – and actions (in pairs)

Desdemona is apparently lying asleep in her bed. What do you think might be her subsequent movements? In some productions she passively awaits her fate; in others, she puts up a spirited struggle, physically fighting back as Othello finally smothers her. To gain a first impression of this final dialogue between husband and wife, take roles as Othello and Desdemona and read lines 23–85 to each other, adding movement and action at appropriate points (the script hints at facial expressions and other reactions).

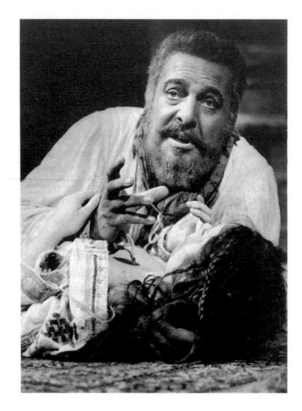

Solicit	pray for forgiveness	**forfend**	forbid
straight	at once	**portents**	bad signs for the future

DESDEMONA Who's there? Othello?
OTHELLO   Ay, Desdemona.
DESDEMONA Will you come to bed, my lord?
OTHELLO Have you prayed tonight, Desdemon?
DESDEMONA   Ay, my lord.   25
OTHELLO If you bethink yourself of any crime
          Unreconciled as yet to heaven and grace,
          Solicit for it straight.
DESDEMONA Alack, my lord, what may you mean by that?
OTHELLO Well, do it, and be brief: I will walk by: 30
          I would not kill thy unpreparèd spirit;
          No – heaven forfend! – I would not kill thy soul.
DESDEMONA Talk you of killing?
OTHELLO   Ay, I do.
DESDEMONA   Then heaven
          Have mercy on me!
OTHELLO   Amen, with all my heart!
DESDEMONA If you say so, I hope you will not kill me.   35
OTHELLO Hum!
DESDEMONA And yet I fear you, for you're fatal then
          When your eyes roll so. Why I should fear I know not,
          Since guiltiness I know not, but yet I feel I fear.
OTHELLO Think on thy sins.
DESDEMONA   They are loves I bear to you.   40
OTHELLO Ay, and for that thou diest.
DESDEMONA That death's unnatural that kills for loving.
          Alas, why gnaw you so your nether lip?
          Some bloody passion shakes your very frame:
          These are portents; but yet I hope, I hope   45
          They do not point on me.

Othello accuses Desdemona of giving her handkerchief to Cassio. She denies this, yet Othello is convinced he has enough proof. He tells her that Cassio has confessed to sexual relations with Desdemona, but now is dead.

1 Send for the key witness!

Desdemona's request to 'Send for the man and ask him' (line 50) is reminiscent of Othello's calling for Desdemona in Act 1 to support his testimony when he is accused by Brabantio of abduction. In that case the Duke agrees to send for Desdemona, who is then able to corroborate Othello's story. Here, Othello does not hear what the key witness (Cassio) has to say and he merely accuses Desdemona of 'perjury'. Othello's view of 'justice' and of 'evidence' has changed in the course of the play (see below and p. 230). But what is his mood at this moment? Some critics argue that for much of this formal dialogue his tone is calm and rational. Do you agree? Consider particularly how he warns of 'perjury' in lines 50–1.

2 'Justice' enacted? (in groups of three)

There is much legal language in this bedroom episode, almost as if it were some kind of courtroom in session, with Othello taking on the roles of both judge and executioner. Pick out any examples of legal-sounding language you can find. Identify what constitutes the case for the prosecution, what the case for the defence, and what is presented as evidence. How does Othello's 'legal procedure' differ from what you know to be conventional practice?

Enact a version of this section of the scene as if it is taking place in a court of law. Play with the script as much as you like, but retain fragments of the original language. Try playing it in different styles and tones (e.g. as a parody of a television courtroom drama). Your experiment may help you decide on effective ways of performing the episode on stage.

---

perjury   untruthfulness, lying on oath
presently   at once
article   item in a list of accusations (a legal term)

conception   suspicion
do groan withal   am pained by, give birth to

OTHELLO   Peace, and be still!

DESDEMONA I will so. What's the matter?

OTHELLO That handkerchief which I so loved and gave thee,
            Thou gav'st to Cassio.

DESDEMONA   No, by my life and soul!
            Send for the man and ask him.

OTHELLO   Sweet soul, take heed.   50
            Take heed of perjury: thou art on thy death-bed.

DESDEMONA Ay, but not yet to die.

OTHELLO   Yes, presently.
            Therefore confess thee freely of thy sin;
            For to deny each article with oath
            Cannot remove nor choke the strong conception   55
            That I do groan withal. Thou art to die.

DESDEMONA Then Lord have mercy on me!

OTHELLO   I say, Amen.

DESDEMONA And have you mercy too! I never did
            Offend you in my life; never loved Cassio
            But with such general warranty of heaven   60
            As I might love. I never gave him token.

OTHELLO By heaven, I saw my handkerchief in's hand.
            O perjured woman! Thou dost stone my heart,
            And mak'st me call what I intend to do
            A murder, which I thought a sacrifice.   65
            I saw the handkerchief.

DESDEMONA   He found it then;
            I never gave it him. Send for him hither;
            Let him confess a truth.

OTHELLO   He hath confessed.

DESDEMONA What, my lord?

OTHELLO That he hath used thee.

DESDEMONA   How? Unlawfully?   70

OTHELLO Ay.

DESDEMONA He will not say so.

OTHELLO   No, his mouth is stopped:
            Honest Iago hath tane order for't.

DESDEMONA O, my fear interprets! What, is he dead?

OTHELLO Had all his hairs been lives, my great revenge   75
            Had stomach for them all.

In spite of her pleas, Othello suffocates Desdemona. He is disturbed by Emilia calling from outside the door.

1 Action – avoiding melodrama (in groups of three or four)

Take parts and act lines 78–106. Make decisions about the pace, timing of stage directions, positioning and delivery of words to suit the dramatic effect you wish to achieve. How do you avoid it becoming melodramatic, and therefore bordering on the ridiculous?

Share your version with one other group, then discuss any differences of interpretation.

'*He smothers her.*' This is how the director of one production interpreted the stage direction. Comment on the dramatic effect of this physical movement.

---

undone ruined
Being done . . . pause now I've started, I can't stop
yawn tear apart (in an earthquake)

the curtains draw (on the Globe stage, the bed was probably in the recess behind curtains – see illustration on p. 186)

DESDEMONA Alas, he is betrayed, and I undone.

OTHELLO Out, strumpet! Weep'st thou for him to my face?

DESDEMONA O banish me, my lord, but kill me not!

OTHELLO Down, strumpet! 80

DESDEMONA Kill me tomorrow; let me live tonight!

OTHELLO Nay, if you strive –

DESDEMONA But half an hour!

OTHELLO   Being done, there is no pause.

DESDEMONA But while I say one prayer!

OTHELLO   It is too late.

DESDEMONA O, Lord, Lord, Lord! 85

                   He smothers her.

EMILIA (*Within*) My lord, my lord! What, ho! My lord, my lord!

OTHELLO What noise is this? Not dead? Not yet quite dead?

      I that am cruel am yet merciful;

      I would not have thee linger in thy pain.

      So, so.

EMILIA (*Within*) What, ho! My lord, my lord!

OTHELLO   Who's there? 90

EMILIA [*Within*] O, good my lord, I would speak a word with you.

OTHELLO Yes – 'tis Emilia – by and by. – She's dead.

      'Tis like she comes to speak of Cassio's death:

      The noise was high. Ha! No more moving?

      Still as the grave. Shall she come in? Were't good? 95

      I think she stirs again. No. What's best to do?

      If she come in, she'll sure speak to my wife –

      My wife, my wife! What wife? I have no wife.

      O insupportable! O heavy hour!

      Methinks it should be now a huge eclipse 100

      Of sun and moon, and that th'affrighted globe

      Should yawn at alteration.

EMILIA [*Within*]   I do beseech you

      That I may speak with you. O, good my lord!

OTHELLO I had forgot thee. O, come in, Emilia.

      Soft, by and by. Let me the curtains draw. 105

      Where art thou?

              [*He unlocks the door.*]

      What's the matter with thee now?

Emilia reports that Roderigo is dead but Cassio lives. Desdemona revives briefly, only to protect her husband in her dying breath. Othello confesses to Emilia and attempts to explain.

---

1 Desdemona: a 'real' character? (in small groups)

Even in her dying breath, Desdemona supports her husband. She tells a lie on her death-bed to protect him from a murder charge. Do you admire her for her faithfulness, or find her action hard to swallow? Do you see her as a dramatic function, a sharp contrast to Othello, rather than as a 'real' person or character?

Discuss your attitudes to the way Desdemona has been portrayed in Scene 2. Focus your discussion on:

- how 21st-century readers might react to Desdemona
- how a reader's gender and culture also affect the way they see Desdemona
- how Desdemona reflects early seventeenth-century attitudes to women and marriage
- how Desdemona embodies or relates to the play's dramatic themes and concerns.

2 Contrasts (in pairs)

Opposite are a number of sharp contrasts in language:

angel v. devil
false v. true
water v. fire
hell v. heavenly
sweet v. harsh.

Locate each pair in the page of script opposite and explore ways of presenting them through movement or tableaux. After this physical activity, talk together about the significance of each pair of contrasts in their dramatic context (e.g. what they suggest about characters, or themes, or mood).

---

error of the moon the moon straying off course (the influence of the moon was said to cause madness)

was wont used to do

Enter EMILIA.

EMILIA O, my good lord, yonder's foul murders done.

OTHELLO What? Now?

EMILIA But now, my lord.

OTHELLO It is the very error of the moon: 110
      She comes more nearer earth than she was wont
      And makes men mad.

EMILIA Cassio, my lord, hath killed a young Venetian
      Called Roderigo.

OTHELLO   Roderigo killed?
      And Cassio killed?

EMILIA   No, Cassio is not killed. 115

OTHELLO Not Cassio killed! Then murder's out of tune,
      And sweet revenge grows harsh.

DESDEMONA O, falsely, falsely murdered!

EMILIA   O Lord! What cry is that?

OTHELLO That? What?

EMILIA Out and alas, that was my lady's voice! 120
      [*She draws the bed-curtains.*]
      Help, help, ho, help! O, lady, speak again!
      Sweet Desdemona, O sweet mistress, speak!

DESDEMONA A guiltless death I die.

EMILIA O, who hath done this deed?

DESDEMONA Nobody; I myself. Farewell. 125
      Commend me to my kind lord. O farewell! *She dies*

OTHELLO Why, how should she be murdered?

EMILIA   Alas, who knows?

OTHELLO You heard her say herself it was not I.

EMILIA She said so; I must needs report the truth.

OTHELLO She's like a liar gone to burning hell: 130
      'Twas I that killed her.

EMILIA   O, the more angel she,
      And you the blacker devil!

OTHELLO She turned to folly, and she was a whore.

EMILIA Thou dost belie her, and thou art a devil.

OTHELLO She was false as water.

EMILIA   Thou art rash as fire to say 135
      That she was false. O, she was heavenly true!

Othello reveals that Iago gave him the details of Desdemona's infidelity. Emilia increasingly questions Iago's part in Othello's story and curses them both. She is unmoved by Othello's threats and calls for help.

---

1 Emilia: a 'collective memory' (in groups of six to eight)

In the page of script opposite, pay particular attention to the role and character of Emilia. Select a word, phrase or line of hers that strikes you as being interesting or memorable. Learn your chosen word(s).

Present your 'collective memory' of Emilia by putting together a group presentation of all your chosen fragments of script. It doesn't matter if some of you have chosen the same words. Combine the words with stylised movement, or some other action. What impression of Emilia emerges from your work? Suggest four or five adjectives to describe her.

2 '. . . honest, honest Iago' (in groups of three)

Emilia's shocked response, and the ten repetitions of the word 'husband', culminate in Othello's exclamation: 'My friend, thy husband, honest, honest Iago.'

a Produce a series of 'sculptures' (using yourselves as the raw material) which are based on any ideas that arise from your interpretation of line 153 within its context in the play.

b Write two or three paragraphs about Iago as a husband, a friend, an 'honest' colleague.

3 'Ha!'

Spend about five minutes writing what you think Othello means by his exclamation 'Ha!' at line 157. Compare your notes with others and discuss what led to your interpretation.

---

else   if you don't believe it
extremity   final punishment (legal term)

chrysolite   a semi-precious stone
made mocks with   mocked
Peace . . . best   you'd better keep quiet

OTHELLO Cassio did top her: ask thy husband else.
O, I were damned beneath all depth in hell
But that I did proceed upon just grounds
To this extremity. Thy husband knew it all. 140
EMILIA My husband?
OTHELLO Thy husband.
EMILIA That she was false to wedlock?
OTHELLO Ay, with Cassio. Nay, had she been true,
If heaven would make me such another world
Of one entire and perfect chrysolite,
I'd not have sold her for it.
EMILIA My husband? 145
OTHELLO Ay, 'twas he that told me on her first;
An honest man he is, and hates the slime
That sticks on filthy deeds.
EMILIA My husband?
OTHELLO What needs this iterance, woman? I say thy husband.
EMILIA O mistress, villainy hath made mocks with love! 150
My husband say that she was false?
OTHELLO He, woman;
I say thy husband. Dost understand the word?
My friend, thy husband, honest, honest Iago.
EMILIA If he say so, may his pernicious soul
Rot half a grain a day! He lies to th'heart. 155
She was too fond of her most filthy bargain.
OTHELLO Ha!
EMILIA Do thy worst.
This deed of thine is no more worthy heaven
Than thou wast worthy her.
OTHELLO Peace, you were best. 160
EMILIA Thou has not half that power to do me harm
As I have to be hurt. O gull! O dolt!
As ignorant as dirt. Thou hast done a deed –
I care not for thy sword – I'll make thee known,
Though I lost twenty lives. Help! help! ho, help! 165
The Moor hath killed my mistress. Murder, murder!

Montano, Gratiano and Iago come to investigate Emilia's cries of murder. She challenges Iago about what he has told Othello about Desdemona. Iago orders her home.

---

1 Four freeze-frames (in groups of five or six)

Imagine freezing the action on stage at four key moments from this page of script:

> 'Disprove this villain, if thou be'st a man.' (line 171)
> 'O monstrous act!' (line 189)
> 'What, are you mad?' (line 193)
> '. . . thou hast killed the sweetest innocent / That e'er did lift up eye' (lines 198–9).

Take roles, and for each 'moment' create a still picture which you can hold for at least thirty seconds. Within each, select a key character who can step out of the freeze-frame and outline their personal thoughts or fears at that precise moment.

Present your four moments to the rest of the class as a series of snapshots.

2 Repetition: dramatic effect (in pairs)

a Certain words are repeated opposite (e.g. 'lie' and 'villainy').
   Talk together about the dramatic effect of each repetition.

b Look in particular at Othello's 'O! O! O!' at line 197.
   Experiment with ways of reading it. What might 'O' mean here?

3 A wife's role changes

''Tis proper I obey him', declares Emilia at line 195, 'but not now.' You may already have worked on Emilia's character through activities on pages 94 and 118. What does line 195 add to your impression of her?

---

charm hold still
forfend forbid

set the murder on caused the
murder

Enter MONTANO, GRATIANO *and* IAGO.

MONTANO What is the matter? How now, general?

EMILIA O, are you come, Iago? You have done well,
    That men must lay their murders on your neck.

GRATIANO What is the matter?   170

EMILIA Disprove this villain, if thou be'st a man.
    He says thou told'st him that his wife was false.
    I know thou didst not, thou'rt not such a villain.
    Speak, for my heart is full.

IAGO I told him what I thought, and told no more   175
    Than what he found himself was apt and true.

EMILIA But did you ever tell him she was false?

IAGO I did.

EMILIA You told a lie, an odious damnèd lie:
    Upon my soul, a lie, a wicked lie!   180
    She false with Cassio? Did you say with Cassio?

IAGO With Cassio, mistress. Go to, charm your tongue.

EMILIA I will not charm my tongue; I am bound to speak:
    My mistress here lies murdered in her bed.

ALL O, heavens forfend!   185

EMILIA And your reports have set the murder on.

OTHELLO Nay, stare not, masters; it is true indeed.

GRATIANO 'Tis a strange truth.

MONTANO O monstrous act!

EMILIA   Villainy, villainy, villainy!
    I think upon't, I think – I smell't – O villainy!   190
    I thought so then; I'll kill myself for grief.
    O villainy, villainy!

IAGO What, are you mad? I charge you get you home.

EMILIA Good gentlemen, let me have leave to speak.
    'Tis proper I obey him, but not now.   195
    Perchance, Iago, I will ne'er go home.

OTHELLO O! O! O!

                  Othello falls on the bed.

EMILIA   Nay, lay thee down and roar,
    For thou hast killed the sweetest innocent
    That e'er did lift up eye.

Othello confesses the murder to Gratiano, who says that Brabantio is dead. Emilia reveals that Iago persuaded her to steal Desdemona's handkerchief and give it to him. Iago tries to silence her.

---

1 Gratiano's reaction: blaming Desdemona? (in pairs)

Gratiano is a relative of Desdemona. What do you think of his response at lines 203–5 on discovering that she has just been murdered? He seems to be blaming Desdemona for Brabantio's death. Do you agree with that interpretation of what he says? If so, what does it suggest about him? If you disagree, how do you interpret his response and character?

2 Different viewpoints on what was 'confessed'

Othello claims that Desdemona committed 'the act of shame' many times with Cassio, and that 'Cassio confessed it'. Remind yourself exactly what Cassio 'confessed' to, and in what circumstances. There are three versions of this 'evidence': Iago's, Othello's and Cassio's. Turn back to Act 4 Scene 1, lines 72–153, to remind yourself of the 'evidence'. Write three paragraphs, one each for Cassio, Othello and Iago. Each paragraph begins: 'This is what I believe happened in the "eavesdropping" episode in Act 4 Scene 1.'

3 What is each character thinking?

At line 221, the stage direction reads: '*Iago draws his sword and threatens Emilia.*' Think about the action on stage at this precise moment. Consider each of the five characters in turn. Suggest what is in each one's mind at this point. For example, there are three other men on stage – why doesn't anyone disarm Iago?

---

mortal fatal
Shore cut
thread thread of life
reprobance state of damnation

recognisance keepsake
north either north wind, or people of
the north

OTHELLO [*Standing up.*]   O, she was foul!
    I scarce did know you, uncle; there lies your niece,   200
    Whose breath indeed these hands have newly stopped.
    I know this act shows horrible and grim –
GRATIANO Poor Desdemon, I am glad thy father's dead:
    Thy match was mortal to him, and pure grief
    Shore his old thread in twain. Did he live now,   205
    This sight would make him do a desperate turn,
    Yea, curse his better angel from his side
    And fall to reprobance.
OTHELLO 'Tis pitiful; but yet Iago knows
    That she with Cassio hath the act of shame   210
    A thousand times committed. Cassio confessed it,
    And she did gratify his amorous works
    With that recognisance and pledge of love
    Which I first gave her. I saw it in his hand:
    It was a handkerchief, an antique token   215
    My father gave my mother.
EMILIA   O God! O heavenly God!
IAGO Zounds, hold your peace!
EMILIA   'Twill out, 'twill out. I peace!
    No, I will speak as liberal as the north;
    Let heaven, and men, and devils, let them all,
    All, all cry shame against me, yet I'll speak.   220
IAGO Be wise and get you home.
EMILIA   I will not.
    [*Iago draws his sword and threatens Emilia.*]
GRATIANO   Fie,
    Your sword upon a woman!
EMILIA O thou dull Moor, that handkerchief thou speak'st of
    I found by fortune and did give my husband,
    For often, with a solemn earnestness –   225
    More than indeed belonged to such a trifle –
    He begged of me to steal it.
IAGO   Villainous whore!

Othello attempts to kill Iago, but is prevented by Montano. Iago stabs Emilia and then escapes. Emilia dies speaking of Desdemona's purity. Othello finds another sword and calls to Gratiano.

1 Slow motion (in groups of five or six)

Iago's abuse of Emilia ('Filth, thou liest!') does not stop her telling the truth, and the scene erupts in a flurry of action. Enact the stage direction at line 233 in slow motion. Decide how you could make the best use of the space you have available, and experiment with different ways of making an intensely dramatic episode.

Turn to the picture of an Elizabethan theatre on page 186 and plot the same action in that space.

2 '. . . honour outlive honesty': what do you think?

Think about Othello's comment: 'why should honour outlive honesty?' (line 243). Write a paragraph explaining what you understand to be the meaning of Othello's words and why they might be considered to be significant in the context of the whole play.

3 Does Emilia get her last wish? (in pairs)

One commentator points out that the men on stage do nothing to save Emilia's life, and indeed, when Montano disarms Othello, he inadvertently saves Iago at the expense of Emilia. In her dying words Emilia asks to be laid next to Desdemona's body, but there is no stage direction to indicate whether this happens or not. No one mentions Emilia again. How significant do you think this is? Talk together about how you would stage what happens to Emilia up to the point when she dies.

4 The dying swan (in pairs)

Find out what you can of the legend that swans sing as they die. Use your research to write notes on how Emilia's image of the swan (lines 245–6) adds to the atmosphere of this final scene.

---

coxcomb fool
Precious a term used to intensify abuse
whipster whippersnapper, youngster
bode foretell

play the swan sing on the point of death
ice-brook's temper steel strengthened by being plunged into an icy stream
naked unarmed

EMILIA She give it Cassio! No, alas, I found it
    And I did give't my husband.
IAGO   Filth, thou liest!
EMILIA By heaven, I do not, I do not, gentlemen.   230
    O murderous coxcomb, what should such a fool
    Do with so good a wife?
OTHELLO   Are there no stones in heaven
    But what serves for the thunder? Precious villain!
[*Othello runs at Iago; Montano disarms him; Iago stabs Emilia from*
                behind and exit.]
GRATIANO The woman falls; sure he hath killed his wife.
EMILIA Ay, ay; O, lay me by my mistress' side.   235
GRATIANO He's gone, but his wife's killed.
MONTANO 'Tis a notorious villain. Take you this weapon,
    Which I have here recovered from the Moor.
    Come guard the door without; let him not pass,
    But kill him rather. I'll after the same villain,   240
    For 'tis a damnèd slave.
                    Exeunt Montano and Gratiano
OTHELLO   I am not valiant neither,
    But every puny whipster gets my sword.
    But why should honour outlive honesty?
    Let it go all.
EMILIA   What did thy song bode, lady?
    Hark, canst thou hear me? I will play the swan   245
    And die in music: [*Sings*] 'Willow, willow, willow.'
    Moor, she was chaste; she loved thee, cruel Moor;
    So come my soul to bliss, as I speak true;
    So speaking as I think, I die, I die.   *She dies*
OTHELLO I have another weapon in this chamber;   250
    It was a sword of Spain, the ice-brook's temper.
    O, here it is. – Uncle, I must come forth.
GRATIANO (*Within*) If thou attempt it, it will cost thee dear;
    Thou hast no weapon, and perforce must suffer.
OTHELLO Look in upon me then, and speak with me,   255
    Or naked as I am, I will assault thee.

Othello, now fully realising he has murdered an innocent woman, expects the punishments of hell. Lodovico and the others return with Iago and Othello attacks him.

---

1 Othello's speech: language

Some commentators have said that the broken and defeated Othello is here attempting to use language in such a way as to reclaim his former glory as a renowned military leader. This is reflected particularly in his use of:

- metaphor
- hyperbole (exaggeration)
- simple, powerful monosyllables
- grand, poetic language.

Identify examples of each of these features in lines 257–79. Write them down and make notes on the dramatic effectiveness of each.

2 Othello's speech: structure (in groups of four or five)

Othello's speech is structured in three parts, corresponding with the three stages of his life: Othello the great warrior, Othello the murderer at his life's end, and Othello tortured in hell. His life's journey is imagined as a sea voyage. Find the three elements of the speech. Make a group presentation, exploring the structure of the speech and its images.

3 Lodovico's entrance: Venetian law restored

With the entrance of Lodovico and Cassio, the controlling force of Venetian law is reintroduced. Lodovico calls on the two defendants as if in a court of law, and presides as if a high court judge. But Othello's violence towards Iago momentarily disturbs that order.

Work out how you would stage the entrance of Lodovico and the others, following the script from line 275 to the bottom of the page. Plot the moves and positioning, using the picture of an Elizabethan theatre on page 186. Write a paragraph justifying your choices.

---

your stop your force as a guard
butt goal, target
sea-mark beacon
Man but a rush aim just a reed

ill-starred ill-fated
compt the Day of Judgement
his feet . . . fable (the devil was supposed to have cloven feet)

[Enter Gratiano.]

GRATIANO What is the matter?

OTHELLO   Behold, I have a weapon:
A better never did itself sustain
Upon a soldier's thigh. I have seen the day
That with this little arm and this good sword   260
I have made my way through more impediments
Than twenty times your stop. But, O vain boast!
Who can control his fate? 'Tis not so now.
Be not afraid, though you do see me weaponed:
Here is my journey's end, here is my butt   265
And very sea-mark of my utmost sail.
Do you go back dismayed? 'Tis a lost fear:
Man but a rush against Othello's breast,
And he retires. Where should Othello go?
[He goes to the bed.]
Now, how dost thou look now? O ill-starred wench!   270
Pale as thy smock! When we shall meet at compt
This look of thine will hurl my soul from heaven
And fiends will snatch at it. Cold, cold, my girl,
Even like thy chastity.
O cursèd, cursèd slave! Whip me, ye devils,   275
From the possession of this heavenly sight!
Blow me about in winds! Roast me in sulphur!
Wash me in steep-down gulfs of liquid fire!
O Desdemon! Dead Desdemon! Dead! O! O!

Enter LODOVICO, *Montano,* CASSIO *in a chair, Iago in the charge of*
OFFICERS.

LODOVICO Where is this rash and most unfortunate man?   280
OTHELLO That's he that was Othello: here I am.
LODOVICO Where is that viper? Bring the villain forth.
OTHELLO I look down towards his feet; but that's a fable.
If that thou be'st a devil, I cannot kill thee.
[He wounds Iago.]

Lodovico takes control and investigates the case. Othello asks Cassio's pardon. Letters found in Roderigo's pockets tell of Iago's plot to kill Cassio and of Roderigo's threat to expose Iago. Iago refuses to give any explanation of his conduct.

1 'I bleed, sir, but not killed'

Iago's line could be uttered in a variety of ways. How would you advise an actor to say those words? Consider the following suggestions to help you make your decision:

- Iago is playing for sympathy.
- He is bitterly sarcastic.
- He is resigned to his fate.
- He is detached and neutral.
- He is utterly defeated, in pain and wants to die.
- He is triumphant, taunting Othello.
- He is chillingly inhuman, hinting at his own indestructibility.

2 Silence

Why does Iago refuse to speak further? Write a paragraph explaining possible reasons for his silence.

3 'An honourable murderer . . .' (in pairs)

Othello claims that he is 'An honourable murderer . . . For naught did I in hate, but all in honour.' How do you think Othello might defend this statement? Role-play an imaginary interview between Lodovico and Othello where this conversation is extended.

4 Two letters

Two letters are found in Roderigo's pocket, both helping to explain Iago's plotting. The first is probably written by Iago and 'imports / The death of Cassio'. The second is a 'discontented paper' written by Roderigo, probably to Iago or Othello. Write the two letters.

Torments torture
in the nick in the nick of time

satisfied him stopped his complaints
caitiff wretch, villain

LODOVICO Wrench his sword from him.

IAGO   I bleed, sir, but not killed.   285

OTHELLO I am not sorry neither; I'd have thee live,
      For in my sense 'tis happiness to die.

LODOVICO O, thou Othello, that wert once so good,
      Fallen in the practice of a damnèd slave,
      What shall be said to thee?

OTHELLO   Why, anything: 290
      An honourable murderer, if you will;
      For naught did I in hate, but all in honour.

LODOVICO This wretch hath part confessed his villainy.
      Did you and he consent in Cassio's death?

OTHELLO Ay.   295

CASSIO Dear general, I never gave you cause.

OTHELLO I do believe it, and I ask your pardon.
      Will you, I pray, demand that demi-devil
      Why he hath thus ensnared my soul and body?

IAGO Demand me nothing; what you know, you know.   300
      From this time forth I never will speak word.

LODOVICO What! Not to pray?

GRATIANO Torments will ope your lips.

OTHELLO   Well, thou dost best.

LODOVICO Sir, you shall understand what hath befallen,
      Which, as I think, you know not. Here is a letter   305
      Found in the pocket of the slain Roderigo,
      And here another: the one of them imports
      The death of Cassio, to be undertook
      By Roderigo.

OTHELLO   O villain!

CASSIO   Most heathenish and most gross!

LODOVICO Now here's another discontented paper,   310
      Found in his pocket too; and this, it seems,
      Roderigo meant to have sent this damnèd villain,
      But that, belike, Iago, in the nick,
      Came in and satisfied him.

OTHELLO   O the pernicious caitiff!
      How came you, Cassio, by that handkerchief   315
      That was my wife's?

Cassio tells how he found the handkerchief, and how Roderigo was used by Iago. Lodovico pronounces Othello's arrest and Cassio's instatement as governor. Othello asks that his whole story should be truthfully told. He stabs himself.

---

1 Punishments (in pairs)

Lodovico sentences Iago to 'cunning cruelty' and 'torment' (torture). Othello is to be kept under close arrest and then tried by the Venetian courts. Decide what you consider fitting punishment for the two men. Give reasons for the treatment that you decide upon.

2 Othello's obituary

Othello's last major speech in the play is in resonant, controlled verse, and amounts to his own obituary. He follows the conventions of obituary writers and includes the following elements:

- his service in Venetian colonial exploits (line 335)
- his emotional/love life (line 340)
- his downfall (lines 341–4)
- his last moments (lines 344–7)
- a past great deed (lines 348–52).

Some readers find it difficult to accept all aspects of Othello's own interpretation of his life. He claims he 'loved not wisely, but too well' and that he was 'one not easily jealous but, being wrought, / Perplexed in the extreme'. Both are contentious remarks, open to challenge. And whilst his claim to have served the state well is true, that 'truth' is from the point of view of Venetians, rather than their foreign subjects.

a Speak lines 334–52 to bring out Othello's feelings.

b Write an alternative obituary. Follow the conventions of obituary writers, but write from the point of view of a Turk. Where would it be critical (and how might the Turkish writer deal with Othello's attitudes: e.g. 'circumcisèd dog')?

---

upbraids tells off
Brave insult
Soft you just a moment

base Indian American Indians were famed for their 'ignorance' about the value of precious gems
traduced insulted

CASSIO   I found it in my chamber;
          And he himself confessed but even now
          That there he dropped it for a special purpose
          Which wrought to his desire.
OTHELLO   O fool, fool, fool!
CASSIO There is besides in Roderigo's letter   320
          How he upbraids Iago, that he made him
          Brave me upon the watch, whereon it came
          That I was cast; and even but now he spake –
          After long seeming dead – Iago hurt him,
          Iago set him on.   325
LODOVICO You must forsake this room and go with us.
          Your power and your command is taken off
          And Cassio rules in Cyprus. For this slave,
          If there be any cunning cruelty
          That can torment him much and hold him long   330
          It shall be his. You shall close prisoner rest
          Till that the nature of your fault be known
          To the Venetian state. Come, bring him away.
OTHELLO Soft you; a word or two before you go.
          I have done the state some service and they know't: 335
          No more of that. I pray you, in your letters
          When you shall these unlucky deeds relate,
          Speak of me as I am; nothing extenuate,
          Nor set down aught in malice. Then must you speak
          Of one that loved not wisely, but too well;   340
          Of one not easily jealous but, being wrought,
          Perplexed in the extreme; of one whose hand,
          Like the base Indian, threw a pearl away
          Richer than all his tribe; of one whose subdued eyes,
          Albeit unusèd to the melting mood,   345
          Drops tears as fast as the Arabian trees
          Their medicinable gum. Set you down this;
          And say besides that in Aleppo once
          Where a malignant and a turbaned Turk
          Beat a Venetian and traduced the state,   350
          I took by th'throat the circumcisèd dog
          And smote him thus.
                    He stabs himself.

Othello dies beside Desdemona. Lodovico awards Othello's possessions to Gratiano, and orders Cassio to decide Iago's punishment. Lodovico leaves to report in full to the Venetian state.

---

1 Lodovico's report

Lodovico states his intention of going immediately to Venice to make his formal report of events to the Senate. Write his report.

2 '. . . he was great of heart' (in pairs)

Othello, in lines 334–52, had imagined what his obituary would be like. Here, Cassio's words about the dead Othello are the closest anyone comes to a real obituary or eulogy. Instead, Othello is hardly mentioned and attention is drawn to Iago. Talk together about what you think the dramatic effect of this is.

3 A final image (in groups of seven to ten)

What last image would you want an audience to be left with in a production of *Othello*? The final stage direction ('*Exeunt*') is for all the remaining actors to go off, but there are important choices for a director to make. Would you have them all leaving together? Would you want the bodies on the bed to be spot-lit or obscured by curtains? Might you wish to end with a tableau involving all or some of the remaining characters? Discuss, and show your final image.

4 Cassio as general, Bianca as . . .? (in pairs)

The last time we saw Bianca was when she was led off at Iago's insistence just after Cassio had been injured. Imagine that Cassio now encounters her as he leaves Othello's house. How would the new general of the occupying force react? Improvise the scene.

---

period conclusion
Spartan dog (the legendary hounds of Sparta in Greece were extremely savage)

fell cruel
censure judgement

LODOVICO O bloody period!

GRATIANO   All that's spoke is marred!

OTHELLO I kissed thee ere I killed thee: no way but this,
 Killing myself, to die upon a kiss.   355

         He [falls on the bed and] dies

CASSIO This did I fear, but thought he had no weapon,
 For he was great of heart.

LODOVICO [*To Iago*]   O Spartan dog,
 More fell than anguish, hunger, or the sea,
 Look on the tragic loading of this bed:
 This is thy work. The object poisons sight;   360
 Let it be hid.

     [*The bed-curtains are drawn.*]
     Gratiano, keep the house
 And seize upon the fortunes of the Moor,
 For they succeed on you. To you, lord governor,
 Remains the censure of this hellish villain:
 The time, the place, the torture, O, enforce it! 365
 Myself will straight aboard, and to the state
 This heavy act with heavy heart relate.

         Exeunt

Looking back at the whole play
Activities for groups or individuals

1 Fifteen-minute version (in small groups)

Divide yourselves into five groups, each group taking one act of the play. You are going to produce a three-minute version of your chosen act, using only words from the script itself. When you are ready, put each of the five acts together in turn. You have created a fifteen-minute version of the whole play!

As a variation, perform each act in a different style (soap opera, documentary investigation, slapstick comedy, melodrama, etc.).

2 Production matters

Imagine you are planning a production of *Othello*:

a At what point in the play would you have the interval? Why?

b What music would you play as the audience took their seats at the start, or as they left at the end? Justify your choices.

c Design a poster, publicity material ('flyers') and programme cover.

d Write the programme notes for your production.

e Draw up a cast list, indicating which male characters could 'double up' their parts.

3 Coroner's investigation (written version)

Three or four corpses – one suicide and three suspected murders – all in the space of one evening! The coroner in Cyprus would be kept busy investigating the full circumstances of each of the deaths. Compile the coroner's dossier. It includes eye-witness statements, psychiatric reports, post-mortem reports, and any other relevant documentation about the deceased. Include mock-ups of army personnel files, news-paper cuttings and personal letters. Use your imagination! Work in small groups and produce a large display of the various examples of written 'evidence'. (See also pp. 238–9.)

4 Illustrations

Look through all the illustrations in this edition, particularly those in the colour section. Choose three that most appeal to you. Write a sentence about each, saying what it is that you find interesting about the way they interpret the play.

5 The myth of the handkerchief (in large groups)

Work in groups of eight or as a whole class. This activity serves as an active way to revise part of the plot and involves a discussion about the play's metaphorical and cultural meanings.

How significant is Desdemona's 'napkin' which Emilia finds and passes to Iago in Act 3 Scene 3? Trace its history and meaning as it is passed from person to person in the course of the play. (See Act 3 Scene 3, lines 288–330; Act 3 Scene 4, lines 48–96; Act 4 Scene 1, lines 142–91.)

Each person in the group takes on one of the following roles:

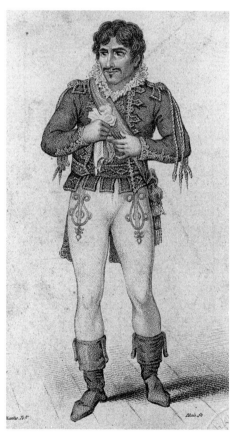

- Bianca
- Egyptian charmer
- Iago
- Cassio
- Othello
- Othello's mother
- Desdemona
- Emilia.

Pass an appropriately decorated handkerchief or tissue from person to person in the correct order; when the 'napkin' is passed to you, state who you are, how you got it and what you believe to be its significance.

Discuss how far the napkin serves merely as a plot device, or whether it becomes richly symbolic as the play progresses. Also talk together about how it links the women characters in the play.

Edmund Kean as Iago (1814).

What is the play about?

Traditionally, answers to this question have focused on 'character' (see p. 223) or themes. **Themes** are ideas or concerns that are dramatically explored or presented in different ways as the play develops. In *Othello* such themes include **jealousy** (the sexual jealousy of Othello, and Iago's professional envy of Cassio); **appearance versus reality** (including honesty/dishonesty, loyalty/disloyalty); **reputation**; **public versus private concerns**; and **racism** (including notions of alienation and belonging).

In recent years, developments in literary theory have led to other ways of understanding Shakespeare's plays, and so provide different answers to the question 'What is *Othello* about?':

Cultural materialist Argues the play offers a subversive critique of the social and political beliefs of Shakespeare's time (and shows how changing beliefs have shaped subsequent readings, see pp. 236–7). For example, racism and sexism in *Othello* are seen as inherent in the way early (and late) capitalist society is structured, rather than simply located in individuals.

Feminist Emphasises the importance of the three women characters and explores the way limits are imposed on their freedom to act. Shows how gender has constructed traditional (male) readings of the play.

New historicist Places the play firmly in its historical context. Othello is a self-made man, and represents a move away from the medieval belief in humans' fixed place in society.

Performance criticism Explores *Othello* as theatre; analysis of productions past and present (see pp. 240–3).

Post-colonial criticism Exposes colonial European notions of race and difference. Othello is presented as both exotic and threateningly savage.

Post-modernist Here, the focus is on the text itself, rather than on its context. It stresses how meaning is hard to pin down, as for example in the words, or concepts of, 'honesty' and 'justice'.

Psychoanalytical Focuses on sub-currents of desire, and repressed sexuality. For instance, Iago's attitudes to sex and women offer a productive starting point for analysis.

Characters

Traditional criticism has tended to focus on Othello as a **tragic hero**. Critics have applied ancient Greek ideas on tragedy (notably those of Aristotle) and assumed that the tragic hero is a mixture of admirable qualities and a **tragic flaw** that proves fatal. Othello's 'flaw' has usually been identified as jealousy, but a different reading (see pp. 237, 240) argues that it is egotism (self-centredness). This type of approach usually treats characters in the plays as if they were living people.

However, there are problems with such readings. It has been argued that Elizabethan and Jacobean playwrights were not concerned with constructing psychologically consistent 'characters'. It may be that the fascination with tragic heroes emerged some time during the nineteenth century – the time of the great Victorian actor-managers, famed for their starring roles. Also, some critics and historians have suggested that Victorian moralists were interested in using Shakespeare's characters as examples for moral guidance.

- In small groups, discuss how you might apply the idea of the tragically flawed noble hero to Othello.
- What 'moral lesson' might a Victorian reader be tempted to draw from the play?
- Using this line of interpretation, how do you explain Desdemona's and Emilia's deaths?

Shakespeare was writing at a time of rapid change socially, politically and economically. Today, many critics argue that his audiences were concerned with **interplay between characters**, and the **interchange of ideas** in the plays.

A good deal of recent literary theory (see p. 222) assumes that the most important aspect of a 'character' is the **dramatic function** they fulfil within the social and political context of the play. As such, characters embody the wider concerns of the play, and they exist only whilst on stage, within the play's dramatically created world.

This section offers a number of activities that will help you explore different views of 'character', combining more traditional ideas about 'characterisation' with broader considerations of characters' thematic, dramatic and political functions.

1 It's a man's world! The representation of women

> Nowhere in Shakespeare are relations between males and females more searchingly, painfully probed. *Marilyn French, 1982*

There are only three women in the play. Each female character is bound up in a relationship with a man. Only one survives.

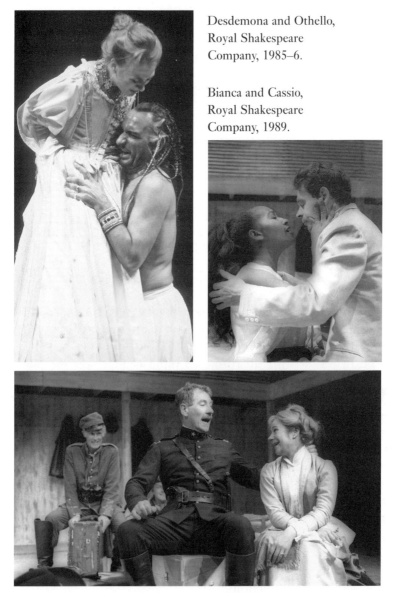

Desdemona and Othello,
Royal Shakespeare
Company, 1985–6.

Bianca and Cassio,
Royal Shakespeare
Company, 1989.

Emilia and Iago, Royal Shakespeare Company, 1989.

What are the roles of these women and how restricted are they by their society? Working in small groups, consider the roles of the three women. Discuss this list of statements in turn, deciding which you agree or disagree with:

- All three women are presented according to *men's* interpretations.
- The women are completely passive.
- Each woman is defined in terms of her male partner.
- Women are fully emancipated in the play.
- Each woman stands for an aspect of 'womanhood' – romantic idealist, practical realist and sex object.
- Each relationship provokes jealousy in one partner.
- Women's roles in the play are ambiguous.
- The women are all portrayed as being rather stupid.
- Men hold all the power in Venetian society.
- Each woman comes from a different social class, and that is significant.
- Women talk the most sense in the play.
- The women are bonded by some notion of 'sisterhood'.
- The women are more trusting than men.
- Men use abusive terms to refer to women; women don't use abusive terms back.
- All three women have identical attitudes to men and relationships.

a Choose two or three quotations from the play which seem to say something important about the presentation of one or all of the women characters. Put the lines together into a short oral, dramatic or written presentation that sums up your conclusions.

b Hot-seat Bianca. Hers is an interesting perspective on events. What questions would you want to ask her?

c It has been argued that each woman's love for a man is much stronger than the relationships they have or feel for each other as women. All three are underestimated and abused by the man they love. Use your experience of *Othello* to write an essay on the claim 'The real tragedy for Desdemona, Emilia and Bianca is that their marital and emotional bonds take precedence over their common cause as women.'

2 How Othello develops (in groups of five)

In the course of the play Othello apparently changes from the 'noble Moor' to a 'devil' and a 'murderous coxcomb'. His way of speaking shifts from calm authority in Act 1 Scene 2, line 59:

Keep up your bright swords, for the dew will rust them.

to tortured confusion by Act 4 Scene 1, lines 40–1:

Pish! Noses, / ears, and lips. Is't possible? – Confess? Handkerchief? O devil!

Members of the group take one act each and research Othello's role in the following ways:

- Briefly summarise what Othello does in the space of the act.
- Note down what you think are significant descriptions of Othello made by other characters.
- Say how Othello relates to one other character – pick out a short piece of dialogue which seems significant.
- Pick out one or two of Othello's speeches which you consider to be particularly dramatic.
- Study Othello's use of language in your chosen speeches/dialogue, looking closely at the imagery and other features that could suggest his emotional state.

When each person has completed their individual investigation, pool your research from Act 1 to Act 5. Discuss any changes you see in Othello in terms of action, relationships and language. Explore presenting your findings diagrammatically (e.g. graphs, flow diagram, storyboard).

Lastly, consider if this research provides all the evidence you need to show how Othello changes over the course of the play. Does it tell the 'full story'? What other aspects of Othello's development might you have investigated?

3 Photographs (in pairs)

a Create a 'photograph' of Iago with one other character. The second person's identity should be obvious from their posture, position and facial expression. Show your photograph. The rest of the class guess who Iago's companion is.

b When all pairs have shown their photographs, the whole class discusses why some characters were easier to guess than others, and what all the photographs reveal about Iago (e.g. whether there were differences in the way he was portrayed by each pair).

4 Iago – a fantasy profile (in groups of three)

Iago is a malcontent, a man with a grudge. He puts on the outward appearance of the bluff, honest soldier, but behind that false exterior he lies to, mentally tortures and betrays Othello. Yet for over four hundred years this malicious joker has fascinated audiences. The following activities invite you to think about him in today's world.

Play around with the character of Iago. If he were a real, live person, what:

- would be his favourite film?
- would be his favourite book and/or magazine?
- would be his favourite television programme?
- would be his favourite type of music?
- daily newspaper would he read?
- football (or other sports) team would he support?
- would he do for a living?
- would his leisure activities be?
- political party might he support?
- would be his views of key current affairs?

Present your group's ideas back to the rest of the class. Be prepared to explain *why* you made those choices for him.

5 Cassio: a press conference (preparation in small groups)

One student takes the part of Cassio, others of government advisers (perhaps Montano and Lodovico) and at least one spin-doctor. Prepare a formal statement for Cassio to read out at a press conference; also prepare answers to likely press questions. (What questions might Cassio *refuse* to answer?)

Other students take on the roles of newspaper and television news reporters (decide whether 'popular' or 'serious'). Prepare questions about recent events, Cassio's view of Othello and others, Cassio's military career, his motivation, interests, feelings, private life and so on. What kind of information will your readers/viewers be interested in?

Organise the press conference and role-play the event as a whole class – perhaps video it.

Next, put together a group display consisting of 'clippings' about recent events in Cyprus. These might include front-page stories (e.g. destruction of Turkish fleet in storm, drunken brawl, murder); political analyses of Venetian military leaders; an in-depth interview/profile of Cassio; gossip column / scandalous rumours and so on.

The language of *Othello*

1 Dramatic language

Shakespeare was writing for theatre conditions that were very different from those common today: open-air stages, no electric light; little in the way of scenery, few props. Playwrights therefore had to create atmosphere and setting through language. Here are some examples from *Othello*. In each case identify where the quotation comes from and who is speaking. Then find other examples in the text:

- **Stage directions** 'Look where she comes!'; 'Iago beckons me'.
- **Setting the scene** 'What from the cape can you discern at sea?'; 'on the brow o'the sea / Stand ranks of people'; 'Strike on the tinder, ho!'; 'Light, I say, light!' (indicating it's night-time).
- **Voicing a character's 'thoughts'** This could be done through one of two stage conventions, either the **Aside** or the **soliloquy**. For examples of how a soliloquy might be staged see, for instance, pages 44 and 88. A number of Asides reveal inner thoughts and sometimes emphasise dramatic irony (other characters on stage cannot hear what is said): 'I am not merry, but I do beguile / The thing I am by seeming otherwise'; 'He takes her by the palm'; 'By heaven, that should be my handkerchief!'.

2 Verse and prose (in pairs)

Verse Traditionally spoken by high-status characters. Othello's early speeches are in iambic pentameters (lines with a five-beat rhythm). Lines are often run on (**enjambement**) as ideas are developed in a coherent and confident way (e.g. Act 1 Scene 3, lines 76–94). By contrast, Iago's speeches are often end-stopped or with mid-line **caesura** (pause); this helps to suggest he is a plain-speaking man.

Prose Traditionally used by comic or low-status characters. The mood and tone of a scene can be changed by switching from verse to prose. Iago skilfully alternates between the two. His use of prose gives the impression of informal talk, taking others into his confidence.

a Trace Othello's speech-making through the course of the play. Where does his syntax (sentence structure) begin to fall apart? How is his state of mind reflected in his language?

b Look carefully at two scenes in which Iago speaks in prose. Present your ideas about the effect of it.

3 Imagery

Imagery conjures up vivid pictures or associations in the mind, and creates a richly symbolic and visual dimension for the play. In *Othello* certain image clusters recur.

Animals

- Usually insulting, especially when used by Iago: e.g.: 'an old black ram / Is tupping your white ewe'; 'Plague him with flies'.
- As Othello comes under Iago's influence, he echoes Iago's choice of image: e.g.: 'I had rather be a toad / And live upon the vapour of a dungeon'; 'as prime as goats, as hot as monkeys'.
- Exposed as a villain, Iago is called 'inhuman dog' and 'viper'.

Poison and disease

Disease reflects the supposed corruption of Venetian society, and becomes a metaphor for the corruption of Othello's mind:

- Iago's words act as poison in the play: 'poison his delight'; 'pour this pestilence into his ear'.
- Othello's jealousy acts like poison: 'If there be cords or knives, / Poison or fire . . . I'll not endure it.'
- Othello asks Iago for real poison: 'Get me some poison, Iago, this night'.
- Ironically, in Act 1 Othello is falsely accused by Brabantio of drugging Desdemona: 'corrupted / By spells and medicines'.

Hell and the devil

The play resonates with numerous references to hell and damnation:

- Iago to Brabantio: 'the devil will make a grandsire of you'.
- Brabantio to Othello: 'Damned as thou art, thou hast enchanted her'.
- Iago about himself: 'Divinity of hell! / When devils will the blackest sins put on, / They do suggest at first with heavenly shows / As I do now.'
- Othello on vengeance: 'Arise, black vengeance, from thy hollow cell'.
- Othello on Desdemona: 'the fair devil'.
- Emilia to Othello: 'thou art a devil'.
- Iago is revealed to be 'that demi-devil'; 'this hellish villain'.

- ◆ In small groups, make a collage on large sugar paper which you feel best captures key images from the play.

4 Images: Othello avoiding reality? (in groups of four)

Look back at Othello's 'cause' speech, uttered as he enters Desdemona's bedchamber, about to kill her (Act 5 Scene 2, lines 1–22).
This speech is rich in visually striking images. One writer has suggested that Othello cannot face the reality of his own role, the living
woman before him and his intended act, so he finds symbols for each
in an attempt to idealise his situation. Explore this interpretation by
locating the following images and explaining briefly the effect of each:

Image	How it is being used
a carved alabaster effigy on a tomb	
light	Metaphor for life. 'Snuff out'= euphemism for killing. Desdemona is personified as light – opposite to hell
a rose	
the figure of Justice (usually depicted with sword and scales)	

a Create a series of tableaux which visually capture the speech.

b Look again at Othello's final speech (Act 5 Scene 2, lines 335–52).
Identify the images he uses and explain their effect. Talk together
about whether you think his imagery here may be another
example of avoiding the reality of his situation.

5 An *Othello* glossary

During the play, Iago's actions completely redefine the word 'honest'.
Othello redefines the meaning of 'justice'. These are not the only
words that change their meaning or effect through the play.

Compile an *Othello* glossary, defining words in terms of the way
they come to be used or enacted as the play progresses. Here are
some suggested entries you might have in your glossary:

- justice
- civility
- savage
- whore
- honesty
- ocular proof

For each give examples of their usage. Some may be used only once
(e.g. 'ocular proof'), but subsequent action shows their redefinition.

Is *Othello* a racist play?

The central character of the play could be said to be:

- mentally unstable
- physically aggressive
- sensual
- insanely jealous
- highly gullible.

His main action in the play is to strangle a white woman. He is black.

A clear example of offensive racial stereotyping?

Certainly, there is some historical evidence of racial stereotyping in Shakespeare's England. There were enough black residents (mainly from the African continent) to prompt Elizabeth I to express her discontent at the great numbers of 'Negars and blackamoors which are crept into the realm'. Travel writers portrayed the natives of Africa as barbarous, lawless and 'a people of beastly lyvinge'. One contemporary writer on the history and people of Africa claimed that 'whomsoever they finde but talking with their wives they presently go about to murther them . . . by reason of jealousie you may see them daily one to be the death and destruction of another' (from Eldred Jones, *Othello's Countrymen*, 1965).

What the critics say

In 1693, Thomas Rymer published *A Short View of Tragedy*. He saw the moral of *Othello* to be 'a caution of all Maidens of Quality how, without their parents' consent, they run away with Blackamoors'. He goes on to draw comparisons between the imagined Venetian society of the play and his own seventeenth-century England: 'With us a Blackamoor might rise to be a trumpeter . . . With us a Moor might marry some little drab, or Small-coal Wench . . . certaynly never was any Play fraught like this of *Othello* with improbabilities.'

Just over a century later, Samuel Taylor Coleridge expresses a similar view: 'It would be something monstrous to conceive this beautiful Venetian girl falling in love with a veritable negro.'

Many influential twentieth-century writers on *Othello* concentrated on debating Othello's precise ethnic origins, taking great pains to prove that Othello would have been Arabic in appearance (see illustration below). A. C. Bradley (*Shakespearean Tragedy*, 1904) explains why he saw this to be an important point: 'Perhaps if we saw Othello coal-black with the bodily eye, the aversion of our blood . . . would overpower our imagination.'

F. R. Leavis (*The Common Pursuit*, 1952) ascribes 'voluptuous sensuality' and 'sensual possessiveness, appetite' to the central character, and comments that 'the stuff of which he is made begins . . . to deteriorate and show itself unfit'.

Are they right to read the play in this way?

The Moorish ambassador to Queen Elizabeth I (1600–1). Compare this picture of a 'noble Moor' with other portrayals of Othello in this edition.

'Far more fair than black'
Language, race and culture in the play

On page 12, you were asked to explore the way language carries and reinforces the prejudices of the dominant social group. It's easy to recognise the blatant and intentional racist abuse in much of Iago's and Roderigo's dialogue ('the thick-lips', or 'an old black ram / Is tupping your white ewe'). But language often works more subtly in carrying meaning. This section extends the activity from page 12 and explores more fully how language can be culturally loaded.

1 Definitions (in pairs)
Look up the word 'black' in a dictionary. Note down how many different uses there are of the word. Now do the same for 'white' and 'fair'. Divide the definitions into *positive* and *negative* uses. If you look up these words in the *Oxford English Dictionary*, in your school or college library, you could also research the earliest recorded dates of particular usages. Discuss your findings with the whole class, making links and comparisons between the three sets of definitions.

2 Meanings
Discuss in what sense the Duke is using the word 'black' in:

If virtue no delighted beauty lack,
Your son-in-law is far more fair than black.   *Act 1 Scene 3, lines 285–6*

Then talk together about how you think Othello is intending 'black' to be interpreted in the following two examples:

Her name, that was as fresh
As Dian's visage, is now begrimed and black
As mine own face.   *Act 3 Scene 3, lines 387–9*

Arise, black vengeance   *Act 3 Scene 3, line 448*

Identify other uses of 'black' in the play and discuss their meanings in the context of who uses the word, and when.

3 Portrayals (in pairs)
The conventional image of hell is of a place of evil, torture and darkness. In early church paintings devils were always portrayed as

black. This portrayal is very evident in Emilia's raging at Othello for killing Desdemona: 'O, the more angel she, / And you the blacker devil!' (Act 5 Scene 2, lines 131–2).

In Shakespeare's *Macbeth* the three witches are called 'secret, black, and midnight hags', and the tyrant Macbeth himself is referred to as 'black Macbeth'. 'The devil damn thee black' is hurled as a curse upon a servant. Here, blackness is linked strongly with evil.

Make a collection of similar references in *Othello* which link blackness with the devil.

4 Other writers (in pairs)

Consider the following poem, written in 1973 by the South African writer Stanley Mogoba, and compare Mogoba's usage of the words 'black' (and 'white') with that in *Othello*. You might also like to compare William Blake's 'The Little Black Boy' in the same way.

White Lies

Humming Maggie.
Hit by a virus, the Caucasian Craze,
sees horror in the mirror.
Frantic and dutifully
she corrodes a sooty face,
braves a hot iron comb
on a shrubby scalp.
I look on.

I know pure white, a white heart,
white, peace, ultimate virtue.
Angels are white angels are good.
Me I'm black, black as sin stuffed in a snuff-tin.
Lord, I've been brainwhitewashed.

But for Heaven's sake God, just let me be.
Under cover of my darkness let me crusade.
On a canvas stretching from here
to Dallas, Memphis, Belsen,
Golgotha, I'll daub a white devil.
Let me teach black truth.
That dark clouds aren't a sign of doom, but hope. Rain. Life.
Let me unleash a volty bolt of black,
so all around may know black right.

5 Black and white imagery (in pairs)

At the heart of the play is the marriage of a black man and a white woman, seen by many of the play's characters to be 'against all rules of nature'. Black and white imagery emphasises this opposition throughout the fabric of the play's language. As has been explored in the previous two pages, in the cultural and historical context of the play black and white can be equated with dark and light, hell and heaven, good and bad.

The contrast between black and white is further intensified by Shakespeare's use of **antithesis**: the setting of word against word, or phrase against phrase (as in 'fair' against 'black', 'black ram' against 'white ewe'). Shakespeare uses this device frequently in all his plays, probably because antithesis expresses conflict, and conflict is the essence of all drama. It is used in different ways throughout *Othello* (as when 'hand' is set against 'heart', see p. 130, and in Othello's 'sweet revenge grows harsh'). But it is the insistent opposition of black against white that so powerfully pervades the whole play.

Whereas Othello is black-skinned and often referred to by his colour or ethnicity ('the Moor', 'sooty bosom'), it is white-skinned Iago who turns out to be the devil and who immerses himself in images of hell and night. In contrast, Desdemona's fairness is emphasised and, even at the end of the play, Othello refers to her as a 'pearl' and as 'light'.

The first scene of the play, where Iago's evil plan is first hatched, takes place at night. The play moves through storm into daylight, then moves back to night-time for the final tragic events.

Some commentators have suggested that Othello's inherent bravery and virtue mean that at the beginning of the play he is able to overcome colour prejudice. As he is corrupted by Iago and his relationship with Desdemona is 'blackened' by lies, Othello becomes more conscious of himself as black, and begins to conform to prevailing racist stereotypes. He, too, comes to regard 'black' as a negative term: 'Her name, that was as fresh / As Dian's visage, is now begrimed and black / As mine own face.'

♦ Using only black-and-white illustrations, photos, display paper and other resources, create a collage out of words, quotations and pictures which explores the central opposition between black and white in the play.

Critics' forum

On these two pages are extracts from influential *Othello* critics. You will discover that the readings offered are very different, in some cases quite contradictory. Working in small groups, read through each extract and discuss what evidence from the play the particular writer in each case might be using to support their view. Try to suggest what other influences each reader brings to their interpretation of the play (e.g. Christianity, 'empire') and what theoretical perspective they might be adopting (see p. 222).

Imagine *Critics' Forum* is a late-evening television arts programme, chaired by Melanie Bookworm. In it, a group of professional critics with very differing views is brought together for a discussion on a particular work of literature. Tonight it is *Othello*. One student (as Ms Bookworm) chairs the debate, the rest choose a critical stance from the extracts given, and each argues their case. Remember, you have to know the play really well and you'll have to do thorough preparation beforehand.

[Othello] does not belong to our world, and he seems to enter it we know not whence – almost as if from wonderland. There is something mysterious in his descent from men of royal siege; in his wanderings in vast deserts and among marvellous peoples; in his tales of magic handkerchiefs and prophetic Sibyls; in the sudden vague glimpses we get of numberless battles and sieges in which he has played the hero and has borne a charmed life; even in chance references to his baptism, his being sold to slavery, his sojourn in Aleppo.

And he is not merely a romantic figure; his own nature is romantic.

So he comes before us, dark and grand, with a light upon him from the sun where he was born.

A. C. Bradley, 1904

Othello, in his magnanimous way, is egotistic. He really is, beyond any question, the nobly massive man of action, the captain of men, he sees himself as being . . . In short, a habit of self-approving, self-dramatisation is an essential element in Othello's make-up, and remains so at the very end.

It is, at the best, the impressive manifestation of a noble egotism . . . This self-centredness doesn't mean self-knowledge: that is a virtue which Othello, as soldier of fortune, hasn't had much need of.

F. R. Leavis, 1952

Among the tragedies of Shakespeare *Othello* is supreme in one quality: beauty. Much of its poetry, in imagery, perfection of phrase, and steadiness of rhythm, soaring yet firm, enchants the sensuous imagination.

Othello is like a hero of the ancient world in that he is not a man like us, but a man recognised as extraordinary. He seems born to do great deeds and live in legend. He has the heroic capacity for passion. But the thing which most sets him apart is his solitariness. He is a stranger, a man of alien race, without ties of nature or natural duties.

Helen Gardner, 1955

The action of *Othello* opens out to include the audience, and their perception of the struggle of good and evil. They do not go home hoping they will never meet an Iago, but rather understanding something of the nature of evil and how soon bright things come to confusion . . . We no longer feel, as Shakespeare's contemporaries did, the ubiquity of Satan, but Iago is still serviceable to us, as an objective correlative of the mindless inventiveness of racist aggression. Iago is still alive and kicking and filling migrants' letterboxes with excrement.

Germaine Greer, 1986

In loving and marrying each other, Othello and Desdemona instinctively act according to principles of racial equality and sexual freedom which are still not normative, still far from generally accepted and practised even in our own day, let alone in Shakespeare's.

Shakespeare's tragic protagonists are all overpowered by the prevailing social and ideological tides which sweep them unawares out of their depth, rather than by some metaphysically predestined misfortune or by some flaw, whether culpable, haphazard or innate, in the composition of their characters.

Kiernan Ryan, 1989

From the opening scenes of the play, we quickly note how Othello experiences his identity in contradictory terms set by the Venetians . . . Generations of western critics largely ignored these ideological underpinnings of Othello's identity and focused instead on the Moor's character in terms of psychological realism. However, as the literary history of the play testifies, they had difficulty in reconciling Othello's role as a tragic hero with his blackness . . . Othello self-destructively internalizes the prevailing racism, while Desdemona . . . remains an idealized, virtuous woman – keeping alive the image of a besieged, white femininity so crucial to the production of the black man as a 'savage'.

Jyotsna Singh, 2004

The relation between violence and the ideological power of the state may be glimpsed in the way Othello justifies himself, in his last speech, as a good Venetian: he boasts of killing someone. Not Desdemona . . . but a 'malignant and a turban'd Turk' who 'Beat a Venetian and traduc'd the state'. Othello says he 'took by the throat the circumcised dog / And smote him thus'. And so, upon this recollection, Othello stabs himself, recognizing himself, for the last time, as an outsider, a discredit to the social order he has been persuaded to respect.

Alan Sinfield, 2004

Coroner's investigation
A role-play activity for the whole class

Time: a month after Othello's death.

Place: a coroner's court in Venice.

This group activity will help you revise your knowledge and understanding of the whole play. Create a whole-class role-play around an imaginary coroner's investigation. It provides plenty of scope for getting everyone imaginatively involved in an active investigation of characters' relationships, motivations and the public and private aspects of the play.

The following notes will help focus each participant's preparation for the role-play. Take time to prepare your character and their side of the story, then set the room out as a court. The coroner presides over the hearing and assesses the evidence at the end of the role-play.

Coroner
- Work in a small group with the assistant/usher(s), etc.
- What questions will you put to each character?
- What concrete evidence exists? Any exhibits to use in court (e.g. weapons/letters)?
- Consider how you will shape your questions to elicit full answers (as opposed to 'yes'/'no' replies).

Coroner's assistant
- Assist coroner in running the proceedings.
- Establish an order of events and present it on paper.
- Keep a record of the proceedings of the court.

Montano
- What contact did you have with Othello/Cassio/Iago? Impressions?
- Any important/significant events you witnessed first hand?
- Did Othello live up to his reputation?

Duke of Venice
- How will you behave in court?
- Which characters did you know well?
- What relevant evidence do you have for the court?
- How do you see your position in relation to the whole Cyprus venture now?
- Do you feel any responsibility for what has happened?

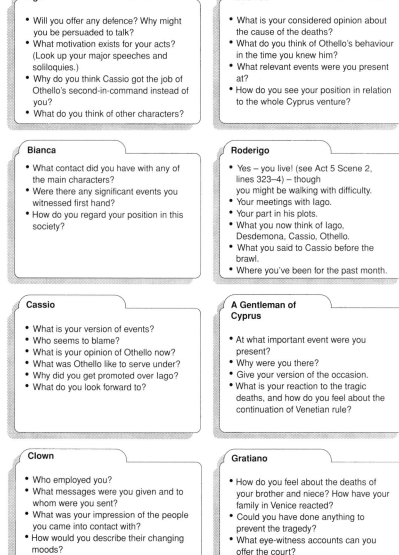

Iago

- Will you offer any defence? Why might you be persuaded to talk?
- What motivation exists for your acts? (Look up your major speeches and soliloquies.)
- Why do you think Cassio got the job of Othello's second-in-command instead of you?
- What do you think of other characters?

Lodovico

- What is your considered opinion about the cause of the deaths?
- What do you think of Othello's behaviour in the time you knew him?
- What relevant events were you present at?
- How do you see your position in relation to the whole Cyprus venture?

Bianca

- What contact did you have with any of the main characters?
- Were there any significant events you witnessed first hand?
- How do you regard your position in this society?

Roderigo

- Yes – you live! (see Act 5 Scene 2, lines 323–4) – though you might be walking with difficulty.
- Your meetings with Iago.
- Your part in his plots.
- What you now think of Iago, Desdemona, Cassio, Othello.
- What you said to Cassio before the brawl.
- Where you've been for the past month.

Cassio

- What is your version of events?
- Who seems to blame?
- What is your opinion of Othello now?
- What was Othello like to serve under?
- Why did you get promoted over Iago?
- What do you look forward to?

A Gentleman of Cyprus

- At what important event were you present?
- Why were you there?
- Give your version of the occasion.
- What is your reaction to the tragic deaths, and how do you feel about the continuation of Venetian rule?

Clown

- Who employed you?
- What messages were you given and to whom were you sent?
- What was your impression of the people you came into contact with?
- How would you describe their changing moods?
- Consider how you might act/speak in court (terrible puns, for instance?).

Gratiano

- How do you feel about the deaths of your brother and niece? How have your family in Venice reacted?
- Could you have done anything to prevent the tragedy?
- What eye-witness accounts can you offer the court?

Other roles (if needed)   Jury members, court ushers – could be involved in helping others to prepare their roles, or be responsible for creating exhibits (letters, etc.).

Othello in performance

Since its first recorded performance in 1604, *Othello* has remained a popular stage play. However, one of the earliest critics of the play, Thomas Rymer (1693), dismissed it as 'a Bloody Farce' because he thought that too much hinged upon 'so remote a trifle as a handkerchief'.

Key critical discussion in the twentieth century tended to focus upon whether Iago or Othello command the greatest stage presence. Largely, this debate is bound up with differing interpretations of Othello, shaped by the critical writings of A. C. Bradley (1904) and F. R. Leavis (1937). In brief, Bradley argued that Othello was essentially noble, and was brought down by Iago's villainy. In contrast, Leavis saw Othello as self-centred and self-dramatising, all too ready to believe Iago's hints and lies. Bradley viewed Iago as a more complex, fascinating character, but Leavis asserted that Iago 'is not much more than a necessary piece of dramatic mechanism'.

From around the 1980s, and in the twenty-first century, attention has been increasingly directed towards cultural, post-colonial and feminist/gender readings of the play influenced by developments in literary theory (see pp. 222, 236 and 237).

There is no substitute for seeing a live performance of the play at the theatre, as well as comparing different film or video versions in order to gain an appreciation of the living play as opposed to simply reading the script. The following activities are all designed to enable you to consider the play in performance.

1 Openings

As a skilled playwright Shakespeare knew he had to catch the interest of his audience right at the start of each play. Therefore in most plays we often find vigorous dialogue, intriguing situations and conflict introduced in the first scene. Scene 1 of *Othello* is no exception. Consider how the opening moments are portrayed in three different film/video versions of *Othello*. For example:

- Trevor Nunn's 1990 Royal Shakespeare Company production starts briefly with an empty stage in half-light; a striking visual contrast is immediately established with Iago in dark military uniform and Roderigo dressed in a light-coloured linen suit and panama hat.
- Oliver Parker's 1995 Hollywood film opens with a lengthy title sequence, the camera tracking a gondola's journey through

night-time Venice. A shrouded pair of figures is seated close together; the woman's face is occasionally glimpsed, but the man is masked. The scene cuts to the Senate where war is being discussed. Cut back to a secret wedding scene, Iago and Roderigo as two surreptitious onlookers. It is only now that some of Iago's opening dialogue is introduced.

- Orson Welles chose to begin his 1952 black-and-white film version with Othello's funeral procession, overlooked by a caged Iago; in this version the play is visually framed by its tragic outcome, the main action becoming a kind of flashback.

◆ Imagine you are making a new film version of *Othello*. How will your film begin? Where will it be set? What music or sound effects will you use? What atmosphere are you seeking to create? Will you want to reorder/cut the script?

2 Casting: traditions of 'blacking-up'

Traditionally Othello has been played on stage by white actors 'blacked-up'. Perhaps the most famous example on the London stage was Laurence Olivier's performance in 1964 (above), seen by many theatre critics as the definitive Othello.

Modern understandings of 'race' and cultural politics have led to less favourable criticisms of Olivier's performance, which is now regarded by many as relying on a racist stereotype. Heavily influenced by F. R. Leavis's reading of the play (see pp. 232 and 237), Olivier portrayed Othello as a sensuous and barely civilised egotist.

Another famous portrayal of Othello, however, was that of the black American actor, singer and political activist, Paul Robeson (right), in the mid-1940s. His performance has generally come to be regarded as the antithesis of Olivier's in that it emphasised the 'noble', sympathetic aspects of Othello.

Nowadays, most audiences expect to see a black actor playing Othello. An interesting experiment, however, was the 'photonegative' staging by the Washington Shakespeare Theatre (1997), where Othello (above) was played by a white actor and all other parts by black actors.

Ira Aldridge, the first black actor to play major Shakespeare roles (c. 1850).

◆ Discuss what effect you think different casting decisions might have on the way a modern audience 'reads' a performance of *Othello*. You might want to look back at photographs in this edition of black and white actors playing Othello as you talk.

3 Adaptations

Eighteenth-century adaptations

In the eighteenth century it was popular to rewrite certain of Shakespeare's tragedies (e.g. *Romeo and Juliet, King Lear*) in order to give them a happy ending. Imagine you are a stage adapter and have been asked to give *Othello* a happy ending. How will you do it? At what point in the play do you have to begin to make changes?

◆ Make notes outlining your alterations, including some examples of your new script.

Modern adaptations

Tim B. Nelson's 2001 film version updated and transferred *Othello* to a modern American high-school setting.

In a made-for-television adaptation (first screened on UK television in 2001), scriptwriter Andrew Davis transposes the story to modern London: Ben Jago, deputy Metropolitan Police Commissioner, is passed over for promotion in favour of his black colleague, John Othello. Michael Cass is assigned bodyguard duties when Othello and his wife, Dessie, are racially harassed . . .

◆ Present a file of other ideas you have for either a modern-dress production of Shakespeare's *Othello* or an updated drama based upon the *Othello* story.

William Shakespeare
1564–1616

1564 Born Stratford-upon-Avon, eldest son of John and Mary Shakespeare.

1582 Marries Anne Hathaway of Shottery, near Stratford.

1583 Daughter, Susanna, born.

1585 Twins, son and daughter, Hamnet and Judith, born.

1592 First mention of Shakespeare in London. Robert Greene, another playwright, described Shakespeare as 'an upstart crow beautified with our feathers . . .'. Greene seems to have been jealous of Shakespeare. He mocked Shakespeare's name, calling him 'the only Shake-scene in a country' (presumably because Shakespeare was writing successful plays).

1595 A shareholder in The Lord Chamberlain's Men, an acting company that became extremely popular.

1596 Son Hamnet dies, aged 11.
Father, John, granted arms (acknowledged as a gentleman).

1597 Buys New Place, the grandest house in Stratford.

1598 Acts in Ben Jonson's *Every Man in His Humour*.

1599 Globe Theatre opens on Bankside. Performances in the open air.

1601 Father, John, dies.

1603 James I grants Shakespeare's company a royal patent: The Lord Chamberlain's Men become The King's Men and play about twelve performances each year at court.

1607 Daughter, Susanna, marries Dr John Hall.

1608 Mother, Mary, dies.

1609 The King's Men begin performing indoors at Blackfriars Theatre.

1610 Probably returns from London to live in Stratford.

1616 Daughter, Judith, marries Thomas Quiney.
Dies. Buried in Holy Trinity Church, Stratford-upon-Avon.

The plays and poems
(no one knows exactly when he wrote each play)

1589–95 *The Two Gentlemen of Verona, The Taming of the Shrew, First, Second and Third Parts of King Henry VI, Titus Andronicus, King Richard III, The Comedy of Errors, Love's Labour's Lost, A Midsummer Night's Dream, Romeo and Juliet, King Richard II* (and the long poems *Venus and Adonis* and *The Rape of Lucrece*).

1596–9 *King John, The Merchant of Venice, First and Second Parts of King Henry IV, The Merry Wives of Windsor, Much Ado About Nothing, King Henry V, Julius Caesar* (and probably the *Sonnets*).

1600–5 *As You Like It, Hamlet, Twelfth Night, Troilus and Cressida, Measure for Measure, Othello, All's Well That Ends Well, Timon of Athens, King Lear.*

1606–11 *Macbeth, Antony and Cleopatra, Pericles, Coriolanus, The Winter's Tale, Cymbeline, The Tempest.*

1613 *King Henry VIII, The Two Noble Kinsmen* (both probably with John Fletcher).

1623 Shakespeare's plays published as a collection (now called the First Folio).